LYNETTE ROBERTS was born in Buenos Aires of Welsh family in 1909 and died in West Wales in 1995. She published two collections of poems in her lifetime, both from Faber and Faber: *Poems* (1944) and *Gods with Stainless Ears* (subtitled 'A Heroic Poem'; 1951). She married the Welsh writer and editor Keidrych Rhys.

PATRICK McGUINNESS lives in Caernarfon, Wales, and works at Oxford, where he is Professor of French and Comparative Literature. He is a Fellow of the Royal Society of Literature, a Fellow of the Learned Society of Wales, and was made *Chevalier des arts et des lettres* by the French government. His books include two novels, three collections of poems, a memoir and several academic books.

CHARLES MUNDYE is Professor of Modern Literature in the Creative Industries Institute at Sheffield Hallam University. He is President of the Robert Graves Society and Fellow of the English Association.

Lynette Roberts c. 1940.
(Photograph reproduced by kind permission of Angharad
and Prydein Rhys.)

Lynette Roberts

edited by Patrick McGuinness
& Charles Mundye

A Letter to the Dead

Collected Poems

CARCANET CLASSICS

First published in Great Britain in 2025 by
Carcanet
Main Library, The University of Manchester
Oxford Road, Manchester, M13 9PP
www.carcanet.co.uk

ISBN 978 1 80017 505 1

Book design by Andrew Latimer, Carcanet
Typesetting by LiteBook Prepress Services
Printed in Great Britain by SRP Ltd, Exeter, Devon

MIX
Paper | Supporting
responsible forestry
FSC
www.fsc.org FSC® C014540

The publisher acknowledges financial
assistance from Arts Council England.

Supported using public funding by
ARTS COUNCIL
ENGLAND

CONTENTS

Poems (1944)

Gods with Stainless Ears: A Heroic Poem (1951)

Uncollected and Unpublished Poems

Further Uncollected and Unpublished Poems

Appendix

Lynette Roberts holding a wild rabbit, taken just after her poetry reading at Wadham College, Oxford, Spring 1952. (Photograph reproduced by kind permission of Angharad and Prydein Rhys.)

Turtle doves, by Lynette Roberts.
(Photograph and image reproduced by kind
permission of Angharad and Prydein Rhys.)

Everyone who knew my mother, Lynette Roberts, remembers the same qualities in her: she was warm, loving, positive, incredibly generous, open-minded and unconventional, and had a great sense of fun and mischief. They remember her curiosity and powers of observation, her love of dancing, her energy and zest for life.

Because she was in and out of mental hospitals for the last twenty-five years of her life and lost touch with many friends, it was good for me to hear their stories. For example, the painter and writer Celia Buckmaster, who had been one of her bridesmaids, and helped Lynette with her flower arranging business, told me how one day Lynette decided they needed a holiday. Lynette looked through the atlas and was attracted to Madeira. On research it turned out Madeira was the only place where the Bristle Footed Worm remained – that, of course, intrigued her so off they went, travelling cargo. Lynette found a small house high up the hill and a woman called Angelina to work for them. It was during those long days of freedom that Lynette found her vocation as a poet. She sent a telegram to London announcing 'Have found my voice at last'.

The painter Sheila Healey knew Lynette in Buenos Aires and London. 'Lynette was very warm and kind,' she told me. 'She befriended people and gave them courage. Her flat in Charlotte Street was completely original – she did amazing things with colour. She opened the door to colour to me when we looked at Indian miniatures in the V&A. I also think of her as very enthusiastic. When she was interested in something she studied it intensely.'

Lynette always longed for a simple home, with a fire and a table – a place to look after friends in need – but much of her life was unsettled and nomadic, in rented rooms and a caravan. When she left my father, our address became The

Caravan, The Graveyard, Laugharne. Later in Bells Wood, Hertfordshire, we spent a whole summer catching butterflies and dragonflies, draping muslin round the caravan to keep them captive so we could draw them. The caravan's final resting place was Chislehurst Caves, where Lynette tried to set up an underground art gallery. While we were there she bought me and my brother Prydein an old gypsy caravan which we painted red and yellow.

Eventually her lovely sister Win bought us a house. Here Lynette grew old-fashioned roses and pinks, checking which had the best scent and finding out their history – reference books were always covered with her notes and sketches. She made spaghetti and hung it on the clothes airer to dry. Our red wine glasses had been bought with her Derby winnings: at 33-1 the odds weren't good but she loved the name Never Say Die – a motto she always quoted. She was almost always broke, owing money all round: one morning a cheque arrived and that evening we were on the boat train to Paris.

While she was dying, in rural Wales, she kept reverting to Spanish – though not her first language it was the language of her childhood. At one point we needed a dictionary to understand her. Then we read her poems and she was happy. She'd have been delighted to see her work published again, but she wouldn't have been surprised. She always knew her own worth.

Angharad Rhys
2005

INTRODUCTION

I

The Argentine-born Welsh writer Lynette Roberts published two books of poems as dramatic, varied, dense, elliptical and inset with verbal novelty as any experimental poetry in the twentieth century. T.S. Eliot, her friend and editor at Faber, praised her work, complimenting it by that most Eliotic of criteria: that it communicated before it made sense. Robert Graves, who drew on her expertise as he researched for *The White Goddess*, wrote: 'Lynette Roberts is one of the few true poets now writing. Her best is the best.' Dylan Thomas was best man at her wedding, Wyndham Lewis drew her portrait, and she was for a while on the peripheries of bohemian London. Her first collection, *Poems*, appeared in 1944, when she was thirty-five. The second, *Gods with Stainless Ears*, subtitled 'A Heroic Poem', came out in 1951. By her mid-forties she had stopped writing, had a severe mental breakdown, and become a Jehovah's Witness. She took no further interest in her work or literary reputation. By the time of her death, aged eighty-six in 1995, only a few people had heard of her. Her poetry, out of print for nearly half a century, was unknown beyond a small circle of poets and critics resourceful or privileged enough to lay hold of first and only editions of her books.[1] Her prose, including a war diary, an autobiography and uncollected or unpublished articles and memoirs, was forgotten.

The opening of *Poems*, 'Poem from Llanybri', is a welcome-poem to soldier and fellow-poet Alun Lewis:

If you come my way that is…
Between now and then, I will offer you
A fist full of rock cress fresh from the bank
The valley tips of garlic red with dew
Cooler than shallots, a breath you can swank

In the village when you come. At noon-day
I will offer you a choice bowl of cawl
Served with a 'lover's' spoon and a chopped spray
of leeks or savori fach, not used now,

In the old way you'll understand. [...]

A portal to the book, it imagines the poetic encounter
as a hospitality extended and a hospitality repaid. This is
poetry as dialogue, poetry as rooted tradition: a celebration
of community, both in the village, here described for its
uniqueness, and within the circle of poets. It takes pleasure in
the Welsh words and phrases – 'cawl', 'savori fach' and place
names such as 'Cwmcelyn' – but also in the Welsh speech-
patterns that make their way into English: *if you come my
way that is…* . 'Poem from Llanybri' celebrates poetry both
as living language and as heightened, ceremonial language. It
is fresh, direct, seemingly artless in its tone; but even as it is
powered by future verbs, it is reaching back, to the 'old ways',
the old customs. It asserts continuity of tradition, speech and
community: 'Can you come? – send an ode or elegy/ In the old
way and raise our heritage'.[2] That small word, 'our', is revealing
too: Roberts was born in Argentina, educated at art school in
London, and had been in Wales, married to a Welshman, less
than two years. Though her parents' families, Australian for
generations, had originally come from Wales, she was Welsh
by a combination of choice and imaginative will. 'Poem from

Llanybri' is a cosmopolitan's claim to a rooted culture that is also a culture of rootedness.

The originality and compressed variety of *Poems* emerges when we compare 'Poem from Llanybri' with the last poem in the book, 'Cwmcelyn'. It opens with an extract in Welsh, from the Book of Revelation, in Bishop Morgan's 1588 Welsh Bible. The English comes in the notes at the back of *Poems*, which are grandly titled 'Notes on Legend and Form'. By the time of *Gods with Stainless Ears*, the notes will occupy fourteen pages of translations and explanatory, scholarly and polemical elucidations (directly useful, as well as providing an intertextual forcefield beyond the poem). There then follows this, which surely reads as freshly and surprisingly now as when the 1944 reader first laid eyes on it:

> Air white with cold. Cycloid wind prevails
> On ichnolithic plain where no print runs
> And winter hardens into plates of ice;
> Shoots an anthracite glitter of death
> From their eyes – these men shine darkly.

When it appeared seven years later as the last section of *Gods with Stainless Ears* (and the 1951 reader will have been a very different kind of reader), 'Cwmcelyn' is the culmination of a narrative at once mythic and futuristic, a poem as different from 'Poem from Llanybri' as could be written by the same author. The contrast – between a poem that goes out to meet its reader and invites them into a recognisable, though gently idealised landscape and community, and 'Cwmcelyn', an apparently high modernist barrage of linguistic special effects, exotic referentiality and futuristic drama – is between the 'modernist' and the 'traditional', the 'elitist' and the 'democratic', the 'obscure' and the 'accessible'. With Lynette

Roberts, the two can be found between the covers of one slim first collection.

II

Lynette Roberts was born on 4 July 1909 in Buenos Aires. Her father, Cecil Arthur Roberts, came from Welsh-descended family, originally from Ruthin, north-east Wales. Cecil had gone to Argentina from Australia, where his family had lived since 1840, after training as a railway engineer. He became head of Western Railways in Argentina (one of Lynette Roberts's poems, 'Argentine Railways' is about his work), and a prominent member of the expatriate community. The family lived comfortably, owning yachts and racehorses, though Dylan Thomas's initial belief that Lynette had 'rich Welsh parents in South America (oil-diving or train-wrecking)'[3], was inaccurate. By the time she settled in Britain, Roberts was far from wealthy – she was no Nancy Cunard or Edith Sitwell, and her poetry bears little comparison with that parallel tradition we could call 'heiress modernism'. Lynette's mother, Ruby Garbutt, was also of Welsh origin – her family had come from Pembrokeshire. Lynette had two sisters, Winifred and Rosemary, and a brother, Dymock. Dymock was sent to school at Winchester, but after a mental breakdown was in a mental institution in Salisbury from the age of sixteen. In *Gods with Stainless Ears* the poem's speaker poignantly remembers 'my brother./ His Cathedral mind in Bedlam'.

Lynette Roberts first came to London with her parents during the First World War, in which her father fought and was wounded, before returning to Argentina, where she and her sisters attended convent school. On 3 July 1923, the day before Lynette's fourteenth birthday, her mother died of typhoid. In an unpublished talk on her South American poems, Lynette wrote that her mother had become fatally ill after drinking water from a contaminated well. Soon after this, the girls were sent to Bournemouth for their schooling. Cecil Roberts later remarried his childhood sweetheart Nora Sloan, who left her husband in Scotland and obtained a divorce in Uruguay to be free to marry him. In the 1930s, Lynette moved to London to study at the Central School of Arts and Crafts. During this period she roomed in Museum Street and Newman Street, in Fitzrovia. With her friend Celia Buckmaster, she travelled to Madeira; later, soon before the outbreak of war, she travelled to Hungary and Germany with another friend from Argentina, Kathleen Bellamy, who wrote reports for the Argentine newspaper *La Nacion* which Lynette illustrated. Roberts trained to be a florist with Constance Spry, and set up a flower arranging business called Bruska. She was for a while engaged to Merlin Minshall, intelligence officer, amateur racing driver and the man often claimed to have been the inspiration for Ian Fleming's James Bond (Minshall worked for Fleming, and published his autobiography, *Guilt-Edged*, in 1977). Roberts broke off the engagement when she met her future husband, the Welsh writer and editor, Keidrych Rhys, whom she encountered at a *Poetry London* event in London in 1939 organized by Tambimuttu, the magazine's influential editor. Rhys, Lynette recalled in her autobiography, 'was charming and spoke like a prince'. Dylan Thomas remembered Lynette as 'A curious girl, a poet, as they say, in her own right [...] with all the symptoms of hysteria'.[4] Alun Lewis was less snide: writing to his parents he described 'a queer girl, very gifted, [who] wears a red cloak and is unaccountable.'[5] Rhys was the flamboyant and resourceful editor of *Wales*, a journal of poetry and criticism that led a hand-to-mouth existence belied by the stature of its contributors and the energy of its promotion. He published a book of poems, *The Van Pool and Other Poems*, in 1942, and edited *Poems from the Forces* in 1941; *More Poems from the Forces* came two years later, followed by *Modern Welsh Poetry* (Faber, 1944). *Modern Welsh Poetry* is a landmark in Welsh writing in English, containing work by Dylan Thomas, Vernon Watkins, Emyr Humphries, David Jones, Idris Davies, R.S. Thomas and others. Rhys also founded the short-lived Druid Press, which published R.S. Thomas's first book, *The Stones of the Field* in 1946. Born to a Welsh-speaking farming family near Llangadog in Carmarthenshire in 1913, and christened William Ronald Rees Jones, he had legally adopted the name 'Keidrych' in 1940, calling himself after a stream that ran near his home. In one of his poems, the grandly titled 'The Prodigal Speaks', Rhys dramatised himself as follows:

> Yes born on Boxing Day among the childlike virgin hills
> [...]
> Middle of war; hamlet called Bethlehem; one shop; chapel.
>
> Almost a second Christ! say; only son of a tenant-
> Farmer of hundred odd acres growing corn for red soldiers
> Merrily with a daft boy from an industrial school who
> Spoke in a strange tongue across our great Silurian arc of sky.[6]

Lynette may have had this poem in mind when, in Part V of *Gods with Stainless Ears*, she evoked the soldier-hero, based on an idealised Keidrych, as 'He, of Bethlehem treading a campaign/ Of clouds, the fleecy cade purring at his side' (the word 'cade' meaning the holy Lamb).

The couple married in Llansteffan (the English version of the name is Llanstephan), a village on the Tywi estuary, on 4 October 1939. Keidrych's parents disapproved of the marriage, and made no secret of it. Dylan Thomas, his best man, mischievously described the wedding to Vernon Watkins as 'distinguished mostly by the beauty of the female attendants, the brown suit of the best man [Thomas had borrowed it from Watkins], the savage displeasure of Keidrych's mother, & Keidrych's own extremely hangdog look & red-rimmed eyes'.[7] Lynette's bridesmaids were Kathleen Bellamy and Celia Buckmaster. Keidrych and Lynette rented a cottage in the village of Llanybri, a few miles from Llansteffan, where they lived, with frequent visits to London, throughout the war. After a miscarriage in March 1940, Lynette gave birth to two children: Angharad, in May 1945 and Prydein, in November 1946. In July 1940, Keidrych was called up to work on coastal defences, and his tours of duty included postings to the Orkneys, Yarmouth and Dover.

It was in Llanybri that Lynette Roberts produced her most original and characteristic work: as well as her two books of poetry, she wrote a novel called 'Nesta' which was never published. We know from her letters to Graves that the book was set in medieval Wales (Roberts referred to it in her bibliography as 'A Historical Novel on Welsh Medieval History') and that it was 'modernistic' in punctuation and narrative treatment. Graves called it a 'work of genius in its wild way', but disapproved of its disregard for historical accuracy, its experimentalism, and its anachronisms. Nesta, or Nêst in Welsh, was the grandmother of Gerald of Wales and daughter of Rhys ap Tewdr, the last independent prince of South Wales. Known as the 'Helen of Wales', she had many lovers, and several children from different fathers, including Henry I of England. In 1108 she was kidnapped by Owain ap Cadwgan of Cardigan, and the incident started a war.[8] Judging from Graves's letters, he found Roberts's notion of a 'historical novel' very different from his own: 'Lynette is always breaking in with "hoodoo", "frou-frou", "aluminium", "Knossos", S. America, modern painters & so on', he complained. Eliot, who considered the book for Faber, described it as 'a quite extraordinary affair' in a letter of 11 April 1945. Roberts also published, in 1944 with Keidrych's Druid Press, a pamphlet called *Village Dialect*, containing stories and an article on country dialect, in which she ranges over a variety of material (from Elizabethan English to Pierre Loti's *Pêcheur d'Islande* via Joyce's *Finnegans Wake*), and claims to have 'arrived at the essence of all languages of the soil'.[9]

Throughout her time in Llanybri, Roberts kept a diary – quirky, observant, funny, but always deeply engaged in the culture of the place and its people. Characteristic of her attitude is optimism and toughness of mind, and though she has a complicated person's tendency to idealise the simple life, she is free of the kind of pseudo-Celtic sentimentality to which she, an outsider, might easily have succumbed. After a visit by Ernest Rhys she complains of his obsession with the Celtic twilight: 'He was still caught up in its aura when he met us, and, frankly, this nauseated me.' Elsewhere she writes of her belief in traditional crafts, before specifying: 'I do not mean the retention of arty crafty work of the past, but rather the modern craft that is contemporary and is required for practical use in our time.' She describes air raids, the arrival of evacuees, the daily grind of village life and its sustaining friendships; but also uses the diary to keep track of her eclectic researches: on butterflies, cattle, wild flowers and birds; on coracles, architecture, gravestone lettering and Renaissance painters. Several of these researches culminated in essays and articles: on Renaissance painters for *Life and Letters To-Day* or on coracles and Welsh architecture for *The Field*. Whether commenting on culture and politics ('the word *tradition* is really a substitute for fear') or sketching her neighbours ('Mrs Treharne […] lay or sat in her four-poster bed like a pickled Elizabethan'), the diary is not just a pleasure to read but an invaluable document on life on the 'home front'. It is often poignant too, about the loneliness and quiet extremity of her existence:

> I feel chequered with energy. Full of positive red squares and black negative ones. What shall I do? One moment I feel I could draw the moon from its zenith and the next I am unbearably listless, can find nothing to interest me in this bare stone village. [...] I feel cramped and barred from life. Could it be that I dislike the ties of married life, that I resent *having* to cook four times a day, wash up, see to the kitchen fire [...]? All this when I am 'with child'. [...] Now quick again, I feel full of bubbles in the head. (7 March 1940)

Roberts encountered Tambimuttu, Henry Treece, George Barker, Roy Campbell, Kathleen Raine and others, poets associated with the New Romantic and 'Apocalypse' groupings. She also knew the Anglo-Welsh poets – not just Dylan Thomas, but R.S. Thomas, Glyn Jones and Vernon Watkins. She was familiar, largely through translation, with Welsh-language poetry from the earliest literature to the work of her contemporaries, and several of her own poems experiment with the *englyn*, a traditional Welsh strict metre form. Roberts also read, and attended readings by, Auden, MacNeice and Day Lewis, and the influence of these poets has been underexplored – on her conception of the long poem for instance, not to mention her interest in the moving image, film and sound and mass media. Of the established modernists she knew and read Eliot and David Jones, as well as the work of poets and critics, like Laura Riding and Graves, who set themselves against modernism. Her diary, letters and autobiography contain many fine, lapidary or humorous vignettes of the literary world of the time: Cecil Day Lewis is 'like a temperate book on a shelf'; MacNeice, 'bastard-looking:

excellent delivery of sinewy and satirical verse'; R.S. Thomas, 'a gloomy sort of person – who like most intelligent ministers today doesn't believe in the church that he preaches'. One of Lynette's most effusive admirers was Edith Sitwell, with whom she corresponded for several years from the early 1940s, and to whom she dedicated *Gods with Stainless Ears*. Lynette's unpublished account of a tea party with the Sitwells suggests that, despite her affection for Edith, she was not comfortable in the Sitwellian *milieu*. 'Yesterday a wretched day of my life', she begins, elaborating:

> We walked over to the cool and ornate marble piece to find spread over the whole surface Edith Sitwell. Madame Tussaud. Wax. Out of the past. Out of a picture. I was shaken more than I had expected to be. And it was over some considerable time before I could register all that I saw.[10]

In 1943, Roberts began a correspondence with Robert Graves. Their letters contain a fascinating insight into the composition of *The White Goddess*, to which Roberts contributed material and advice on sources, and for which she is acknowledged in the foreword to the book. The previous year, in 1942, she had sent some poems to T.S. Eliot at Faber, and a few months after a manuscript of *A Heroic Poem*, later to become *Gods with Stainless Ears*. Eliot was interested, though found it 'stiff going' and suggested she send him a volume of short poems. He asked for the 'Heroic Poem' again in 1948, and it was published three years later. In the dustjacket notes to *Poems*, Eliot wrote:

> She has, first, an unusual gift for observation and evocation of scenery and place, whether it is in Wales or her native South America; second, a gift for verse

construction, influenced by the Welsh tradition, which is evident in her freer verse as well as in stricter forms; and third, an original idiom and tone of speech.

The acknowledgements to the book reveal the range of journals she published in: George Orwell's politically engaged *Tribune* contrasts with the exotic, aesthetic home of the New Romantic and Apocalypse poets, Tambimuttu's *Poetry London*; the urbane *Horizon* of Cyril Connolly contrasts with James Laughlin's modernist *New Directions*, recently founded to promote Ezra Pound, William Carlos Williams, H.D. and others. From the memoirs and letters of the time, Roberts emerges as a kind of insider's outsider, well-connected but somehow out on a limb: 'the one and only Latino-Welsh modernist', as one of her best critics, Nigel Wheale, puts it.[11] As a special interest group, a sort of 'fusion-identity', this is certainly an unusual category to fall into.

Life at Llanybri was very different from the London literary scene. Keidrych was often away, and after going AWOL from the army (*Gods with Stainless Ears* obliquely refers to this in Part II where the gunner is interned and appears before the army board), he was transferred to the Ministry of Information for the last three years of the war. One of Lynette's most painful experiences came in summer 1942, when the rumour began in the village that she was a spy. This is the subject of her poem 'Raw Salt on Eye':

> Hard people, I will wash up now, bake bread and
> hang
> Dishcloth over the weeping hedge. I can not raise
> My mind, for it has gone wandering away with him
> I shall not forget; and your ill-mannered praise.

By 1948, the marriage with Keidrych had broken up. Lynette left Llanybri and moved temporarily to a caravan in Laugharne, the village that inspired Thomas's 'Under Milk Wood'. Her address, written at the bottom of several of her unpublished poems, was 'The Caravan, The Graveyard, Laugharne'. The couple divorced in 1949, and she returned to London, where she lived in Kent Terrace NW1 and in a caravan in Bells Wood, Hertfordshire, close to where the children went to boarding school. Since *Poems* and *Gods with Stainless Ears*, she had put together another full collection, and continued to publish in magazines and journals. The manuscript for 'The Fifth Pillar of Song', containing eighty-odd pages of new poems (and several earlier ones excluded from *Poems*), was sent to Eliot in 1951. It was turned down two years later. Between 1950 and 1952 Lynette continued to give poetry readings (her bibliography lists readings at the Institute of Contemporary Art and the Oxford University Poetry Society) and took part in radio programmes on the Welsh Regional Service and the Third Programme. Poems continued to appear in journals – *Poetry* (Chicago), *Poetry* (London), *The Listener* – until 1953, but by now her career as a poet had effectively ended. In December 1952, a verse play, 'O Lovers of Death', was broadcast (no recording survives) on the Welsh Regional Service. In February 1953 *El Dorado*, a 'radio ballad' about Welsh colonists in Patagonia, was broadcast on the Third Programme and repeated twice. Other projects – anthologies, editions, essays – came to nothing. In 1954 she published her last book, *The Endeavour*, a novel about Captain Cook's expedition.

In 1955–6 Roberts set up the Chislehurst Caves art project in Kent, which ended after an accident in which a cave ceiling collapsed and seriously injured the sculptor Peter Danziger. The paintings exhibited on the cave walls were by the Guyanese artist Denis Williams. In 1956, and partly as a result of the project's failure, Roberts had a mental breakdown, and in the same year her sister Win bought her a house near Chislehurst. It was the first home of her own. Later that year, while still recovering, Roberts became a Jehovah's Witness, and remained one for the rest of her life. In 1970 she returned to Llanybri, moving into a cottage in Spring Gardens. Suffering from schizophrenia, she was committed four times under the Mental Health Act to St David's Hospital, Carmarthen. After her first stay in hospital, she moved to Carmarthen, and then in 1989 to Towy Haven residential home in Ferryside, overlooking Llansteffan on the other side of the bay. In December 1994 she fell and broke her hip while dancing, and later had a heart attack in hospital. She died of heart failure on 26 September at Towy Haven, and was buried in Llanybri churchyard.

III

One way into Lynette Roberts's work is 'Swansea Raid'. It appeared first in *Life and Letters To-Day* in 1941 (as 'From a New Perception of Colour', subtitled 'And I shall take as my Example the Raid on Swansea') and was reprinted with some differences in *Village Dialect*:

> I, that is Xebo7011 pass out into the chill-blue air and join Xebn559162 her sack apron greening by the light of the moon. I read around her hips: 'BEST CWT: CLARK'S COW-CAKES, H.T.5.' I do not laugh because I love my peasant friend. The night is clear, spacious, a himmel blue, and the stars minute pinpricks. The elbow-drone of jerries burden the sky and our sailing planes tack in and out with their fine metallic hum.
>
> Oh! look how lovely she is caught in those lights! Oh!

From our high village on the Towy we can see straight down the South Wales Coast. Every searchlight goes up, a glade of magnesium waning to a distant hill which we know to be Swansea.

Swansea's sure to be bad; look at those flares like a swarm of orange bees.

They fade and others return. A collyrium sky, chemically washed Cu DH2. A blasting flash impels Swansea to riot! higher, absurdly higher, the sulphuric clouds roll with their stench of ore, we breathe naphthalene air, the pillars of smoke writhe and the astringent sky lies pale at her sides. A Jerry overhead drops two flares; the cows returning to their sheds wear hides of cyanite blue, their eyes GLINTING OPALS! We, alarmed, stand puce beneath another flare, our blood distilled, cylindricals of glass. The raiders scatter, then return and form a piratic ring within our shores. High explosives splash up blue, white, and green. We know all copper compounds are poisonous, we know also where they are.

Bleached, Rosie turns to fetch in the cows. I lonely, return to my hearth, there is a quiet clayfire with blue flames rising that would bring solace to any heart.[12]

'I' breezily corrects herself from first person pronoun to number, and the tone from the start is excited rather than fearful. The voices are rendered in direct speech, speech that is tender and comradely, emphasising how, beneath the impersonality of numbers, human relations continue intact (direct speech fragments in Roberts tend to be identity-emphatic, and not – as in much modernist poetry – identity-scrambling). At the end of 'Swansea Raid', the names return, as dust settles after an explosion. Place, people and things rebecome themselves: 'Rosie returns to fetch the cows'; 'I lonely' goes back indoors;

the fire is no longer the fire of flares and explosions but an intimate domestic fire. This may be a text about fracturing, scattering and dispersal; but it is also about the resumption of life, of community and social relations. It also displays the orders – elemental/mythic (moon), artificial/technological (explosions and flares), and domestic (hearthfire) – in and between which Roberts's poetry as a whole moves. Central too to its conception is the interplay of axes: we have the vertical, the defining axis of lyric poetry (images of verticality such as assumption, descent, flight, geological drilling abound throughout Roberts's work, along with intimations of moral uplift, freefall, abjection and dejection); then the horizontal, the vector of a more 'naturalist', observational approach. It is also perhaps the axis of historical time (whether imagined as linear or elliptical), of myth and of futuristic anticipation. And like much of Roberts's poetry, however stylised, oblique or encrypted, it is set in a real place, in the midst of a real event, among real people.[13]

'Swansea Raid' also reveals Roberts's characteristic verbal association and linguistic play: 'pass out' sounds military, while 'glade of magnesium' sets off the natural world against the scientific, a frequent device in her work. The flares are like 'orange bees', but this is no 'bee-loud glade', though the planes' menacing thrum stands in eerie consonance with the Yeatsian image of repose. There is even bilingual wordplay: in 'Jerries burden the sky' the plane's heavy buzzing is expressed through an anglicised echo of the French verb, *bourdonner*, to buzz, in turn taken up by the word 'drone'. Ready-made phrases or images are given a twist, diverted into something curious, jolting or sinister such as the text-fragment, seen in a flash, advertising 'Cow Cakes' and 'read around her hips'. Like the rest of Roberts's poetry, 'Swansea Raid' is lexically omnivorous: painterly, technical, dramatic, full of strange words and shiny magpie diction, the glittering new language of technological knowhow is spliced with the language of the farm. Among Roberts's key words, appropriately enough, are 'alloy' and 'compound', useful words to bear in mind when confronted with her use of language and treatment of subject.

Poems is grounded in a variety places: West Wales, South America, London. Roberts ranges freely over myth and history (whether Welsh, Greek or Incan), drawing them back to the domestic and the private. In her work, we are as likely to encounter railroads and air raids as milking pails and dishcloths drying on hedges, submerged Incan temples as Cow and Gate lorries. Characters from Homer or the Mabinogi exist in the same poems, and in the same imaginative continuum, as cow cakes and Marie Stopes. There are semi-mythical places and science-fictional locations, archaisms jostle with technical locutions, pastoral comes up against the futuristic. There are moments of vatic arousal and romantic nationalism, epigraphs in Welsh, references to Maeterlinck and Hokusai alongside the Dogs of Annwn, Aertex clothing and Singer sewing machines. There is never the same poem twice, and her range – public, private, intimate, free and tightly formal – is remarkably broad. Some of her alleged obscurity, and much of her oblique or inverted syntax, is down to her tendency to transcribe, unaltered, the idioms and phrases she hears all around her. While many of her phrases seem cryptic, elliptical or contorted, many are simply unmediated, direct speech. Her fascination, on the one hand, with dialect (even if it is an idealised version of the 'language of the soil') and, on the other, with the rarefied or specialist lexicons of science or botany or art history, seem of a piece with modernistic attempts to bypass the linguistic middle-ground. Roberts's tone is by turns hieratic, ceremonial, matter-of-fact and immediate. Often it is all at once. Even her poem-titles are mysterious and compelling: 'Raw Salt on Eye', 'Ecliptic Blue', 'Fifth of the Strata', 'Xaquixaguana'.

Lynette Roberts is in an obvious and precise sense a war poet. Her poetry describes bereavement, privation and loss, the brokenness and fracturing of experience both for the combatants and for those left at home. But she is also a poet of the hearth, of community, of continuity and survival. She does not idealise the domestic world: it is extreme, heartbreaking, cruel, and perhaps her greatest achievement in *Poems* is the conviction with which she describes women's life in wartime. Troubled scenes of domesticity recur in her work, and the depth of contentment depicted in 'Poem from Llanybri' is not typical. Roberts is uniquely able to express the way modern war is reflected and refracted, projected and screened or watched from afar. And as in 'Swansea Raid', it is also in constant danger of being turned into something spectacular. Her poems often register the liminal moments when danger tips into spectacle and spectacle into danger. In 'Earthbound' the poem's speaker describes sitting at her make-up table and hearing of the death of a local boy:

> I, in my dressing gown,
> At the dressing table with mirror in hand
> Suggest my lips with accustomed air, see
> The reflected van like lipstick enter the village
> When Laura came, and asked me if I knew […]

The preoccupation with reflections is characteristic of Roberts's subject as well as her imagery, from the handmirror at the dressing-table to the 'Sun splintered on waves' of Part I of *Gods with Stainless Ears*. The home front is not a refuge so much as a screen onto which the drama of war is projected and scattered, real but estranged, intangible but touching all aspects of life. Hence perhaps her poetry's insistence on images of reflections and refractions, of film, news broadcasts and sound recording. In this context we may think of Keith Douglas's poem 'How to Kill', in which the poem's speaker sights the enemy soldier 'in the dial of my glass'. He gives the order to fire: 'Being damned, I am amused/ to see the centre of love diffused/ and the waves of love travel into vacancy'.[14] 'How to Kill' is built around metaphors of distance: the technology of death ensures one can kill from far away, just as the 'damned' speaker is emotionally distanced from his own action. It is real and unreal: the glass brings the image closer but keeps its reality at bay, while the words 'diffusion' and 'waves' (Douglas was surely evoking the language of radio and cinema broadcasting here), insist on war experience, even for the combatant, as something projected, technologically mediated and disembodied. There is a marked insistence on such images in Roberts's poetry too. 'Catoptric' (produced by or relating to mirrors or reflections) is one of her many unusual words, and her poems abound in images of glass, prisms, shiny metals and alloys, water, ice, mirrors and polished surfaces. In his review of Keith Tuma's *Anthology of Twentieth-Century British and Irish Poetry*, the poet John Wilkinson discusses Roberts as an example of what he calls 'frostwork': 'window glass which is semi-opaque through its decoration; that is, poets whose writing exhibits a sustained balance between linguistic surface and reference to an internal or external world'.[15] For Wilkinson, Roberts is a test case in the perennial debate: between poets who write as if language were the clear pane that renders the world as it is, and those for whom language not only alters what we see, but is a part of it, needing itself to be rendered.

In her diary Roberts describes the event on which 'Earthbound' is based, and how she and one of the village's evacuees make a wreath for the dead boy. The image is of two outsiders engaged in an act of community. Though the mirror scatters and inverts at the start of the poem, the wreath is circular and cyclic:

We made the wreath standing on the white floor;
Bent each to our purpose wire to rose-wire;
Pinning each leaf smooth,
Polishing the outer edge with the warmth of our
hands.

The circle finished and note thought out,
We carried the ring through the attentive eyes of the
street:
Then slowly drove by Butcher's Van to the 'Union
Hall'.

The poem sets the whole against the broken, the circle against the fragment, peace against war, without lapsing into melodrama or sentimentality. *Poems* is crossed with bereavement. 'Lamentation' opens with Lynette's view of herself as the outsider: 'To the village of lace and stone/ Came strangers. I was one of these/ Always observant and slightly obscure'. It goes on to connect her own loss, the miscarriage of her child and the 'emptiness of crib', with the devastation caused by an air raid that has killed animals on the farm :

O the salt loss of life
Her lovely green ways.
The emptiness of crib
And big stare of night
The breast of the hills
Yield a bucket of milk:
But the crane no longer cries
With the round birds at dawn
For the home has been shadowed
A storm of sorrow drowned the way.

The lost child is a small but insistent presence in her poems, often figured as a shadow (most obviously in 'The Shadow Remains'). In Part IV of *Gods*, the child announced in Part I has been miscarried:

> I, rimmeled, awake before the dressing sun:
> Alone, I pent up incinerator, serf of satellite gloom
> Cower around my cradled self; find crape-plume
> In a work-basket cast into swaddling clothes
> Forcipated from my mind after the foetal fall:
>
> Rising ashly, challenge of blood to curb – compose –
> Martial mortal, face a red mourning alone.
> To the star of third magnitude O my God,
> Shriek, sear my swollen breasts, send succour
> To sift and settle me. […]

In other poems it is the mythical and the legendary dimensions that seem to shadow daily life. 'The Circle of C' opens in a matter-of-fact tone out of keeping with the poem's arcane subject:

> I walk and cinder bats riddle my cloak
> I walk to Cwmcelyn ask prophets the way.
> 'There is no way they cried crouched on the hoarstone
>   rock
> And the Dogs of Annwn roared louder than of late.'

It is a puzzling poem, but her notes on it are (like many of her notes) offered in good faith:

The ghosts of dogs, heard and seen in the sky. Invariably connected with Hell and Death omens. They appear in early triads, and in the first story of the Mabinogion [...] I have used this image as an interpretation of the raiders droning over the estuary and hill; their stiff and ghostly flight barking terror into the hearts of the villagers.

This is typical of Roberts's use of unusual references: she has (mostly) a clear idea of the connections between images and ideas, and her method of association, if sometimes hard to follow, is not designed to mystify us or make us toil through thickets of notes. That it sometimes fails is more down to lapses of method or confusion of effect than a deliberate attempt to write 'obscure' poetry. Compared with the notes, say, of T.S. Eliot, in parts more delphic even than the mysteries they elucidate, or those of David Jones or Ezra Pound, Roberts's notes are artless and straightforward (this does not of course stop her from failing to provide notes for passages that need them). 'The Circle of C' moves from the mysterious prophetic mode (she is told that her lover 'will come not as he said he would come/ But later with sailing ice, war glass and fame') back into the ordinary, domestic world. The movement back to the home fire is similar to that of 'Swansea Raid':

> I left the Bay, wing felled and bogged
> Kicked the shale despondent and green
>
> Heard Rosie say lace curtained in clogs
> I've put a Yule log on your grate.

Life is experienced as a sort of doubleness, unfolding in a mythic-domestic continuum. In poems like these, it's as if the everyday was myth's lived double. Roberts's poems constantly make the connection between quotidian existence and the legendary or mythical forms they echo or project. In Part II of *Gods with Stainless Ears*, the geese 'sleeve their own/ Shadows'. It is one of the poem's many extraordinary yet precise images, and provides a way of thinking about the relationship between past and present and future, about myth and daily life, and about the poet and her many projected selves. Roberts often identifies with historical or mythical characters, such as Rhiannon and Branwen from the Mabinogi, strong women wronged, trapped, outcast, or reduced to domestic drudgery; women who lose their children and are failed by their husbands. In *Gods with Stainless Ears*, the woman is at the Singer sewing machine – a 'perfect model scrolled with gold, // Chromium wheel and black structure, firm on/ Mahogany plinth' – making an aertex shirt for her soldier lover. This is a machine-age Penelope awaiting her returning warrior.

The language of *Gods with Stainless Ears* is already emerging in poems such as 'Spring', poems pitched somewhere between the futuristic and the pastoral:

> The full field.
> The stiff line of trees.
> The antiseptic grass – dew shining
> The green,
> Spraying from shorn hedgerows
> Sodium earth dug hard;
> Bound by the fury of earth's lower crust.
>
> Black bending cattle nose to the warmth
> Pebble sheep pant to a lighter tune.
> To high air sustained
> To high springing air.
> To blue-life-mist rising from the flaming earth.

If myth is time plumbed, then geology is place plumbed – Roberts is fond of the language of geology and archaeology, of strata and rock formations, the Palaeozoic and the Cambrian. Often, as in *Gods with Stainless Ears*, it is the aerial view that dominates, the airman's or the bird's eye view, and poems proceed by dazzling climbs and swoops: planes and birds, emotions and states of mind, all partake of that energising verticality. But, as in 'Spring', there is also the view from the grass blade, from the sustaining earth – poetry that seeks depth as well as height, aiming for the core as well as the zenith.

To a sense of place, Roberts adds an organic vision of community. In her South American poems she pays the same attention to cultural details, to the architecture and customs of the native people, as she does to those of the Welsh community she lives in. Whether writing about Welsh cottages, Incan temples or huts with corrugated roofs, Roberts is guided by a sense of the intimate bond between people, landscape and habitation. In an article for *The Field* called 'Simplicity of the Welsh Village' (the word 'simplicity' is a touchstone in her writing), Roberts claims that Wales's 'extensive peasant democratic tradition [...] will harmonise with modern architecture', and makes an audacious connection between peasant architecture and the uncompromising modernism of Le Corbusier and Frank Lloyd Wright. Her poetry makes similar connections between the old and the new, the ancient and the modern. In the same article, she describes the differences between Wales and England as inherent in their different cultures, landscapes and psychologies:

> The first [difference], to my mind, is colour: the blue slates and greener pastures, the two predominant colours of the Celt, the sharp outline of the whitewashed farms and houses as they stand against the skyline; the way in

which the walls project geometrical planes of light that resemble still-life models of squares and cubes. This cold austerity is suddenly upon us, and contrasts so vividly with the rich, mellow tones of English farmhouses, that we are estranged and left singularly apart.[16]

For Roberts, this geometrical, angular vision is entirely compatible with the centuries-old architecture of the Welsh village – her painterly eye is capable of seeing both abstract and figurative, the soft contours and the hard edges of her landscape. In *Gods with Stainless Ears* the village is 'scintillating/ Like mothball white on a hill' and the air 'planed' into 'euclidian cubes'. That positive use of the word 'estranged' is telling too: in a sense, her poetry insists on unfamiliarity, estrangement and foreignness as part of the experience of the poem's meaning, rather than as uncomfortable incidents on the way to clarity. In the notes to *Gods with Stainless Ears* she writes 'I have intentionally used Welsh quotations as this helps to give the conscious impact and culture of another nation'. The poet who talks about 'my village' and 'our heritage' is also alive to the richness of the unfamiliar or defamiliarised. In the same article she goes on, evoking the magnesium light of flash photography, to describe the 'penetrating power of the white sunlight of Wales' as an explosive revealer of forms:

> This last condition of magnesium light alters the whole panorama of Wales [...]. It is a light which glazes every building, stone and tree [...]. It is the clear condition of light, I believe, that has helped more to effect that change that exists between England and Wales than any other defect or attribute. The fresh and burnished illumination of colour is partly due to this light.

The rain, the continual downpour of rain, may also compensate us indirectly, by giving us that pure day which precedes it, which everyone in Wales must know. During those intervals the rain water is reflected back to us through a magnetic prism of light. The sea, which surrounds two-thirds of Wales, throws up another plane of light. And a third shaft of light reaches us at a fuller angle through the sun.[17]

Even at its most dazzling, eclectic or overcharged, Roberts's poetry bears witness to a spectrum of female experience which rarely makes it into poetry about war – or not as something violently, colourfully lived, as distinct from merely endured. Under their myth-plated exteriors, Roberts's poems treat childbirth and miscarriage, loneliness and disappointed expectation, exiguous rations and neighbourly slights. All these subjects turn up in her poems with an intensity of expression and originality of diction we find nowhere else. No poetry better expresses that amalgam of drudgery and enforced, fretful inertia, or that particular species of actively-experienced passivity that characterises an ordinary woman's life in wartime. When Roberts gives an epic scale to the domestic, it does not traduce, inflate or efface the domestic – it extends it. Poetry is the mirror in which ordinary life looks to find itself reflected in myth.

IV

'Cwmcelyn' appears at the end of *Poems* because Eliot felt that there were not enough poems to make up a volume. In a letter of 17 November 1943 he suggests that she include a section of 'the long poem' to bring it up to length. He also considers, then rejects, the idea of publishing both books in one. *Gods with Stainless Ears* was largely complete before *Poems* appeared, despite being published six years later (in her preface Roberts writes that it was written over two years, 1941–3). It is legitimate to suppose that between writing and publication the book underwent some changes. The most significant of these is the insertion of prose 'arguments' at the start of each section, recommended by Eliot to help the reader with the poem's narrative. By the time these were written, Roberts had divorced Rhys, and this explains, in particular, the differences between the 'argument' and the narrative content of Part V. There have also been a few revisions of punctuation and vocabulary. One particular instance of this, noted by Nigel Wheale in his essay 'Beyond the Trauma Stratus', is where Part V of *Gods* replaces 'chinese fields of tungsten' from the 1944 version of 'Cwmcelyn' with 'chinese blocks of uranium'. It is a minor detail, but a revealing one: the revision reflects an increased awareness of developing nuclear politics that suggests Roberts's interest in keeping the poem as up to date as possible.

'The subject is universal, and the tragedy one of too many', Roberts writes in her preface, the language composed of 'congested words and images, and certain hard, metallic lines':

> when I wrote this poem, the scenes and visions ran before me like a newsreel. […] But the poem was written for filming, especially Part V where the soldier and his girl walk in the fourth dimension and visit the various outer strata of our planet.

Roberts was not the first to imagine poetry and film joined – Auden and Britten had collaborated in the mid-1930s on GPO films such as 'Night Mail' and 'Coal Face' (1936).

Though Roberts may certainly have learned something from their approach, theirs was a collaboration: Britten wrote a score to accompany lines by Auden which are no more or less intrinsically 'filmic' for being written for film. Film was for them part of the medium; for Roberts it was part of the conception. In her account of tea with the Sitwells we get an insight into what she had in mind not just for the poetry of the future, but for the way it would be disseminated:

> We spoke of the next war... I suggested that during that no doubt people would attend films of poetry with unseen voice as opposed to the poetry reading [...] I said I hoped poetry would soon be filmed.

This idea of the 'unseen voice' fits well with the narration of *Gods* – the poem is told by the woman, from inside and outside her own story, while the prose 'arguments' at the beginning of each section are impersonal and have the scene-setting function of script or screenplay directions. They do more than summarise the story (without them some of the poetry would be ambiguous beyond safe surmising); they also explain poetic conceits, sound effects ('Machine-gun is suggested by the tapping of a woodpecker...'), and image-sequences as if for camera rather than reader. It would be difficult to find a long poem more cinematically imagined – rather as the Symbolist dramas of Maeterlinck or Mallarmé were conceived for the theatre of the intellect, so *Gods with Stainless Ears* may be a script for the cinema of the mind. In 'Beyond the Trauma Stratus', Nigel Wheale embeds the poem in its era. This is a poem, as Wheale explains, full of 'anxieties about post-war social development' such as nuclear power and the Beveridge Report, with a busy meshwork of context behind its grand gestures of transcendence.[18]

Briefly (and reductively) put, *Gods with Stainless Ears* tells, through 680-odd lines of mainly five-line stanzas, prose 'arguments', epigraphs and notes, a dreamlike war narrative of shifting perspectives and timezones. Set around the West Wales Coast, its protagonists are a man and a woman – the 'soldier and his girl'. It is in many ways autobiographical: the soldier's number is Rhys's war number, the details of the woman's life map directly onto Lynette's, and the poem is peopled with local characters from Llanybri and Llansteffan. Part I introduces the scene and the setting; Part II begins with an elegy for a lost airman played on a gramophone; Part III describes the soldiers getting ready for action and the gunner 'standing apart, through maladjustment of mind and spirit rejecting his girl'; Part IV starts with the girl speaking of her miscarriage; in Part V the protagonists are assumed upwards into a futuristic world, only to be returned to the world they left, changed forever.

The unfolding of narrative in epic is hieratic, stately, processional; the unfolding of narrative in newsreel is jerky, spliced, whirring. *Gods with Stainless Ears* overlays both modes to extraordinary effect. In the 'argument' to the poem's first part, Roberts writes:

> The poem opens with a bay wild and somewhat secluded from man. And it is in front, or within sight of this bay that the whole action takes place: merging from its natural state into a supernatural tension within the first six stanzas. War changes its contour.

The opening is a poetic tracking shot:

> Today the same tide leans back, blue rinsing bay,
> With new beaks scissoring the air, a care-away
> Cadence of sight and sound, poets and men

Rediscovering them. Saline mud
Siltering, wet with marshpinks, fresh as lime stud

Whitening fields, gulls and stones attending them;
Curlews disputing coverts pipe back: stem
Plaintive legs deep in the ironing edge, that
Outshines the shale, a railway line washed flat,
Or tin splintered from a crab-green cave.

This is Saint Cadoc's Day. All this Saint Cadoc's
Estuary: and that bell tolling, Abbey paddock
Sunk. – Sad as ancient monument of stone.
Trees vail, exhale cyprine shade, widowing
Homeric hills, green pinnacles of bone.

The new beaks of the birds 'scissor' the air; a few stanzas later
there are 'aluminium beaks', announcing the planes overhead.
The poem insists on the exactness of its setting – the coast,
the railway line, the shops and pubs. The local merges
into the mythical: the Second World War merges into
Cattraeth, the great murderous battle described by the poet
Aneirin in the *Gododdin* as 'Evans shop' says that the soldiers
are 'training for another Cattraeth'; the hills become 'Homeric';
and even John Roberts, the coracle man of Llansteffan (about
whom Roberts writes in her diary and *Village Dialect*), merges
into Charon, boatman of the Styx.

Gods is a modernist long poem, but not just in the
Poundian sense of a 'poem including history'. Rather, it is a
poem including the future, a poem that tells a story, with a
forceful narrative drive, and which bears witness to its time:

[…] To what age can this be compared?
Men slave, spit and spade. Glean life pure.

Accelerate oxidised roads. Drill new hearts and
   hearths
Impale the money-goaders' palisade. And you

Of acetated minds, workers with xantheine
Faces, revolutionise your land; holding
The simple measures of life in your hand,
Remembering navies and peacocks never sail
Together in the aftermaths of disaster.

This is the modernism of anticipation, not nostalgia. Despite
the Poundian tone of 'Impale the money-goaders' palisade',
there is something optimistic about this poem, even amid the
ravages, the personal loss, the death and decimation of the
'pilotless age'. 'To what age can this be compared?' the voice
asks, and it is not an ironic question. The answer is all ages and
none: the poem takes place both in a unique time and place
and in a vast mythic-historic continuum.

Roberts uses the familiar resources of science fiction:
a technological cladding around mythical paradigms. Nature
here exists in the machine age, while descriptions of modernist
architecture (chromium cenotaphs, steel escalators, aluminium
rails) are as vividly up-to-date as they are imagined. Even the
poem's flora are metallic forms forged in nuclear-age smithies:

Corymb of coriander, each ray frosted
Incandescent: by square stem held, hispid,
And purple spotted. Twice pinnate with fronds
Of chrome. Laid higher than the exulted hedge;
By pure collated disc of daisy glittering

White on red powdered stem […]

'Ceraunic Clouds', 'zebeline stripes', 'chemical paradox', 'ciliated moon', 'febrifuge', 'paleozoic sentinels', 'crystallized cherubic stars' give just a tiny sampler from Roberts's language in *Gods with Stainless Ears*.

The poem also announces a coming into consciousness of possibilities: political, scientific and social. There is even a romantic nationalist underpinning. Roberts incorporates the poem 'We must uprise O my people' from *Poems* into Part II of *Gods with Stainless Ears*, seeming to promise, so far as Wales is concerned, some post-war nationalist unfinished business. In Part I, the English soldiers take down the Welsh flag, only for the flag's colours to reinvest themselves into the earth:

> 'Pull down the bastard.' 'Pull down the flag.'
> The flag torn down. Emerald on
> Unfortunate field and red flaw its great
> Perfection; without sound crept back like myth
> Into folds of earth: grew greener shafts of resilience.

There are shades here of both Saunders Lewis, poet and playwright and founder-member of Plaid Cymru, and of Dylan Thomas. At the end of Part V of *Gods*, the soldier 'frees dragon from the glacier glade', and the poem ends with a Wales in frozen limbo about to be released. The heroism may be Girl's and Boy's Own stuff, but it is meant, and it looks ahead to the post-war climate rather than back to the world of lost princes. To Roberts's European and Anglo-American modernist contexts, we must also add the context of Welsh literary and cultural awakening. She is what would today be called a 'nationalist' or a 'culturalist': she insists on the uniqueness of Welsh culture and is conscious of the ease with which the small country could be – and was being – swallowed up. In her article on Patagonia she wrote of Wales being 'oppressed partly by her own misdirection and partly by outside jurisdiction'; in a 1952 *Times Literary*

Supplement review of Welsh writing, she warned: 'what the Welsh dragon lacks at present is fire; […] the younger generation must rediscover the source of that fire before the particularities of the Celtic imagination are once again submerged in an Anglicised culture'.[19] Both she and Keidrych Rhys were drawn to the radical nonconformist and pacifist tradition of Welsh culture, and Roberts's time in West Wales coincides with the strengthening of Welsh Nationalism as a political programme. In her diary she expresses anger at the proposed forced requisition of land in Preseli in Pembrokeshire by the War Office – a major galvanising issue for post-war Welsh nationalism.

In Part V, the soldier and the girl rise up together:

> We by centrifugal force … rose softly ….
> Faded from bloodsight. We, he and I ran
> On to a steel escalator, the white
> Electric sun drilling down on the cubed ice;
> Our cyanite flesh chilled on aluminium
>
> Rail. Growing taller, our demon diminishing
> With steep incline […]

They climb 'through moist and luminous dust', to 'a ceiling and clarity/ Of *Peace*' with 'Sweet white air varied as syllables'. The woman-speaker is 'contented in this fourth dimensional state', but the couple are forced to return. As the 'argument' has it 'the world demands their return':

> Earthwards like arctic terns the spangled
> Mirrors still on our wings. Colder. Continuous as
> *newsreel*,
> Quadrillion cells spotting the air, stinging
> The face like a swarm of bees. Lower. A vitreous green

> Paperweight – the sky is greenglaze with snow flying
>
> Upwards zionwards. Such iconic sky bears promise.
> Dredging slowly down, veiling shield of sky hard.
> Cold. Austere. Tumbled over each other lurched
> Into the dark penumbra; then, through a
> Rift as suddenly, the solid stone of earth
>
> Rushed up; hit us hard as household iron [...]

Travelling down through 'currents/ of ice, emerald streams and blue electric lakes' they return to the post-war desolation of a 'bleak telegraphic planet', finding a 'Mental Home for Poets' in the now-derelict bay. There are perhaps associations of the Fall, but the divergence between the 'argument' and the final stanzas of the poem cause problems: the 'argument' is pessimistic and suggests the sundering of the couple and failure of liberation and renewal. The girl, alone, 'turns away: towards a hard new chemical dawn', the soldier 'walks meekly into the mental home'. In the poem, however, the feel is on the contrary optimistic, defiant, vibrant:

> Salt spring from frosted sea filters palea light
> Raising tangerine and hard line of rind on the
> Astringent sky. Catoptric on waterice he of deep love
> Frees dragon from the glacier glade,
> Sights death fading into chillblain ears.

This volume also presents a selection of Lynette Roberts's uncollected and unpublished poems, many of which were intended for the volume that never appeared, 'The Fifth Pillar of Song'. Eliot's rejection of the book is understandable. Though there are many original or successful poems, it is uneven and confused. Its best poems are those, like 'The "Pele" Fetched in' or 'Saint Swithin's Pool', which have simplicity and depth, and in which there is a sense of the cosmic embroiled in the everyday. The poems chosen here are intended to represent the best of the unpublished or uncollected work, though a few examples of the latter category are included to give the reader a sense of the whole. The final section of the book contains three texts. The first is the 'ballad for voices' *El Dorado*, a breathlessly told, Wild-West-style adventure about the murder of Welsh colonists by a group of Indians in 1883-4. *El Dorado* was a poem for radio, and should be considered as such: it has colour, adventure and pace, but it does not measure up – as poetry – to the rest of Roberts's work, and is not a gaucho *Under Milk Wood*. Also in the appendix is an article by Roberts on Patagonia, first published in *Wales*, in which she discusses the incident retold in *El Dorado*, and the text of a radio talk she gave on her South American poems.

V

It seemed inevitable that Roberts's poetry would be charged with 'obscurity', a charge often levelled against women poets of a modernist bent – Mina Loy, Marianne Moore, Laura Riding, to mention just three (it is always the men who are 'learnèd' and the women who are 'obscure'.) In a letter of 3 December 1944, Graves wrote to Roberts to air his own doubts:

> Eliot and Pound have set a bad example. Your lines all work out surely, I grant you, which is very rare in the present slapdash pseudo-intelligent world; and

of course in *Cwmcelyn* you are doing what every poet I suppose must do once at least: show his or her awareness of what a frightful mess the world of ideas has got into because of Science taking the bit between its teeth & bolting. You are saying 'To interpret the present god-awful complex confusion one must unconfusedly use the language of god-awful confusion'... [T]here are a great many small points I'd like to question you about: such as your views on how much interrelation of dissociated ideas is possible in a single line without bursting the sense...[20]

Graves could hardly disguise his ambivalence. Her reply is remarkable for its self-assurance:

It is a long heroic poem. I cannot change it; but I believe a stricter technique would have reduced the poem and clarified what I wanted to say. On the other hand it would have been less pliable and adventurous and may have constrained that which I had purposely set out to do: which is to use words in relation to today – both with regard to sound (ie: discords ugly grating words) & meaning.[21]

A similar uncertainty about Roberts's diction underlies Eliot's query about 'Poem' (later the opening of Part II of *Gods*): 'The words *plimsole*, *cuprite*, *zebeline* and *neumes* seem to exist but I think that bringing them all into one short poem is a mistake', he tactfully suggests in a letter of 24 November 1943. The following month he accepts these words, telling her that he is convinced by her reasons – 'I like your defence of your queer words and now accept all of them, but I am still not happy about *zebeline*'.[22] Eliot's are editor's queries, but Graves's are more obviously grappling with something larger. The point of view Graves puts forward in his letter to Roberts is articulated in many of his critical interventions, from the *Survey of Modernist Poetry* (1927) which he wrote with Laura Riding, to the Clark Lectures of 1954. For Graves, 'modernism' is essentially a fractured response to a fractured world: for all its innovative bluster, it is tired, pessimistic and passive. It reveals something of Lynette Roberts's faith in what she was doing that she should have stood her ground so single-mindedly against poets of the stature of Graves and Eliot.

In a review of *Gods with Stainless Ears*, the *Times Literary Supplement* critic complained that 'the vocabulary needs a chemical glossary', going on to dismiss 'the contrast between the high tragic tones of the poet and the naivety of her incidents' as 'irresistibly ludicrous' (16 November 1951). The review is dismissive, but the reviewer has a point about the poem's contrasts: between grandiloquence and something altogether more artless or innocent. Tony Conran, in an essay on Roberts in his book *Frontiers in Anglo-Welsh Poetry*, offers perhaps the most perceptive comment made on what we could call Roberts's contextual lack of context:

> As with other primitives [Conran talks about John Clare and Emily Dickinson] these poets' viewpoint is eccentric to their culture's literary norm, though perhaps derivable from it. The primitive's isolation is in a sense a reflection of the isolation of all modernist art. That is perhaps why Henri Rousseau lived happily beside the cubists. But it is not necessarily the same thing as modernism, though most primitives would certainly claim to be 'modern'. Modernists create an environment in which primitives can come to the fore; so much so that 'primitive' and modernist can often be regarded as two sides of the same coin.[23]

Conran is right, not just in the detail of Lynette Roberts's place in the poetic tradition, but in the more sweeping suggestion he makes about the relationship between the modernist and the primitive. We need not go along with the term 'primitive' – even if Conran is careful to use it in inverted commas – because after all Roberts was educated, well-read, artistically trained, and, for all her 'outsiderness', moved in literary circles, but we can see what he means. We might prefer the term 'naïve' in the specific sense of the naïve painters, the tradition of Henri 'Douanier' Rousseau. A painterly poet, Lynette Roberts was herself a painter in the naïve tradition – one of her finest paintings, of Llanybri old chapel, depicts an angel circling above the village, with the bay in the background and enormous leeks rearing out from the vegetable patch. The painting is framed with a home-made border, designed by Roberts and based on the apron worn by Rosie, her neighbour. Often intricate, exact and harmonious, the 'naïve' painting is also eclectic in its combinations of images, and plays fast and loose with perspective and proportion, facets which, in poetry, might be compared with tone, and specifically with irony, itself the manipulation of emotional distance. Roberts is certainly not ironic; she is never above her subject, and her subject is never beneath poetry. She writes a 'Heroic Poem' and she *means* heroic. The past is no refuge but a fund of analogies, an archive of correspondences; and there is no fear of the future. Her subject is *today which is tomorrow* (*Gods with Stainless Ears*, Part V). Her work has no trace of cultural pessimism – on the contrary – and hers is not a poetry of 'shored fragments'. It may be 'difficult' – indeed it seeks out difficulty as much as it seeks to 'speak of everyday things with ease' (as she writes in 'The Shadow Remains') – but it is not contorted with self-reflexiveness, knowing allusions, or arcane learning. Even the speech fragments, however cut loose from their sources, are transcribed from real utterance, so that raw, unmediated speech coexists with the most overwrought language. This is not the stylised demotic of *The Waste Land*. She also has an enabling – and in the best sense unsophisticated – belief in language's sufficiency. We cannot imagine Pound or Eliot writing in their diaries: 'I experimented with a poem on Rain by using all words which had long thin letters [so that] the print of the pages would look like thin lines of rain.' Writing poetry is not 'a raid on the inarticulate' with shoddy equipment, but a way of bringing word and World into alignment. Her extraordinary freedoms of scale, subject and imaginative conception, her omnivorous diction and imagistic special effects, may at first glance appear similar to those of other modernist poets, but they are unique to Roberts, and to what we could call her 'home-made' world.

How to 'place' Lynette Roberts? And do we need to? *Poems* and *Gods with Stainless Ears* are unique books. Their freshness and originality are difficult to overstate, and cannot simply be explained by means of an intersection of influences and the convergence of biographical and cultural-historical circumstances. Certainly her work can be seen in the context of modernism, in whose second generation Roberts belongs. It obviously shares something with that of Pound and Eliot, but perhaps the nearest to her in vision and conception is David Jones, another poet who created from, and was created by, war and Wales. Her fascination with dialect and her cosmopolitan's idealisation of the simple life, combined with a contrasting taste for new-fangled, specialised or abstruse vocabulary, suggests something along the lines of Conran's modernist-primitive symbiosis. Roberts's work is set within a few square miles of coastline, among a particular people, their customs and their idioms. Roberts has a sense of the absolute

Llanybri Old Chapel by Lynette Roberts

coterminousness of past-in-present-in-future, intertwined as in a Celtic pattern: the archaic is a luminous guide to the contemporary, the mythical is a map of the real. Hers is a world, as she writes in Part I of *Gods with Stainless Ears*, 'where past/ Is not dead but comes uphot suddenly sharp as / Drakestone'. In her fascination with archaeology and geology, her sense of place as the layering of time, we might see unexpected (and strictly limited) similarities with the

Charles Olson of *Maximus*. In her modernism of the local she perhaps recalls (again in a limited but precise way) the William Carlos Williams of *Paterson*. In other respects – its tendency towards emphatic alliteration and assonance, its rhapsodic descriptions, vatic registers and grand abstractions – her poetry belongs to the 1940s, alongside the work of the 'Apocalypse' and New Romantic poets. As well as the poets of this period, Roberts shares something with the artists, specifically with painters such as Ceri Richards and Graham Sutherland, who worked on the peripheries of the literary scene of the time. Most strikingly perhaps, her poetic aerial views are also reminiscent of Eric Ravilious, war artist with the RAF, whose dramatic coastlines and images of planes and submarines make interesting comparison with Roberts's. Her work is also part of the twentieth-century flowering of Welsh poetry in English, the tradition of Dylan Thomas, Glyn Jones, Vernon Watkins, R.S. Thomas. Like these poets, Roberts has learned from the Welsh-language tradition, not just in verse technique but in literary heritage and cultural politics. Add to all this the work of Auden and MacNeice, and we have a poetry bristling with contexts, alive to its time and place even as it dazzlingly dramatises and reimagines them – a poetry open to influence and example while perfecting its own distinct voice and vision.

Patrick McGuinness
2005

1   Though Roberts is little-known, the critical work on her has by and large been insightful. *Poetry Wales* devoted an invaluable special issue (1983, 19/2) to her, containing essays by Anthony Conran and John Pikoulis, extracts from her autobiography and her correspondence with Robert Graves. For essays and articles on Roberts, see especially: Tony Conran, 'Lynette Roberts: War Poet', in *The Cost of Strangeness: Essays on the English Poets of Wales* (Llandysul: Gomer, 1983); 'Lynette Roberts: The Lyric Pieces' (*Poetry Wales*, 1983, 19/2); and 'Lynette Roberts', *Frontiers in Anglo-Welsh Poetry* (Cardiff: University of Wales Press, 1997); John Pikoulis, 'Lynette Roberts and Alun Lewis', (*Poetry Wales* 1983, 19/2); 'The Poetry of the Second World War', in *British Poetry 1900–50*, ed. Gary Day and Brian Docherty (London: Macmillan, 1995). Nigel Wheale, 'Lynette Roberts: Legend and Form in the 1940s', *Critical Quarterly* (1994, 36/3); '"Beyond the Trauma Stratus": Lynette Roberts' *Gods with Stainless Ears* and the Post-War Cultural Landscape', *Welsh Writing in English*, vol. 3 (1997). Among poets, her work has been of interest principally to those of an 'experimental' or 'avant-garde' temper. For a profound and updated engagement with Roberts's themes and manner, see John Wilkinson's poem 'Sarn Helen', subtitled 'Homage to Lynette Roberts and for Friends in Swansea'.

2   Lewis's poem for Roberts was 'Peace' in *Raiders' Dawn* (1941), an unsettling and oblique poem with a final note of optimism. She told him 'My poem is real i.e. true of the everyday things I do. Yours is mythical', and the poetic exchange is all the more poignant for the fact that three years later Lewis would be dead. Alun Lewis's letters to Roberts and Keidrych Rhys appear in *Wales* (February/

March, 1948, VIII/28). For an account of the friendship between Lynette Roberts and Alun Lewis, see John Pikoulis's essay in the *Poetry Wales* special issue on Lynette Roberts. In the same issue Tony Conran's essay 'Lynette Roberts: The Lyric Pieces' discusses Roberts's connections with the Welsh-language poetic tradition.

3   *The Collected Letters of Dylan Thomas*, ed. Paul Ferris (London: Dent, 1985), p. 418.

4   Ibid.

5   Quoted in *Poetry Wales*, Lynette Roberts special issue, p. 14.

6   Keidrych Rhys, *The Van Pool and Other Poems* (London: Routledge, 1942), p. 9.

7   *Collected Letters of Dylan Thomas*, p. 419.

8   I am grateful to Wynn Thomas for pointing this out to me.

9   *Village Dialect*, (Carmarthen: Druid Press, 1944), p. 12. In July 1944 Dylan Thomas wrote 'Lynette, who cannot read Welsh, is revising the standard nineteenth-century book on Welsh prosody, and also annotating a work on the hedgerows of Carmarthenshire. I hope she becomes famous & that they will name an insect after her' (*Collected Letters*, p. 518).

10 Unpublished typescript, untitled and dated 2 September 1943.

11 Nigel Wheale, 'Lynette Roberts: Legend and Form in the 1940s', p. 5.

12 *Village Dialect*, p. 24.

13 The same raid was witnessed by the artist Arthur Giardelli who comments on the mismatch between Roberts's poem (which he describes as having the feel of a Paul Nash painting) and the reality it both works on and climbs free of: 'It isn't like my experience at all […] exceedingly dramatic but to me about complete devastation: fires still burning, smoke, the dash of water out of a pipe hour after

hour. [...] It is a superb poem, but she's using her intellect, her imagination and vision' (Arthur Giardelli, *Paintings Constructions Relief Sculptures: Conversations with Derek Shiel* (Bridgend: Seren, n.d.), pp. 68–9.

14 Keith Douglas, 'How to Kill', *The Complete Poems* (London: Faber, 2000), p. 119.
15 'Frostwork and the Mud Vision' *The Cambridge Quarterly* (2002, 31/1), p. 98, a review of Keith Tuma's *Anthology of Twentieth-Century British and Irish Poetry* (New York: Oxford University Press, 2001).
16 'Simplicity of the Welsh Village', *The Field*, 7 July 1945, p. 8.
17 Ibid., p. 9.
18 Nigel Wheale, 'Beyond the Trauma Stratus', p. 99.
19 'The Welsh Dragon, *Times Literary Supplement*, 29 August 1952, p. xxxi.
20 *Poetry Wales* Lynette Roberts special issue, p. 82.
21 Ibid., p. 84
22 The Eliot-Roberts correspondence dates from summer 1942 to December 1953, and is unpublished.
23 Anthony Conran, *Frontiers in Anglo-Welsh Poetry*, p. 166.

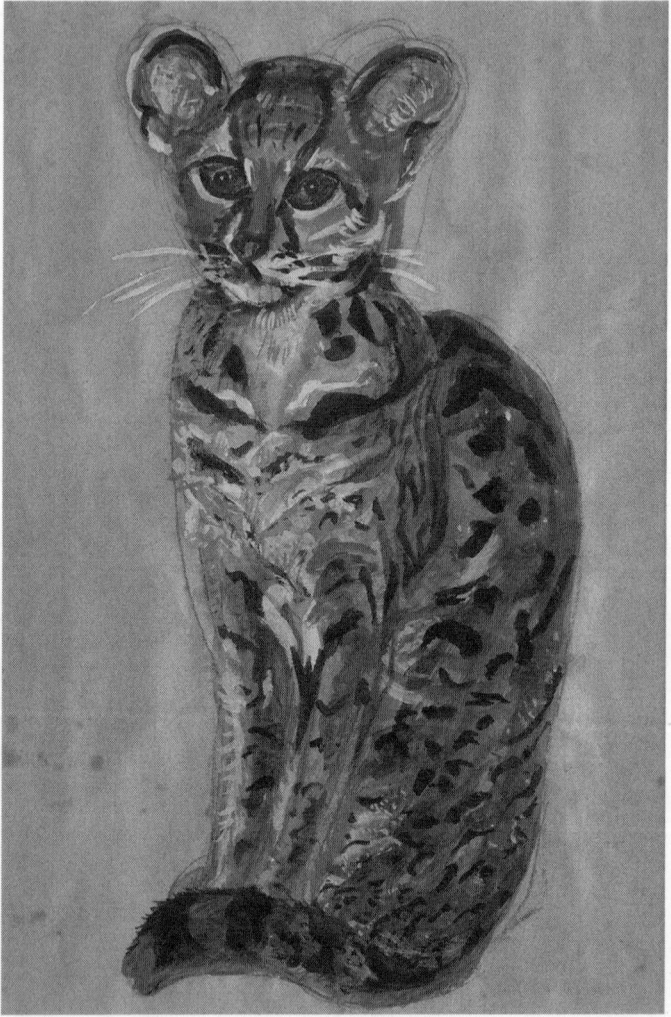

Margay (wild cat), by Lynette Roberts. (Photograph and image reproduced by kind permission of Angharad and Prydein Rhys.)

ACKNOWLEDGEMENTS

Our greatest debt of thanks goes to Lynette's daughter, Angharad Rhys, who has supported the first, and this new edition of collected poems, with her endless encouragement, knowledge and good humour. No one who has worked on Lynette Roberts can fail to be grateful to her critics and advocates. Most notably Tony Conran, Nate Dorward, Keith Tuma, John Pikoulis, Nigel Wheale and John Wilkinson have all in different ways made compelling cases for her stature and interest, and kept the memory of her remarkable poetry alive. *PN Review* first published 'A Letter to the Dead' and republished several previously uncollected poems. Chris Miller, Angharad Price and M. Wynn Thomas gave invaluable advice on matters of interpretation, contextualisation and translation, and Osi and Hilary Osmond were inspiring guides to the landscapes of Lynette's poems: *diolch o galon i chi gyd.*

Patrick McGuinness and Charles Mundye

2025

NOTE ON THE TEXT

Poems (1944) and *Gods with Stainless Ears* (1951) are presented here as they originally appeared, with Roberts's own notes at the back of each volume. Poems previously uncollected by Roberts are arranged by chronological date of publication. Many of Lynette Roberts's papers are held in the Harry Ransom Center at the University of Texas at Austin. Unpublished poems are taken from manuscripts in the Harry Ransom Center, the Robert Graves Archive at St John's College Oxford, and from papers in the possession of the Lynette Roberts Estate. The earliest most complete manuscript is used as the basis wherever this has been possible to establish, ignoring later emendations. Obvious errors of spelling and typography have been corrected, spelling and presentation have been made consistent, and some older conventions have been modernised. The editors' notes are in the conventional place at the back of the book.

POEMS

1944

Lynette Roberts on her father's yacht in Argentina. (Photograph reproduced by kind permission of Angharad and Prydein Rhys.)

POEM FROM LLANYBRI

If you come my way that is...
Between now and then, I will offer you
A fist full of rock cress fresh from the bank
The valley tips of garlic red with dew
Cooler than shallots, a breath you can swank

In the village when you come. At noon-day
I will offer you a choice bowl of cawl
Served with a 'lover's' spoon and a chopped spray
Of leeks or savori fach, not used now,

In the old way you'll understand. The din
Of children singing through the eyelet sheds
Ringing smith hoops, chasing the butt of hens;
Or I can offer you Cwmcelyn spread

With quartz stones from the wild scratchings of men:
You will have to go carefully with clogs
Or thick shoes for it's treacherous the fen,
The East and West Marshes also have bogs.

Then I'll do the lights, fill the lamp with oil,
Get coal from the shed, water from the well;
Pluck and draw pigeon with crop of green foil
This your good supper from the lime-tree fell.

A sit by the hearth with blue flames rising,
No talk. Just a stare at 'Time' gathering
Healed thoughts, pool insight, like swan sailing
Peace and sound around the home, offering

You a night's rest and my day's energy.
You must come – start this pilgrimage
Can you come? – send an ode or elegy
In the old way and raise our heritage.

THE SHADOW REMAINS

To speak of everyday things with ease
And arrest the mind to a simpler world
Where living tables are stripped of a cloth;

Of wood on which I washed, sat at peace:
Cooked duck, shot on an evening in peacock cold:
Studied awhile: wrote: baked bread for us both.

But here by the hearth with leisured grace
I prefer to speak of the vulgar clock that drips
With the falling of rain: woodbine tips, and yarrow

Spills, lamp, packet of salt, and twopence of mace
That sit on the shelf edged with a metal strip,
And below, brazier fire that burns our sorrow,

Dries weeping socks above on the rack: that knew
Two angels pinned to the wall – again two.

PLASNEWYDD

You want to know about my village.
You should want to know even if you
Don't want to know about my village.
My village is very small. You could
Pass it with a winning gait. Smile.
They stand in corners plain talking,
Flick the cows passing down our way.
The women – that's the men,
Pull their aprons over their heads.
They put another around their hips,
Blue sprigged white… so…
Another to cover the one underneath
Pity to spoil: 'Best Hundredweight of
Cow Cakes': sacking stitched and homemade.
Now we are used to such things
Never laugh at their ways for
Our own asides carry a larger tale.
We sit and sit in a cornered rut
We pine for our love to thin the rhythm
From out of our hearts
WAR. 'There's no sense in it.
Just look at her two lovely eyes
Look at those green big big eyes
And the way she hangs her tail.
Like a weasel. Ferret. Snowball
Running away on the breast of a hill.
WAR. There's no sense in it
For us simple people
We all get on so well.
Hal-e-bant.

The cows are on the move.
I must be off on the run:
Hal-e-bant. *pussy drwg*.
Hal-e-bant Fan Fach
Hal-e-bant for the day is long
We must strengthen it:
Ourselves:
To the cows
Fetch them in.'

LOW TIDE

Every waiting moment is a fold of sorrow
Pierced within the heart.
Pieces of mind get torn off emotionally,
In large wisps
Like a waif I lie, stillbound to action:
Each waiting hour I stare and see not,
Hum and hear not, nor, care I how long
The lode mood lasts.
My eyes are raw and wide apart
Stiffened by the salt bar
That separates us.
You so far;
I at ease at the hearth
Glowing for a welcome
From your heart.
Each beating moment crosses my dream
So that wise things cannot pass
As we had planned.
Woe for all of us: supporting those

Who like us fail to steel their hearts,
But keep them wound in clocktight rooms,
Ill found. Unused. Obsessed by time.
Each beating hour
Rings false.

RAW SALT ON EYE

Stone village, who would know that I lived alone:
Who would know that I suffered a two-edged pain,
Was accused of spycraft to full innate minds with loam,
Was felled innocent, suffered a stain as rare as Cain's.

Amelia Phillips, who would know that I lived lonely,
Who would know old shrew that your goose's wing
Did more for me than the plucked asides of daily
Nods: yet I had need of both to prove my sting.

Cold grate, who would know that I craved my love;
Who would know the pain fell twice; could realize
My loss. Only the coloured cries of stars can prove
The cold rise of dawn – understand and advise.

White village, I lost my love. – He went floating
Brushing the wet seas. He stood like a soldier trapped
And thought of me but could not speak. Fighting
Hard he stood, freeing nations the old enemy cramped.

Hard people, will wash up now, bake bread and hang
Dishcloth over the weeping hedge. I can not raise
My mind, for it has gone wandering away with him
I shall not forget; and your ill-mannered praise.

I walk and cinder bats riddle my cloak
I walk to Cwmcelyn ask prophets the way.

'There is no way they cried crouched on the hoarstone rock
And the Dogs of Annwn roared louder than of late.'

'Red fever will fall with the maytide blossom
Fever as red as your cloak. Woe to all men.
Food-ties will mellow in the bromine season
Then willowed peace may be brought.'

But what of my love I cried
As a curlew stabbed the sand:

And we cut for the answer. They said
'He would come not as he said he would come
But later with sailing ice, war glass and fame:
Grieve not it is better so.'

I left the Bay, wing felled and bogged
Kicked the shale despondent and green

Heard Rosie say lace curtained in clogs
I've put a Yule log on your grate.

LAMENTATION

To the village of lace and stone
Came strangers. I was one of these
Always observant and slightly obscure.
I roamed the hills of bird and bone
Rescuing bees from under the storm:
Five hills rocked and four homes fell
The day I remember the raid so well.
Eyes shone like cups chipped and stiff
The living bled the dead lay in their grief
Cows, sheep, horses, all had got struck
Black as bird wounds, red as wild duck.

Dead as icebone breaking the hedge.
Dead as soil failing of good heart.
Dead as trees quivering with shock
At the hot death from the plane.

O the cold loss of cattle
With their lovely big eyes.
The emptiness of sheds,
The rick stacked high.
The breast of the hills
Will soon turn grey
As the dogs that grieve
And I that fetched them in:
For the good gates are closed
In the yard down our way.

'But my loss. My loss is deeper
Than Rosie's of Chapel House Farm
For I met death before birth:

Fought for life and in reply lost
My own with a cold despair.
I hugged the fire around the hearth
To warm the beat and wing
Yet knew the symbol when it came
Lawrence had found the same.
I threw the starling hard as stone
Into the breaking earth...'

Dead as icebone breaking the hedge
Dead as soil failing of good heart.
Dead as trees quivering with shock
At the hot death from the plane.

      O the salt loss of life
      Her lovely green ways.
      The emptiness of crib
      And big stare of night.
      The breast of the hills
      Yield a bucket of milk:
      But the crane no longer cries
      With the round birds at dawn
      For the home has been shadowed
      A storm of sorrow drowned the way.

BROKEN VOICES

Here a perfect people set – on red rock,
      White and grey as gull met
    Pure to plough, each prince hamlet
    Of slate strong as rate ticket.

Now one mouth twisting twelve tongues – of the flock
      Unlocked the padlocked lungs:
    Slung a trail of steaming dung
    Blocking path of two not sung.

Stained virgin village with dearth – for the mock
      Like strumpet jet, rocked mirth
    And farmer: brought no more worth
    Than winding sheet of sour berth.

When gossip kneads to grave crust, – with feared shock
      Runs into fox of dust,
    Then shall the two minds discussed
    Remain bold with new sung trust.

EARTHBOUND

I, in my dressing gown,
At the dressing table with mirror in hand
Suggest my lips with accustomed air, see
The reflected van like lipstick enter the village
When Laura came, and asked me if I knew.

We had known him a little, yet long enough:
Drinking in all rooms, mild and bitter,
Laughing and careless under the washing-line tree.

The day so icy when we gathered the moss,
The frame made from our own wire and cane;
Ivy in perfect scale, roped with fruit from the same root:
And from the Pen of Flowers those which had survived the frost.

We made the wreath standing on the white floor;
Bent each to our purpose wire to rose-wire;
Pinning each leaf smooth,
Polishing the outer edge with the warmth of our hands.

The circle finished and note thought out,
We carried the ring through the attentive eyes of the street:
Then slowly drove by Butcher's Van to the 'Union Hall'.

We walked the greaving room alone,
Saw him lying in his upholstered box,
Violet ribbon carefully crossed,
And about his sides bunches of wild thyme.
No one stirred as we offered the gift. No one drank there again.

SPRING

The full field.
The stiff line of trees.
The antiseptic grass – dew shining.
The green,
Spraying from shorn hedgerows.
Sodium earth dug hard;
Bound by the fury of the earth's lower crust.

Black bending cattle nose to the warmth.
Pebble sheep pant to a lighter tune.
To high air sustained.
To high springing air.
To blue-life-mist rising from the flaming earth.

On aconite shade and xerophyte fern
Dull sheep lie:
That heat 'Lamb's Ear'.
That heat farmer's head.
That heat rick and roar,
Into a raging flame.

From innermost earth.
From fire underground.
From fire out of sight.
From rising fire in the sky
To Spring.
All glory,
And faith in mankind.

RHODE ISLAND RED

Spade jackets and tapping jackdaws on boles of wood,
    Song of joy I sing.
Prim-pied under sky full of fresh livelihood,
    Smile for eye of man.
Outhouses sweet with air stand whitened by the flood,
    Of sun blanching spring.
In plate green meadows sheepdog and farmer brood,
    On galvanised can.
Calling cattle from celandine and clover to mood,
    Song of joy I sing.

ECLIPTIC BLUE

In the cold when sea-mews flake the sky
With their curmurring fight for the eye
Of food on water blue, I think of snow.
              I think alone.

I think of the sea its tall high waves
Of the eyes that it seeks, of the lives
That say the waves seek dead, it is not so
They are not dead.

For sea gives more than it takes and spreads
No stain of death on life of man, but treads
The dead for further flight, as sea-mews know,
              As sea-mews go.

POEM

We must uprise O my people. Though
Secretly trenched in sorrel, we must
Upshine outshine the day's sun: and day
Intensified by the falling prism
Of rain shall curve our smile with straw.

Bring plimsole plover to the tensile sand
And with cuprite crest and petulant feet
Distil our notes into febrile reeds
Crisply starched at the water-rail of tides.
On gault and greensand a gramophone stands:

In zebrine stripes strike out the pilotless
Age: from saxophone towns brass out the dead:
Disinter futility, that we entombing men
Might bridle our runaway hearts.
On tamarisk, on seafield pools shivering

With water-cats, ring out the square slate notes.
Shape the birdbox trees with neumes. Wind sound
Singular into cool and simple corners,
Round pale bittern grass, and all unseen
Unknown places of sheltered rubble

Where whimbrels, redshanks, sandpipers ripple
For the wing of living. Under tin of earth
And wooden boles where owls break music:
From this killing world against humanity,
Uprise against, outshine the day's sun.

WOODPECKER

In elm no bird of jade
Shall creep with cold grey toes
For where I am when the spray
Of green sunlocks the bay
Married to song, mocks the day
    In town no bird.

In town no bird alloy
Shall graze my heart's shy grace,
For here at the lathe when the ring
Of steel threads the spring
For a chromium plane, I sing
    In town no bird.

In town no bird, O greenscarlet
Fate on a white-eyed quest,
A black stave quavers the brain
Drills and derides the reign
Of shells with laughter's bane,
    In town no bird.

In town no bird, too late
To shrive with hot house tears,
For now with jazz in sky alone
Among the purr of metal wings
A coloured band resounds my grief
    In town no bird.

CURLEW

A curlew hovers and haunts the room.
On bare boards creak its filleted feet:
For freedom intones four notes of doom,

Crept, slept, wept, kept, under aerial gloom:
With Europe restless in his wing beat,
A curlew hovers and haunts the room:

Fouls wire, pierces the upholstery bloom,
Strikes window pane with shagreen bleat,
Flicking scarlet tongue to a frenzied fume

Splints his curved beak on square glass tomb:
Runs to and fro seeking mudsilt retreat;
Captured, explodes a chill sky croon

Wail-ing... pal-ing... a desolate phantom
At the bath rim *purring burbling trilling soft sweet*
Syllables of sinuous sound to a liquid moon

Till window, wide, frees thin mails of plume,
Fluting voice and shade through cloud's moist sleet:
A curlew hovers and haunts the room.

MOORHEN

That this, so common an event
In so deplorable a State
Should draw a wreath of joy
From our pale reeded hearts:
That she, without interference
Or compound political tags,
Can, so easily, paddle out
Her freshest brood of sleek black hens:
Stealing the water's shine with elm-
Webbed stretch, the ribbons of sun
Winding around their necks:
Timely jerks purling through
Grisailles of rain – shocking the air
With scarlet bill and garter.
A bank rat sharpening his teeth
Might up on his haunches to listen:
A wise owl with rabbit ears
Could hardly frown at all this fuss.

SEAGULLS

Seagulls' easy glide
Drifting fearlessly as voyagers' tears:
Quay and ship move as imperceptively,
Without knowing we weep.

Cry gulls who recall
An ocean of uncertainty;
Greed of rowing men
Mere flies at the ship's sides.

Last bargains roped and reached:
And as imperceptively regretted,
Tears of fury and stupidity
Reel down the runnels of those cheeks.

FIFTH OF THE STRATA

And the sea will insist
Persuade a path to follow,
Longs eagerly to cover
The green valley pastures:
To flow forward along
The sunken ribbed coomb
And dry river-bed... endlessly.
And it will succeed
Tomorrow follow
All gravel roads
And rise slowly around
The Dragon's scaled Fort;
To leave nothing of Wales
But white island shining
The crest of Snowdon
Glittering with dark wintry-ice.

Find no woe in this:
For this is tomorrow.
And before tomorrow
England will be
For thousands of years
Lying below us
A submerged village
Like weeping Halkin;
When other and better banks
Dry from ocean beds,
Built of crystalline rock
And sharp shell and shale
Will arise for our freedom
For *our* feet to follow:
And this shall be always,
As it is never.

So that magnetism pierces each blight
And shallow ring: sends a scaffold of light
Through suspended hills, drinks truculent sight

And water-silk of day, floating splashing
Eyelashes on about air, swilling
Swallows clean against Sunday, clearing

Breasts whiter than butterflies low over sill;
Who glazed this day? Fetched labourers to spill
About soil, spading like hairpins to till

Of earth. Who gently lifts a strawberry set,
Opens row to shine streamlets of violet sweat,
Sun concentrating on circlet of dust a banquet

Of warmth: tends garden twine unravelled on path,
Liquid gleam round each raceme of grass, an aftermath
That quavers like parakeet fresh out of its bath.

Who polished this day? String of mackerel and glue
Sized and scoured sky to its finest grain of blue:
Flashed motor spirit through each splint of wing: drew

And transfixed man at his most monstrous art of war:
Picked out world mildew and muddled indifference; saw
Heart, pressure of steel, culled into a shadowed claw

Sharpen infinity, and all trees of branched iron,
Leaves elliptical pinnate sprayed thinly over rinsed apron
Of space, their metallic hue so starkly crisp, enamel legion

Of the partial eclipse: darkening nature
Finding a ferret of lines in each feature:
Who clipped this white-eyed splendour? Barbed-wire-fixture.

Meat cover on slab of slate prosecuting inkstand
Cold basin and porcelain plate. Day's bristol shine: a band
Of empty beer bottles, wine jars green for thirst. So reprimand

And commemorate, for this day will come again, war and day,
Imprisoning each other with shylock glint: betray
Clashing bayonets, hold up of sunny sideboard and pay.

Who ran with the sun sandpapered the way? You
Under arcade of bracelet blue: or was it the view
That clarified Thursday, September nineteen forty-two.

HOUSE OF COMMONS

When rose-hips red as braziers shine from the hedge
And spring with natural grace over quick snapping sill,
I suggest to you, is fear the backbone of a pledge,

The spine-cord of tradition, frail people on edge:
Those, who sit upstairs and make old promises with skill,
When rose-hips red as braziers shine from the hedge

And are taut and jumpy to catch from the ledge
So that to fill a promise means leaping the water-mill,
I suggest to you, is fear the backbone of a pledge;

That they do not hasten the experiment, but hedge
And let a brandy hen with its vermilion gill,
When rose-hips red as braziers shine from the hedge

Outshine them both, do what they would not with courage
Cross the wet mill and find the rare Dusky Crane's Bill.
I suggest to you, is fear the backbone of a pledge

That people mild as ducks seem put out by the sedge,
By things so natural, preferring drudge and privilege.
When rose-hips red as braziers shine from the hedge
I suggest to you, is fear the backbone of a pledge?

CROSSED AND UNCROSSED

Heard the steam rising from the chill blue bricks,
Heard the books sob and the buildings huge groan
As the hard crackle of flames leapt on firemen
              and paled the red walls.

Bled their hands in anguish to check the fury
Knowing fire had raged for week and a day:
Clung to buildings like swallows flat and exhausted
              under the storm.

Fled the sky: fragments of the Law, kettles and glass:
Lamb's ghost screamed: Pegasus melted and fell
Meteor of shining light on to a stone court
              and only wing grave.

Round Church built in a Round Age, cold with grief,
Coloured Saints of glass lie buried at your feet:
Crusaders uncross limbs by the green light of flares,
              burn into Tang shapes.

Over firedrake floors the 'Smith' organ pealed
Roared into flames when you proud widow
Ran undaunted: the lead roof dripping red tears
              curving to crash.

Treasure was saved. Your loyalty broke all sight,
Revived the creed of the Templars of old;
Long lost. Others of the Inn escaped duty
              in black hats.

Furniture out, slates ripped off, yet persistently
Hoovering the remaining carpet, living as we all do
Blanketed each night, with torch, keys, emergency basket
                    close by your side.

From paper window we gaze at the catacomb of books,
You, unflinching, stern of spirit, ready to
Gather charred sticks to fight no gas where gas was
                    everywhere escaping.

Through thin library walls where 'Valley' still grows,
From Pump Court to dry bank of rubble, titanic monsters
Roll up from the Thames, to drown the 'storm' should it
                    dare come again.

Still water silences death: fills night with curious light,
Brings green peace and birds to top of Plane tree
Fills Magnolia with grail thoughts: while you of King's Bench
                    Walk, cherish those you most love.

THE SEASONS

Spring which has its appeal in ghosts,
Youth, resurrection, cleansing of the soil,
And in dormant roots already considered,
Stirs, with the sharpening of branches
Challenges heart to do that which it cannot,
Sustain overwork, overthought, overlove.
It clears a path for hope: reinstates
Faith, which we had too easily omitted
With death, in the caustic months of the year.

Summer proclaims joy, laughter before its
Arrival: and deceives us into malice
With its non appearance. It suggests
A romance that we have not received
Sunny balconies in the mind: the seldom
Forgotten perfect island summer with its
Warm haze on flesh, flower, and hide:
The blossoming of their structure, fragrance
And appeal, from their own root recorded.

Autumn comes strutting in like a cockerel,
Red, blue, yellow and brown. It disintegrates
Our purpose of singular thought; destroys
Relationships: and cuts the sap of pride
Ruthlessly. Those who survive retain one heart
And voice. Yet autumn with contrawise motion
Shields the creative mind with covering of leaves,
Settles and matures dormant growth which will
Reappear, under the hard skies of spring.

Winter exceeds the year with impunity:
Devours us of all greed: and freezes
That residue. It upholds that which is not:
Which is, the blaze of summer biting
Into our nature for a future reappeal.
Winter intones loss of all things:
Is the next step to death which is loneliness:
Comfort and warmth to be found around our own
Heart and grate, within the steel ribs of this age.

ORARIUM

He whom my heart sings to
Is gone alone home;
And I am left,
Onela,
Alone in a wood of tears
In the woodlight
Alone.
Birds fly to no purpose
Birds cannot sing
When I am about,
For they dread the tale
Of old,
13 hundred years ago;
When man of God could
And would be saved by God,
Alone.
Over alluvial plains
Through brushwood keeps
And harrowed land,

There lay on pale sweet ground
A head of fire
Open to the wind,
Flaming to the skies
Hallowing the sun
From under the wind.
To desperate wings
And melting tide,
Soundmind lost;
Soundmind never
Accounted for.
Caedmon on the shell tip
Saw, back to Streanaeshalch
With his third eye set on the Abbess Hild,
Waiting for his death,
His telling of the tale,
The old tale,
Retold.

Not for all Heaven was he the loveliest
Lying in cold expectation;
Denying Kings his image in the last round.
His huge woolly head full of sparks and spires.
Not for all Heaven was he the gentlest
Easy to acquire grace and *hebankuningas*,
Mounting pulpits, hands and mind to a wooded measure.
Not for all Heaven was he the bravest
Facing the last storm – alone on the shore,
Fevered with anxiety of another life
Tearing wild angels flitting among his brain,
Falling into precipice of mind and monastery.
Not for all Heaven was this to take place,
But for the good of man: for the simple things he loved:
The heart on green: beasts rising from the earth: for his herds:

For his dream to be retold for his sandcoloured nights
Clothed with the visions of the preceding monks
Chanting over hills; white with their powdered breath
Of pure song and intermediate praise.
Three grouped: stern walls: sky and hills moist:
These familiar sights alone held his brain,
Forced them to bitter images of life and death:
To the tale I tell of deeper times
When man of God could and would
Be saved by God alone. To the moment of darkness
Which fell with the moment of Greater Light:
To the Commanding Vision and Sensitive Mind of God:
To waterpeace and mist: this being the end of all.
This being the God-Head to which he returned,
With his flaming head and proud sorrel chest.

IN SICKNESS AND IN HEALTH

Convent of cold stream.
Convent of white ice stiff on each heart
Break boundary of death.
O strictly forget the accustomed torture.

Turn to fireflames ringing bells for sorrowing souls
Stretched damp out of green bone.
To warmth of blood affinity, dissolved in earth elemental,
Crisp crust of red.
To mauve muslin: flight of hovering flames:
Break fire diaphanous,
Use discipline to feed-guide its flame;

The hearth is yours,
She within it with you over the pain.

Turn solace addressed by care;
The icicle cannot pierce deeper than it has,
And it will dissolve invisibly
As miracles do into thin blue air:
Brush no eyes in passing,
But your own – to leave red rims free from torture.
Death shall not be.
The surrender to another:
The step straight – spare:
Concert of cold stream nursed by another's wing
Who thaws and quenches pain whether hot or cold;
Stepping on clean stones through flood and mudsilt of war,
Sleeping on clear pillow – an angel heads the bed.

BLOOD AND SCARLET THORNS

Who bends the plain to waist of night
And stems the bird to tree of flight,
Who stretches leagues to see a bone
Of bison cast as proud as stone,
Who lengthens maize and sweeps the light
Of grenadine right out of sight;
It is the hard and monstrous plight
Of weeping birth this citron dawn,
       This citron dawn,
A heart breaks through the ice of night
Who is, and bursts a paper kite

That sails the day into a dome
Of joy, and tears, and monotone,
This day maintained: a child was born,
                    A child was born.

RAINSHIVER

Rain freezes our senses.
Our gills fill with a drill motion:
Chills the air and stills the billing birds
To shrill not trill as they should
In this daffodil spring.
We till away, killing pests,
Filling the rills with commercial pills.
We will the sownseed to live in spite of
The swill spouting from the sky.
Rain instils our mind with imperilled dampness;
Rain fells our own skilled discipline
In long stiff strides,
Milling up seedsown with our spilling fists.
Rain falls, drips even from frilled shelves
And envelopes; splashing ink on mourning edges,
Overbrimming pools of wet water;
Rain comes streaming down where there is too much
Falling, drips drops, in wet circles on pond;
Duck dives and bank rats, even they hate
The pelting stinging rain
That beats into their heart
Rings of woe on zinc covered roofs,
On rusty baths and pale iron spikes.

ROYAL MAIL

I would see again São Paulo:
The coffee coloured house with its tarmac roof
And spray of tangerine berries.
I would again climb the mountain cable
And see Pernambuco with its dark polished table,
The brilliance of its sky piercing through the trees
Like so much Byzantine glass or clear Grecian frieze.
As we stumble higher strolling gourds and air-plants
Spring from muscoid branch to barnacle wire:
I would see old man should it come my way,
The mahogany pyramids of burnished berries, gay
With surf-like attitudes of men sitting around
In crisp white suits, starch to the ground.
The peacock struts and nets mimicrying butterflies,
And the fazenda shop clinking like ice in an enamel jug
As you open the door. The stench of wine-wood,
Saw-dust, maize flour, pimentos, and basket of birds,
With the ear-tipped 'Molto bien signorit' and the hot mood
Blazing from the drooping noon. Outside sweating gourds
Dripping rind and peel; yet inside cool as lemon,
Orange, avocado pear.
While in this damp and stony stare of a village
Such images are unknown:
So would I think upon these things
In the event that someday I shall return to my native surf
And feel again the urgency of sun and soil.

THE NEW WORLD

Memory widens our senses, folds them open:
Ancient seas slip back like iguanas and reveal
Plains of space, free, sky-free, lifting a green tree
　　　　　on to a great plain.

Heard legend whistling through the waiting jabirú,
Knew the two-fold saying spinning before their eyes
Breaking life like superstition, they too
　　　　　might become half-crazed.

Staring sitting under the shade of Ombú tree,
Living from the dust: kettles simmer on sticks,
Maté strengthens their day's work like dew
　　　　　on hot dry grass.

So the people baking too close fulfilled time,
Bricks became mud walls and the legend flared high,
Shadows broke, flames frowned and bent the sky
　　　　　proclaiming Indian omens.

Roofs fell clattering in on man and child,
Black framed their faces, from fire not from sun:
While before them land divided announcing
　　　　　stake peggers' loud claim.

Death ate their hearts like locusts over a croaking plain,
Fell tears red as fireflies on the rising dust;
Barbed wire fenced them in or fenced them out,
　　　　　these outcasts of the land.

So the people fled unwanted further on into the land,
On to the Plain of White Ashes where thorns spread
Like the wreath of Christ. Further out on to
                    the ancient Sea of Rhea.

Ombú turned hollow as it stood alone:
Spiders lifted the lids of their homes and slammed them
    back
Sorrow set the plovers screaming at the falling
                    hoofs and feet:

Cinchas bound their eaten hearts: leather sealed their lips;
Ponchos warmed their pumpkin pride: as insects floated,
As windmills grew. Ventevéo! Ventevéo! And further they
                    strove, the harder not to be seen.

Lost now. No sound or care can revive their ways:
La Plata gambles on their courage, spends too flippantly,
Mocks beauty from the shading tree, mounts a corrugated
    roof
                    over their cultured hut.

ARGENTINE RAILWAYS

To you who walked so proudly down the line,
Promoting men from engine plates, skilled
Workers from the sheds: the Board soon killed
The cut you had to socialise the 'decline'.

You, who planned man's bonus among the whine
And shrill of people on the go; filled
The sleeper's clock with admiration; drilled
Time in travelling into a close combine.

But now I prefer to think of you set back
Upon the land, with eucalyptus trees
Shading corral from dust: plan as you please

The round hill into a wholesome farm. 'Their' lack
To accept your methods receive with ease,
For they will come to that in the end or 'freeze'.

XAQUIXAGUANA

In the lake of pools
Where icebergs stand firm on the ground,
And refrain to move for beauty of their image,
Five Temples lie wounded on their sides
Each plundered and more progressive than the last.
I speak of the one with the grey-crusted sleepers
Sitting in the splint-blue cave.
Especially he, of the up-side-down burial
With arrows set like buhls in the rib of the wreck:
Who was this white man of Peru?
And what flat burial did he deserve
To stir their sandstone agave? To face emerald sky
And snarling rocks where the sun's tied up:
Lying stiff among gold filaments and animate clay
Snouting Azrael forms and intricate beads:
Those Huacas spread and exposed under cacti waterbeds,
Green as tunas, weathered with poisoned alizarin darts
Who was this man who stole their store of gold?
Who found down here down Pilcomayo way
Near lion grass and glass birds sailing the lake,
Who was he, that lies buried at the Haravec's feet
Aggrieved by this ice and basaltic sheet?

RIVER PLATE

The pampas are for ever returning
The orange river pounding the sea,
From high dry plain with tint of tea
La Plata spreads, and churns drowning
The dust from the charcas murmuring
At the bare roots of the Ombú tree:
The pampas are for ever returning
Bright green birds into piranha sea.
Over spare-dust and barbed wire slowly
Cattle die from thirst wounds, returning
Like maté ships shivering, bringing
No sound but white bones back to me:
The pampas are for ever returning
Bad bones and dust into an angry sea.

CANZONE BENEDICTO

The bell tolls from umbrella woods:
And we follow with black silk hands
Through round monastery walls to find no one there.

The bees have led us astray:
And on the turning back through death and turpentine halls
We glance tersely at the torturous Stations
Raised by the tall pillars of Rome.

Beyond glass door and circean group of sisters and swine;
Following blue serge and thin button boots;
Passing yellow chair and baskets of endless peel,
We cut our gravel paths and broke through Refectory tables.

From bread and wine interval, nuns of the red medallion
Timed our shoed-exit with glove-stick hands,
And crossed our way with the opulent ways of the Order
So that we, the pale collative faces beat a solemn retreat.

Again past cool black air and caladium altars;
Flicking water and humea into our long white thoughts
Which stretched into veils and caught our hair
On terra-cotta vases held by monandrian palms.

The chimes hastened, echoing our feet on the Aztec mosaic
As we broke light and entered the moist patio,
Its boracic colonnade squared with seraphic blue:
We were there. We were free to talk.

But still to their fury I remained the veronese mask:
The white washed statue.
The calandria in the shade.

CWMCELYN
PART FIVE FROM A LONGER POEM

'... mi a glywais lais y pedwerydd anifail yn dywedyd, Tyred, a gwêl.

Ac mi a edrychais; ac wele farch gwelw-las: ac enw yr hwn oedd yn eistedd arno oedd Marwolaeth: ac yr oedd Uffern yn canlyn gyd âg ef. A rhoddwyd iddynt awdurdod ar y bedwaredd ran o'r ddaear, i ladd â chleddyf, ac â marwolaeth, ac â bwyst-filod y ddaear.

A phan agorodd efe y bummed sêl, mi a welais dan yr allor eneidiau y rhai a laddesid am air Duw, ac am y dystiolaeth oedd ganddynt.

A hwy a lefasant â llef uchel, gan ddywedyd, Pa hyd, Arglwydd, sanctaidd a chywir, nad ydwyt yn barnu ac yn dïal ein gwaed ni ar y rhai sydd yn trigo ar y ddaear?

A gynau gwynion a roed i bob un o honynt;...'

DATGUDDIAD. PENNOD VI

Air white with cold. Cycloid wind prevails.
On ichnolithic plain where no print runs
And winter hardens into plate of ice;
Shoots an anthracite glitter of death
From their eyes – these men shine darkly.

With stiff betrayal, dark suns on pillow
Of snow; but not eclipsed, for out of cauterized
Craters, a conclave of Architects with
Ichnographic plans, shall bridge stronger
Ventricles of faith. They know also

Etonic vows: the abstractions which may arise:
That magnates out of pre-fabricated
Glass, may build Chromium Cenotaphs –
Work and pay for all! Contract aerodromes
To lift planes where ships once crawled, over

Baleful continents to the Caribbean Crane,
Down, to the Southern Christ of Palms
Back on red competitive lines: chaining
Chinese fields of tungsten: above pack-ice
Snaping like wolves on Siberian shores.

Over walls of boracic and tundra torn wounds,
Darkening 'peaked' Fuji-yama, clearing
Cambrian glaciers where xylophone reeds hide
Menhir glaciers and appointed feet.
Out of this hard. Out of this sheet of zinc.

We, by centrifugal force… rose softly…
Faded from blood sight. We, he and I ran
On to a steel escalator, the white
Electric sun drilling down on the cubed ice;
Our cyanite flesh chilled on aluminium

Rail. Growing taller, our demon diminishing
With steep incline. Climbed at gradient
42°; on to a trauma stratus
Where a multitude of birds, each wing
A sunset against a sheet of ice, dipped

And flew throughout our cloth piercing folds
Of pain and fear. Higher through moist
And luminous dust: up breathless to a jungle of
Winedamp, out of gravity and territorial
Sight on to a far outer belt muscling-in

The Earth's curve. On speeding spirals of air
Sailed ketch and kestrel, fighting propeller,
Swastika wings and grey rubber rafts: such
Evidence reconciliating as
Time and shape floated by on swift moving layer.

Out of it. *Out of it.* To a ceiling and clarity
Of *peace.* Sweet white air varied as syllables.
Spray of air fresh, fragrant as beehive glossed
Over with beech. So quiet a terrace to tune-in-to
With prismatic shine on each cell of light:

To laze carelessly in the crown of the sky.
But timeless minds held us victims
To the sour truth. *War and responsibility.*
He, of Bethlehem treading a campaign
Of clouds, the fleecy cade purring at his side:

Sun, serene-sense, tinting page of his face roan,
Bent over glazed chart and wooden table;
With compass and astronomical calculation,
He, again at my side, pricked lines and projected
Latitudes so that we stood we cared not

How, upside-down over South American canes.
Boots proved cumbersome at the height. Bleak battledress
Irritating as old salvaged reed collar:
Black and gravel wings pinned to his heart,
A grief already told. In such radium

Activity – white starlings – suspended
On string like Calder 'stills' – shivered
Like morning stars in the wide open sky.
And I contented in this 4th dimensional state
Passed through, him and the table, pursued

My own work slightly *below* him. In
Sandals and sunsuit lungs naked to the light,
Sitting on chair of glass with no fixed frame
Leaned to the swift machine threading over twill:
'Singer's' perfect model scrolled with gold,

Chromium wheel and black structure firm on
Mahogany plinth… nails varnished with
Chanel shocking! Ears jewelled: light hand
Tipped with dorcas silver thimble, tracing thin
Aertex edge: slim needle and strong sharp

Thread – Coats' cotton 48 – trimmings, and metal
Buttons stitched by hand: excelling always as
Soldier shirt finished floated down to earth.
But cold out night. We wrapt our own mystery
Around us; trailed in cerulean mosquito nets,

As kale canopy lifted from cooler zones below.
Pack of stars in full cry icing the heavens
As we were compelled to descend. Disendowed;
By the State. By will of those hankering
After pig standards of gold. The fall was heavy,

Too sudden for our laughter so that we
Took it with us; dragged it slowly down through
Waled skylanes. Shocked Capricorn and Cancer who
Winked to control us like belisha beacons.
Tacked out of our course into opaline dusk.

A huge silence ashiver: Huge Witness dwells:
In Celestial Study to right and left, lucid
Eyes pay tribute, Angel secretaries with
Paper wings (and paper so scarce) dyed mauvescarlet

With chemical rings: speech blue behind aniline
   minds.

Away from this. Flattery and hypocrisy.
Not even a whisper escaped our lips as we
Continued in sharp descent – old minesweepers
Creaking through boisterous storms, our own God
Within us. Down into xerophilous air, clarion snow

Percolating, oölite flakes warm as
Owl tufts or deciduous leaves falling on
Flesh with the lightness of moths. Without breath
Or bell of joy lurched slipped-slid into icy
Vacuums. Fell out of frozen cylinders. Flew

Earthwards like arctic terns with spangled
Mirrors still on our wings. *Colder.* Continuous as
   newsreel
Quadrillion cells spotting the air, stinging
The face like a swarm of bees. *Lower.* A vitreous green
Paperweight… the sky is greenglaze with snow flying

Upwards zionwards. Such iconic sky bears promise.
Dredging slowly down, veiling shield of sky hard.
Cold. Austere. Tumbled over each other plunged
Into a dark penumbra then through a
Rift as suddenly, the solid stone of earth

Rushed up; hit us hotly as household iron.
Over this maimed and cadaverous globe, the wind
Had streaked each ridge with piercing prongs
Of a curry comb; leaving here and there
A thin sheet of aluminium which shone out

Of the Earth's crust. Over set currents
Of ice, emerald streams and blue electric lakes
Working simultaneously to purify the
World... down driving down... following the thin
Strokes of mapping pens, stretching a page of

Music over vast terrain. This, and stronger
Network of rails, pylons, and steel installations
The only landmark of our territory...
Down, to this bleak telegraphic planet and solid
Pyramids of canvas. Down, gunner and black

Madonna with heart of tin; surrounded
By fluttering greed of ravens, their
Beaks of bone breaking up the wounds of winter;
Croak: a mad voice sunk down a sink. The attendant
Curlews at the forage edge wearing motheaten

Shawls; shagreen legs brittle as ember twigs.
Pipe, plaintive descant sharpening the shale.
From the ascending stirrup to the sun, down,
Dragged down we descended the slimerot ladders,
Rats withdrawing each foot: rust worn where other

Boots had rung. To the Bay known before,
The warm and stagnant wellshafts raising air
Of putrid flesh sunk in desert sands. Stepped out on to
Blue blaze of snow. Barbed wire. No man of bone.
A placard to the right which concerned us;

Mental Home for Poets. He alone on this
Isotonic plain: against a jingle of Generals
And Cabinet Directors determined a

Stand. Declared a Faith. Entered Foreign
Field like a plantagenet King: his spirit

Gorsefierce: hands like perfect quatrains.
Green spindle tears seep out of closed lids....
Mourn murmuring... remembering my brother:
His Cathedral mind in Bedlam. Sign and
Lettering, black grail of quavering curves.

Distrained... mallowfrail... turned to where.
But *today which is tomorrow.*

Salt spring from frosted sea filters palea light
Raising tangerine and hard line of rind on the
Astringent sky. Catoptric on water-ice he of deep love
Frees dragon from the glacier glade,
Sights death fading into chilblain ears.

The Circle of C

Dogs of Annwn: The ghosts of dogs, heard and seen in the sky. Invariably connected with Hell and Death omens. They appear in early triads, and in the first story of the Mabinogion, (Pwyll Prince of Dyved). The legend is no doubt associated with Sirius and the third sea-track of the Phoenicians which may have guided those people to our shore: with Kerberos: and later to emerge as 'Cŵn Ebrill', when curlews crying at night are said to hunt for the souls of the dead. I have used this image as an interpretation of the raiders droning over estuary and hill; their stiff and ghostly flight barking terror into the hearts of the villagers.

Broken Voices

An attempt to apply the strict form of the Welsh englyn to the English language. As far as I know Robert Graves, at the age of thirteen, is the only other poet to have attempted this. Here is an example of englynion by R. Williams Parry, from 'In Memoriam: Morwr':

> Y Tom gwylaidd, twymgalon, – sy'n aros
> Yn hir yn yr eigion:
> Mor oer yw'r marw yr awron
> Dan li'r dŵr, dan heli'r don.

> O ryfedd dorf ddiderfysg – y meirwon
> A gwymon yn gymysg.
> Parlyrau'r perl, erwau'r pysg,
> Yw bedd disgleirdeb addysg.

Fifth of the Strata

Halkin: a village which was submerged near St Ismael, Towy Estuary, about 1606.

Crossed and Uncrossed
For the form in this poem and that of 'The New World' I should like to make acknowledgements to Professor George Thomson: and in particular for the analysis in his 'Book on Greek Metres' of the third and extended line of the sapphic stanzas.

Orarium
Streanaeshalch: Whitby, where Caedmon's monastery once stood. *Hebankuningas*: old Saxon 'the heavenly kings' quoted from an MS found in the Vatican Library, and now believed to be the original passage of Caedmon's 'Genesis' from which the English poem in the book of 'Anglo-Saxon Poetry' was taken. In this poem I have tried to revive an echo of the rhythm and syntax:… 'not is the Kingdom of Heaven like to such flames; this was of all lands the loveliest, that we two here through our Lord's grace have might… where thou to that one not heard, who for us two this calamity has decreed. In that we two the ruler's word have violated…'

Royal Mail
Mimicrying: from the n. mimicry. Here used as a verb, to convey the meaning of both sorrow and mimicking. The butterfly, brazilian blue, is caught by waving a transparent net of peacock blue attached to a long slender pole. This deceives it into the belief that there are other butterflies flitting about on the outer edge of the wood so that it is easily attracted and caught. The commercial use made of their wings; and the fact that 'certain members of the Lepidoptera possess a capacity for sound production' (A.D. Imms, MA, DSc) permitted me to take this liberty.

The New World
Jabirú: stork.

Ombú: botanically a plant: but, to all outside appearances a tree. The fruit resembles white mistletoe berries, the trunk is hollow, and the branches spread and hang like old and young English Oaks. It is the only covering of shade which grows and spreads naturally on the Pampas. There are two legends connected with it. That which W.H. Hudson has dealt with: and the second explained to me at the Convent of the Sacred Heart... where he or she who sits under its shade will eventually become crazy.

Ventevéo: an evil and much feared bird whose call, like the human voice, draws men deeper and deeper into the jungle from where they seldom return. The bird, perching high on the tree at night, penetrates the conscience of the people... come I see you... come I see you. It is said to be under the command of the devil; and its light frame of bones a receptacle for the departed souls of sinners, who unable to find peace, return to flit about restlessly on the earth.

Xaquixaguana

Lake of pools: and *lion grass*: are literal translations of the Patagonian lakes, Nahuel Huapi and Traful.

Sun tied up: Inca idiom from the Quinchua language.

Huaca: consecrated objects preserved with the dead; transferred to the Spanish language and now connected with any superstition attached to a small possession or particular object.

Haravec: Quinchua Language, the tribal poet, chronicler.

River Plate

Piranha: fish which attack cattle and human beings in large shoals and eat them alive. When cattle have to swim across the river, the drovers (peones) usually send over the poorer beasts first, so that if a shoal of piranha are present, they will attack and be absorbed by these, while the healthier herds swim across in safety.

Cwmcelyn
Pronounced Coom-kel-in, meaning 'The Valley of Holly'. Quotation in Welsh from Revelation ch: VI, v. 7–11.

GODS WITH STAINLESS EARS

A Heroic Poem

1951

'This Poem is
dedicated to
Dr Edith Sitwell

A glyweisti a gant Avaon
Vab Taliesin, gerdd gyfion,
Ni chel grudd gystudd calon.

Brân a gant chwedl ar uwchder
Derwen uwch deuffrwd aber,
Trech deall na grymusder.

Gwna y goreu ym mhob angen,
O'r peth fo'n dy berchen,
Gwell no dim gwasgawd brwynen.'

CATTWG DDOETH A'I CANT

PREFACE

This poem was written over a period of two years, 1941–3. Not liking varied metre forms in a long poem, short-lipped lyrics interspersed with heavy marching strides, and not feeling too comfortable within the strict limits of the heroic couplet (wanting elbow room and breathing space), I decided to use the same structure throughout, changing only the rhythm, texture, and tone *internally*. The use of congested words, images, and certain hard metallic lines are introduced with deliberate emphasis to represent a period of muddled and intense thought which arose out of the first years of conflict, e.g. Factory hands and repetitive lines re-occur with the same movement as with a machine. For this I adapted the villanelle (see page [119]). Towards the third year of war, clear, cold, and austere sight is regained, and I have tried to control the stanzas in the fifth part of this poem under these conditions. The subject is universal, and the tragedy one of too many. Here I would add that my own, though part may be expressed, is outside the page.

The background is similar to any rural village: only the surface culture is superimposed or altogether distinct. The sentences at the end of the book are to pierce any obscurity which may arise owing to the isolation of localised folklore; or to make known the legends which belong to this particular part of the world.

Finally, when I wrote this poem, the scenes and visions ran before me like a newsreel. The galley sheets on which I wrote the first draft may be partly responsible for this occurrence. But the poem was written for filming, especially Part V, where the soldier and his girl walk in fourth dimension among the clouds and visit the various outer strata of our planet.

The Caravan   LYNETTE ROBERTS
Laugharne
15 *November* 1949

PART I

'A synnasant oll, ac a ammheuasant, gan ddywedyd y naill wrth y llall, Beth a all hyn fod?

Ac eraill, gan watwar, a ddywedasant, Llawn o win melus ydynt.'

ARGUMENT

The poem opens with a bay wild with birds and somewhat secluded from man. And it is in front, or within sight of this bay that the whole action takes place: merging from its natural state into a supernatural tension within the first six stanzas. War changes its contour. Machine-gun is suggested by the tapping of a woodpecker which gives out the identity of the gunner and provides his nationality, 'a dragon of wings'. Soldiers and armoured corps arrive: military parade and propaganda: factory workers and fatigues. The rural village described within view of this estuary where soldiers wander during the short hours of their leave. The gunners in action, and of one in particular. He, belonging to a Welsh regiment reading a bill by gunlight, and a letter from his girl in which she tells him they are to expect a child. Night falls, and with it comes the wrecking of a plane.

> Today the same tide leans back, blue rinsing bay
> With new beaks scissoring the air, a care-away
> Cadence of sight and sound, poets and men
> Rediscovering them. Saline mud
> Siltering, wet with marshpinks, fresh as lime stud

115

Whitening fields, gulls and stones attending them;
Curlews disputing coverts pipe back: stem
Plaintive legs deep in the ironing edge, that
Outshines the shale, a railway line washed flat,
Or tin splintered from a crab-green cave.

This is Saint Cadoc's Day. All this Saint Cadoc's
Estuary: and that bell tolling, Abbey paddock.
Sunk. – Sad as ancient monument of stone.
Trees vail, exhale cyprine shade, widowing
Homeric hills, green pinnacles of bone.

Escaping from these, tomb and cave, quagmires
Migrate; draw victim eyes with lustre sheen, suck
Confervoid residue from gillette veins: who talk
Now yield, calling others, those who walk
From Llanstephan, Llangain, and Llanybri.

No watereyes squinting or too near madness
Could fail such a trek. In this same old soddenness
In deep corridor graves culverts open; their
Gates kedged in mud, preening feathered air
Elucidating shapes flecked with woolglints

And small affiliated tares. – So walk swiftly by,
For today, *pridian*, tears ravens wings to grate
The bay, and John Roberts covered with ligustrum,
Always sanitary and discreet, rows to and fro from
Bell house to fennel, floating quietly on the tide.

In fear of fate, flying into land Orcadian birds pair
And peal away like praying hands; bare
Aluminium beak to clinic air; frame

Soldier lonely whistling in full corridor train,
Ishmaelites wailing through the windowpane,

O the cut of it, woe sharp on the day
Scaled in blood, the ten-toed woodpecker,
A dragon of wings 1 6 2 0 B 6
4 punctuates machine-gun from the quarry pits:
Soldiers, tanks, lorry make siege on the bay.

Freedom to boot. CONCLAMATION.
    COMPUNCTION.
Kom-pungk'-shun: discomforts of the mind deride
Their mood. Birds on the stirrups of the waterbride
Flush up, and out of time a tintinnabulation
Of voice and feather fall in and out of the ocean sky.

A sanctuary taken – trenched underfoot.
For today, today, the simple bay pined for
Out of reach. The atmospheric bogfoot
Out of season: culverts close their gate,
Machine sets against clay; irons a new uniform.

Trees crisp with Maeterlinck blue, screen
Submarine suns and baskets of bees: but
Men nettled with pie-powdered feet, angry
As rooks on their pernickety beds 'training
For another Cattraeth' said Evans shop.

DISSIMILAR. DISSUNDERED. CRANCH-CRAKE
    CRANCH-CRAKE
ASHIVER. ANHUNGERED ANHELATION.
CERAUNIC CLOUDS CRACK IN THEIR BRAIN.
Who was to be ring carrier for Jerrymandering
Gerontocracy. The officer yellow with argyria?

Soldiers seldom suffered from this; for silver
Scarcely smoothed their palm. CONGRIEVED.
   CONSTRAINED.
CONDEMNED. *Subversive* (?) for humanity blast this
And much else besides. Hell would chill a chitter
Chatter at the sight of their conflowing misery.

SHUN. *Father Precipice of Denbigh Rock,*
Mother Mild of Pembroke Streams, Have mercy on.
Cantation us to shoal deep winter.
Men fall to arms. Men stemmed to die
For the century. Then leap fast to the bone

Take wailing bayonets from the ice of wound.
Emblaze your handrails. Men fall to arms.
Men purred to fight – each other. So can we foresee
Death. Set each life against time. Jagged bitterns:
Gradgrinds all. – Now we ruined in life, bound

For detention in field, again build on lime
And rubble. To what age can this be compared?
Men slave, spit and spade. Glean life pure.
Accelerate oxidised roads. Drill new hearts and hearths.
Impale the money-goaders' palisade. And you

Of acetated minds, workers with xantheine
Faces, revolutionise your land; holding
The simple measures of life in your hand,
Remembering navies and peacocks never sail
Together in the aftermaths of disaster.

Into euclidian cubes grid air is planed.
Propellers scudding up grit and kerosene, braid

Hulls waled 5 miles hollow, spidering each man stark
On steelweb, hammering in rivets ambuscade
Interrupted by sirens screaming tirade.

With machine-strength wearing blinkers and mask,
Will of iron moulding surface to brain chained:
While below in well shafts soldiers squat and cark,
Shell and peel pods and spuds: girders craned;
Into euclidian cubes tempered air is planed.

The brown paper parcels of sappers who ask,
Shelling and peeling: '*How's Jane to-day?*' Barricade
Against blast and red-hot ingots; clatch
Of ricocheting wheels – hell's dim decade
Interrupted by sirens, screaming tirade.

Where each day ingrained is a chained task,
A clatter of clogs, winding of nerves: Fatigues
Thinning into vocal farms, war-limed grey,
Stately as battleships heeled to cove: there forced
Into euclidian cubes carol air is planed.

When daily the water trudge with battering can,
Striding out of snail from sprockets of kale;
Where tractors, carts like nasturiums crack
The windowpane; to rattle of boiling buckets,
Sleeve of plane rippling over hedge:

To each striped tidy plot aproned women work,
Spadeing clay and coal dust into 'pele' jet. To them
To iron bedsteads; kitchens farms cut open
With grates. To calico; village scintillating
Like mothball white on a hill: cresting cascades

And red rock, throwing out a shower of birds,
Woodcutters, and harrowing of gulls. Where
Women titans are weathervanes who fetch
In the cows who wander the valley prints
Greening the squares of their eyes. To men

Ploughing strig and stubble: near geese full of
White 'airs' crisping out their quills, whose
Eyes and ears surrounded with orange cord
Detect and hear the running pads of spiders;
Or better round the slow-slipping dairy-roof

Where rabbits hang punched on the door. To chink
Of ceramic jugs glazed with the lead of years,
Brass and blue glister under paraffin pools
By which everything rubied glows, baize and lace
Curtained to night; intrinsic to seal light

Crouched black on summer sills. Until the watersky
Of dawn flickers a sail-wash shimmering aquamarine
Into TB and disinhumed rooms; where past
Is not dead but comes uphot suddenly sharp as
Drakestone. To them soldiers return; offer chickweed

Love; others scribble the same formula home –
All this cover with blue dome of glass
And engrave the village Llanybri '42:
For OK saltates the cymric hearth and
BBC blares from Bermondsey tongue.

Fine gentle ways fill time's Grave stone
From Stonehenge Blue to Granite's sharp Black.
Old women die folded in skirts, their culture
Entombed: upstarts mock at what was gracious before:
Work out their crudeness on to change and cloth.

Out of whalebone huts gunners drone: 'You,
With the gypsy slit on your ears Vaughan
What do you make of my lover' (!) No answer.
'Who's there in the Chapel Yard who bends?'
Prophets warm in the shade sign black signatures

In the Red Book of Hergest and cross their toes
To confuse the Principality. 'What's that withered
Field?' 'England.' 'Ah.' 'What's that purple pool
Of pansies lingering in so memorial
A town?' 'Culture of London.' 'Oh, so.'

'Pull down the bastard.' 'Pull down the flag.'
The flag torn down. Emerald on
Unfortunate field and red flaw its great
Perfection; without sound crept back like myth
Into folds of earth: grew greener shafts of resilience.

Under the washing line of blue. 'Who's
Speaking now?' 'Who's there in the Chapel Yard
Who bends?' 'Mari Ann is cleaning the graves.'
'Where's the "professor" he should know?' 'If the tide
Swept back for Saint Cadoc where was God

To smooth their corrugated mouths: strike a path
To the Laugharne Pubs?' 'Where's John Roberts,
Old Charon and his Coracle?' 'Who's there low
At the tide who blends?' 'Morgan the poacher,
Setting horsehair with broad bean and hook,

Sly old bugger snaring sheldrake. The State Trapper!'
Breaming boots: bay full of spitshine and brass
Sun splintered on waves – cupping up –
Clear as beer sparkle… 'you've had it, mun'.
'Where's the "professor" he should know?'

He, who comes from Saint Cadoc's Chapter
Giant or Legendary Prince, who loves
One and no other, turns in his mind LEFT – RIGHT
LEFT – RIGHT, tapping boot wry in the dung
Coloured pool wonders which way and why?

Without chevron: yet born under that gyre
Astronomical sign: without chevron: kid
Crests his regimental badge. Poor callid
Cymru; unquestioning, unanswering,
Remaining just the same, braiding wire

With chilling hands, *stands*, under manurial
Showers, till the lurid sun spills across
The sky like a shot Indian. Then to read and relate
By gunlight indelible: '*We incarnate,*
Even if flesh rot you shall have Heaven,

I immured at your side. Serene latch
And cambric joy, floating above you shall
Still overlook pots and pans; yet patch
Your trousers willingly. This is no prodigal,
There is no madrigal but my 'word' cleaved

To your flesh. And you know it so need not fear.'
Indigo, a green mist humouring Ajanta woe.
Cool palm lighting woodbine. Out of pocket: –
Red ink on pink lined paper: 'Bryn Williams Carp
For wire netting and staples 2s and 8d.'

What setting moves mayors to play chess on rocks.
Guns stand manned.
                                        Still stand.
Mind alone,
                        Knocks.

Senile coast beetle browed down to citrine
Rush of sea. Monster night strides up, grating
Rock to rib of death with hide of rusty knuckle.
A pinpoint glows, whirls, grows, whinnying
Larger wheels over the whole damn estuary.

Falling huge, dilating in the too close nightmare,
Their own eyes enlarging the mayors smash rock
Lift skirts and torques and wade out to sea. A whir-
    rying
Of semitic wings. High cordite flash that
Cools the seaboard of the world. Bridling.

Of nerves, THUD   Soundless,
Smoke fumes raise a black hearse that hovers in the
    sky.
Faces forged into icing bags, challenge
The chill fretting in waves to clear the plain,
Leave: crimson steam; scattering of pain on

Euripus wolds. Atonement of blood: seaflooded red.
Fighting scarlet minutes over immeasurable
Earth. Is reflected this day, by sodden
Arterial men crushed under magenta
Monstrosities, blood curdling into dog wail.

How who then. Friend? Chine birds grip to black
Shining cliff, and wing, fowl-of-tar, to rift
In swivelling sea, cold hard as hand on rock:
Sea ride neither matched nor considered in flock.
Go down there far. Into groves of foreign

Glitter. On water mosaic of running tides,
Bitter with sweet birds, and unfortunate flesh; nothing
Fitter than avidity could return such mawkish
Litter. Go down there further and see the lucid
Plane-of-night, strained with piteous men

Drowned in water-swills of crossing waves; lifting
Asteroid heads, so alike, so different from
The petroleum sky: striking death too soon,
And nearer and sooner than they should: this dawn
Mauve as iron, whimpers as the biting jest.

PART II

MAWL I'R HAF

Tydi'r Haf, tad y rhyfig,
Tadwys coed brwysg caead brig,
Teg wdwart feistr tew goedallt,
Twˆr pawb wyd, töwr pob allt.
Tydi a Bair, air wryd,
Didwn ben, dadeni byd.

I'R ALARCH

Yr alarch ar ei wiwlyn,
Abid galch fal abad gwyn,
Llewych edn y lluwch ydwyd,
Lliw gwˆr o nef, llawgrwn wyd…
Gorwyn wyd uwch geirw nant
Mewn crys o liw maen crisiant.
Dwbled fal mil o'r lili,
Wasgod teg, a wisgud ti.
Siecyd o ros gwyn it sydd,
A gown o flodau'r gwinwydd.
Cannaid ar adar ydwyd,
Ceiliog o nef, clog-wyn wyd.

DAFYDD AP GWILYM (c. 1325–85)

ARGUMENT

By the tidal lapping of the water a gramophone remains as the only symbol of a lost airman. The challenge arises to all people to discard their sorrow, break through destruction and outshine the sun. The flowers of the field contrast sharply with the clouding dispiritedness of the soldiers, whose sickness finally develops into gastric trouble and mental neurosis. The healing hand and images of home offered by the girl to her gunner.

> We must uprise O my people. Though
> Secretly trenched in sorrel, we must
> Upshine, outshine the day's sun. And day
> Intensified by the falling haggard
> Of rain shall curve our smile with straw.
>
> Bring plimsole plover to the tensile sand
> And with cuprite crest and petulant feet
> Distil our notes into febrile weeds
> Crisply starched at the water-rail of tides:
> On gault and green stone a gramophone stands,
>
> In zebeline stripes strike out the pilotless
> Age: from saxophone towns brass out the dead:
> Disinter futility that we entombing men
> Might curb our runaway hearts. –
> On tamarisk; on seafield pools shivering
>
> With water-cats, ring out the square slate notes
> Shape the birdbox trees with neumes, wind sound
> Singular into cool and simple corners
> Round pale bittern grass and all unseen
> Unknown places of sheltered rubble

Where whimbrels, redshanks, sandpipers ripple
For the wing of living. Under tin of earth,
From wooden boles where owls break music;
From this killing world against humanity
Uprise against, – outshine the day's sun.

Corymb of coriander: each ray frosted
Incandescent: by square stem held, hispid,
And purple spotted. Twice pinnate with fronds
Of chrome. Laid higher than the exulted hedge;
By pure collated disc of daisy glittering

White on a red powdered stem. By cusp of leaves
Held low to ground; this coriander cane,
Colonnade of angelica, chevril, fennel,
Parsley, aniseed, caraway, yarrow,
All kitchen's frescade culled and tied away;

By this eyelet and low fieldfare herbs are
Accentuated; engraved and brought to light:
To green cymes of guelder rose and flax blue
Meadows of Pembrey sedge. To men allergic,
Gunners: Bogrush, Pricklesedge, stinking Goosefoot,

Foetid Hawk's-beard, Black Horehound, Bloody-veined
Dock, Blue Broomrape, and Bastard Toadflax on dank
Plain of mud cough like Kerberous in midsummer lanes.
Food chyles constricted in their stomach,
Twisting, knotting, and deflexed, rats bolt

Between their teeth. All day the ghosts of ulcer
Hover in front of their paths. With unhealthy
Custom the MO turns a page, lays them aside,
Apart from communication, into pruned
Shuttered wards, curing each for the wrong event!

The MO turns a head. – Long necked in
Achillean sky, geese sleeve their own
Shadows through pools of air. Sailing downstream
Downfast to earth. Hydroplanes splash like
Zinnias on inrushing tides; fussy as moorhens

With tarnished back; whose legs of peeled elm
Trail scarlet garters into the shaking tips
Of reeds. To their aid. To his aid. To my lover.
Under tincture of Myddfai Hills, west of
Bristol glass, gold with bracken dust and black

Cattle motes and all chemical paradox:
XEBO 7011 camouflaged in naval oilskin
In all the gorgeous shades of Hades; –
By seiriol cat with greenfield eyes.
By kitchen rilled with distemper and grass.

By coat stained and saddlestitched by my flowering
Hands. By neighbours like Byzantine Waterspouts: leaning
Out of bedroom windows. By damn tin-blower.
Leaf feathers of the white-eyed woodpecker
Spangled with lime leaves, wearing the

Chuckling red hat! By 7. With magic and craft
To heel. Without abbreviation or contraction
Take thou my lover 4 pints from the 'Farmers' Arms'
Or, if flat, 6 glass tankards from Jones
'Black Horse'. Not supplying either sip homeward

Sloe-gin from Merlin's desk or board 'Cow and Gate'
Lorry. Up to Carmarthen: to the wine merchant; mention
Vicar's name, demand whiskey 'Old Parr',

Mix. Let a mixture be made. Let him my lover
Take one silver tablespoonful out of IN

A little water each fourth hour and the
Acridity of his mind shall be as the crimson
Heart on our fresco wall. – To perfect eyestrain
For your wedgwood eyes, collyrium of well water
From the Ffyn-on-ol-bri springs.

PART III

Ystyriwch eich ffyrdd. Hauasoch lawer, a chludasoch ychydig;
bwytta yr ydych, ond nid hyd ddigon; yfed, ac nid hyd fod yn ddiwall;
ymwisgasoch, ac nid hyd glydwr i neb; a'r hwn a ennillo gyflog,
sydd yn casglu cyflog i gôd dyllog. Fel hyn y dywed ARGLWYDD
y lluoedd;

Ystyriwch eich ffyrdd.

LLYFR HAGGAI. PENNOD I

ARGUMENT

The bay crystallised. Soldiers washing by the light of the moon.
Swansea raid and prayer to Parliament. The gunner standing
apart, through maladjustment of mind and spirit rejecting his girl.
Woefully and with pained frustration. Of their love: wholesome
cottage: his departure abroad. Misunderstanding and unhappiness
of both.

Embrowns himmel hokushai. Manure seeps
In long rags, pavilions hut, camouflages
Arsenical veins with a sprouting
Febrifuge and serial of death; heaves a
Heavier heart of sedimentary hate.

Washing like flies to pin of elbow, soldiers
Under ciliated moon shake off floatings

Of soap; strike code on oxidised zinc; polish
Bayonets clean as the cut of the moon to
Sharpen inactivity. Spark electric cells

Of air into a prism of light as they
Shoulder the blades on parade. A shark wind teethes,
Strips fields; striating black fullstops under hedge;
Bellying-white trees as they stand caustic
And chagrin. Like paleozoic sentinels, stretched high

Above skeleton hills. Dripping rust low on
Blue lined eddies of wind, cold down
To the shafts of their root: to kerb of tide
Where cracked mud quails into Kuan glaze;
To greening dunes where rivulets shine as

Water rises appointing silver streams
To encircle the clay. Mounting ships higher,
Disturbing the colder water of shells. Near
Nightjars undisclosed, where green icy stars
Ripple above the corn this late seaharvest.

'Defending the Navy' they say. Brothers
Who neither coincide nor drink at the same pub.
'Army batons fascist' puff the Navy.
'Aristocrats sinking fast' is the khaki reply.
A convoy timbers the bay. Aubergine hills

Wounded, lie heavily in the dishwater tributary.
Night falling catches the flares and bangs
On gorselit rock. Yellow birds shot from
Iridium creeks. – Let the whaleback of the sea
Fall back into a wrist of ripples, slit,

Snip up the moon sniggering on its back,
For on them sail the hulls of ninety wild birds
Defledged by this evening's raid: jigging up
Like a tapemachine the cold figures February
19th, 20th, 21st. A memorial of Swansea's tragic loss.

Would the Warden of the Marches send us telegrams?
Who would dismiss them with *peace*; throw
Bézique on the table! *A New World*
Before us O Parliament. Be merciful
To our outcast minds shed from cuprite

Pyrite and tin. Bare our pricket hearts
Into a new alloy. Have mercy besides
On us who forged away bayonet and bone.
Standing out from the gun; bleared and solitary,
Shading his broccoli eyelashes; sending death

To no other than the girl he loves, gunner
1620B64 with Post Office pen, dismal heart,
And weak ink, signs and rescinds his love. –

On this vitreous monochrome of a plain
A striped rhizome cat fled across the estuary.

He chosen, blind behind the mourning grid,
Woe, fluttering at the bottom of a cage,
Finds parallel nerves on watersand; dives,
Into the torn prints of his mind, finds hurting lines.
He nearest to the heart stands dead in his

One and a half round the battle-waist suit;
Boots radiating with the exuberant shine
Of coffins among the pale and jumped up press cuttings

Strewn around his feet. O condole. Contrive.
With him in his constriction. He, with a blue

Division of blades in his head: with a
Shivershock of frustration, was a lover,
Or had been until now, who could what the world
Could not, without the aid of Freud, Norman Haire
Or Stopes, offer in his own strange way

Love sweet as a bird – savage as dog at his bone.
Now I wretched woman watch the white shaft
Of light greening the chimney embers,
The ciliated pines chink with ice this
Unwelcome frosty morning. Turn round a kitchen,

Once fragrant and rare as borage flower;
Sweep royal-blue walls; wash white the furniture,
Floor, and odd crockery – draw deep red hangers.
Who cherished love in peace and freedom, knew it
Delicate to hold as open window at dawn.

Where blue-eyed goose met meridian eyes shaded
There is no shine of celandine; our souls
Are cast into galvanised pits. I, crabbed youth,
He cruel negation. Twisted and rough…
Love distrained about the hearth and in running away

To bare our child reached no further than
The kiosk when love's stern face dragged back my will.
Never to be regretted or demolished.
To love, no bed of feathers but crock of thorns.
Yet a ritual; wanting no change. For who would

Strive with impeccable love? To love returning as
Gently as the rain, with grief harnessed
To his shoulders. To love which grew; survived all
Credulous hate. To meet underground as gravelovers do;
O Choice. O my beloved people remember this.

Overseas battling in circles of lust:
Spirit put to no better purpose than
Grain of sand. Overwhich. Backwards and
Forwards soldiers ran. Such battles of mule
Stubbornness; or retreat from vast stone walls,

Brought non-existence of past, present and
Future 1, 2, 1, 2, 1, 2, left, right, left, right,
Accumulating into a monotonous pattern
Of dereliction and gloom. When battles should be
Fought at Home: as trencher-companions. *He at my side.*

PART IV

CRI MADONNA

Un eich amynedd yn ddi-feth,
Un yn eich croes a'ch cri,
Mair, mam Iesu o Nasareth
A' Mari o Llanybri.

DYFNALLT

ARGUMENT

Of birth. Of uneventful birth. Owing to lack of money and to emotional strain death cuts in, double death, loss of lover and child. The struggle for birth under these conditions suggests a comparison with the Madonna, which becomes the nucleus and theme of the whole poem. *That the birth of flesh and blood is everywhere a noble event and that lives of all nationalities must be considered sacred – not to be callously destroyed.* Of the girl's distraction. Humiliation at her double loss. Stanzas of discordant fifths prevail. Cherubs weep, and a desolation and deadness of spirit is felt as after raids. The uselessness of the soldiers' jobs is intensified as they empty latrine buckets in the rain. Making them, since to rebel at this particular time would bring about the country's defeat, *our heroes. The heroes unknown who braved and bore, each a private crucifix.*

I, rimmeled, awake before the dressing sun:
Alone I, pent up incinerator, serf of satellite gloom
Cower around my cradled self; find crape-plume

In a work-basket cast into swaddling clothes
Forcipated from my mind after the foetal fall:

Rising ashly, challenge blood to curb – compose –
Martial mortal, face a red mourning alone.
To the star of the third magnitude O my God,
Shriek, sear my swollen breasts, send succour
To sift and settle me. – This the labour of it…

But reality worse than the pain intrudes,
And no near doctor for six days. This
Also is added truth. Razed for lack of
Incomputable finance. For womb was
Fresh as the day and solid as your hand.

BLOOD OF ALL MEN. DRENCHED ANCESTORS OF WAR
WHETHER GERMAN. BRITISH. RUSSIAN. OR HIDE
FROM SOME OTHER FOREIGN FIELD: REMEMBER AGAIN
BLOOD IS HUMAN. BORN AT COST. REMEMBER THIS
ESPECIALLY YOU TAWDRY LAIRDS AND JUGGLERS OF MINT.

So double hurt was hard to console. Heart hatched
Shrived nerves each day in valley clove. Stretched
Mind tight into scarlet umbrella. Slatched
Nowhere the deflated ropes of blood. Wrenched
Harbouring heartbreak that is a crack grailed.

O where was my consoler. Where O where
You double beast down. Callous Cymru.
O love beaten. By loss humiliated.
Stretched out in muslin distress. Bound
By an iron wreath scattered with coloured beads.

O my people immeasurably alone.
No ringfinger: with the tips of my nails glazed

With sorrow with solemn gravity. Crown tipped
    sideways;
Ears blown back like lilac; with set face
And dry lids, waiting for Love's Arcade.

O LOVE was there no barddoniaeth?
No billing birds to be – coinheritor?

The night sky is braille in a rock of frost.

Why wail ribbon head. Crystallised cherubic
Cluster of stars. Why weep spilling splints to
Steelgraze the sky. Why shrillcold cerulean
Flesh with identity tacked hot on your wing.
Why dribble prick-ears, scintillating in an up

And down nailmourn. Tumbling to earth an icy
    precision
Of pins, distilling flies and peacock fins,
Tears in flames on fire, scorching air as they
Splash into heavier spills of quavering
Silver, drops, seels resinate woe, chills hedge and

Chilblain glades. Grisaille freezes the sense; crines
The gills into a drill motion; stills-shrills
The singing birds to kill; Drips rills
From envelopes, pustule eyes and hat. With
Urinal taint instils mind with a perilled dampness;

Fells skilled discipline to halls of humidity
Engraving clothes to trail balustrades without
Flesh; to a wilderness of pavements blue crayoned
With telegrams, where by a trick of air, owners
And cats remain, trying in mid-air to force riseup

Their own smashed brick. These men have brothers,
Are wived. And in dredging buckets of steam
Through stable-showers, men sway with the slush,
Dreamwhile teeming out cables and rope
Stretch barb wire tight across the crimped moon.

Wringing out moisture from mind and mouth,
Pulverising a haze to gauze their contorted feature,
Inebriate mouths cratered: others with lime fresh
On briared cheeks cut Easter Island shadows, elongating
Into weathered struts that strain all clouds for height.

On the lowering of the Dandelion Sun brail umbrage
For their pall: for those hovering above us tall as a
Siren's wail... pocked and pale as pumice stone...
Mother-shrivelled with tansy tears: and those from
Accumulators, with eyes vacant as motor horns

Who shutter out the bleakness and blink in their
Own way. In quiet corners men yawn out death.
Commiserately sodden. Here rain contravariant:
Here in discord and disobedience:
Probable mutiny and desertion: night splashes up

Mullions in heavy hayloads: lights up shiny
Pailettes on rawset faces: spits up frogs
And tins to fidget their bowels. Dodging
Pillars of rain; pails overbrimming swishswashing;
Drenching rifty suits, their steel shoulders subscribing

Thin laminations of grief. O my people here
With labour illused and minds deranged...
Through rivets of light; *Here are your Heroes.*
While high up, swallowsoft...
Marine butterflies flood out the whole estuary.

'… mi a glywais lais y pedwerydd anifail yn dywedyd,
Tyred, a gwêl. Ac mi a edrychais; ac wele farch gwelw-las:
ac enw yr hwn oedd yn eistedd arno oedd Marwolaeth: ac
yr oedd Uffern yn canlyn gyd âg ef. A rhoddwyd iddynt
awdurdod ar y bedwaredd ran o'r ddaear, i ladd â chleddyf,
ac â newyn, ac â marwolaeth, ac â bwystfilod y ddaear.

A phan agorodd efe y bummed sêl, mi a welais dan
yr allor eneidiau y rhai a laddesid am air Duw, ac am y
dystiolaeth oedd ganddynt.

A hwy a lefasant â llef uchel, gan dddywedyd, Pa hyd,
Arglwydd, sanctaidd a chywir, nad ydwyt yn barnu ac yn
dïal ein gwaed ni ar y rhai sydd yn trigo ar y ddaear?

A gynau gwynion a roed i bob un o honynt;'

DATGUDDIAD. PENNOD VI

ARGUMENT

The same bay plated with ice. Industrial war progressing and
the anxiety for after-war commerce and competitive air-lines.
The soldiers recognising this futility, but also, not without some
faith in social and economic changes. The gunner returned,
and faithful to his girl, they rise through the strata of the sky
to seek peace and solace from the sun. Their love in harmony
on cloud in fourth dimensional state. But memory bringing
with it a consciousness of war – responsibility – they work
towards this end. Fail. For the world demands their return,
and down through the lower strata of the earth they travel, to

the wounded bay where no human contact is found, only pylons, telegraph wires, and a monstrous placard which reads: 'Mental Home for Poets'. The gunner interned under pressure, resolves to free the dragon, and take fate in his own hands. The symbol having been already introduced in Part I of this poem when the woodpecker seen as a 'dragon of wings' introduced the gunner's identity. He walks meekly into the Mental Home. The girl turns away: towards a hard and new chemical dawn breaking up the traditional skyline.

Air white with cold. Cycloid wind prevails.
On ichnolithic plain where no step stirs
And winter hardens into plate of ice:
Shoots an anthracite glitter of death
From their eyes, – these men shine darkly.

With stiff betrayal; dark suns on pillows
Of snow. But not eclipsed, for out of cauterised
Craters, a conclave of architects with
Ichnographic plans, shall bridge stronger
Ventricles of faith. They know also

Etonic vows: the abstractions which may arise:
That magnates out of prefabricated
Glass, may build Chromium Cenotaphs –
Work and pay for all! Contract aerodromes
To lift planes where ships once crawled, over

Baleful continents to the Caribbean Crane,
Down, to the Southern Christ of Palms.
Back on red competitive lines: chasing
Chinese blocks of uranium: above pack-ice
Snapping like wolves on Siberian shores.

Over wails of boracic and tundra torn wounds,
Darkening 'peaked' Fuji-yama, clearing
Cambrian caves where xylophone reeds hide
Menhir glaciers and appointed feet.
Out of this hard. Out of this sheet of zinc.

We by centrifugal force... rose softly...
Faded from bloodsight. We, he and I ran
On to a steel escalator, the white
Electric sun drilling down on the cubed ice;
Our cyanite flesh chilled on aluminium

Rail. Growing taller, our demon diminishing
With steep incline. Climbed at gradient
42°; on to a trauma stratus
Where a multitude of birds, each wing
A sunset against sheet of ice, dipped

And flew throughout our cloth piercing folds
Of pain and fear. Higher through moist
And luminous dust: up breathless to a jungle of
Winedamp, out of gravity and territorial
Sight on to a far outer belt muscling-in

The Earth's curve. In such spirals of air
Sailed ketch and kestrel, fighting propeller,
Swastika wings and grey rubber rafts: this strange
Evidence reconciliating as
Tide and shape floated by on swift moving layer.

Out of it. Out of it. To a ceiling and clarity
Of *Peace*. Sweet white air varied as syllables.
Spray of air fresh, fragrant as beehive glossed

Over with beech. So quiet a terrace to tune-in-to
With Catena shine round each cell of light

To laze carelessly in the Crown of the Sky;
But timeless minds held us victims
To the sour truth. *War and responsibility.*
He, of Bethlehem treading a campaign
Of clouds the fleecy cade purring at his side:

Sun, serene sense, tinting page of his face roan.
Bent over wooden table and glazed chart
And with compass and astronomical calculations
He, again at my side, pricked lines and projected
Latitudes so that we stood we cared not

How, upside down over South American canes.
Boots proved cumbersome at the height. Bleak battledress
Irritating as old salvaged reed collar;
Black and gravel wings pinned to his heart,
A grief already told. In such radium

Activity – white starlings – suspended
On string like Calder 'stills' – shivered
Like morning stars in fresh open sky
I contented in this fourth dimensional state
Past through, him and the table, pursued

My own work slightly *below* him. In
Sandals and sunsuit lungs naked to the light,
Sitting on chair of glass with no fixed frame
Leaned to the swift machine threading over twill:
'Singer's' perfect model scrolled with gold,

Chromium wheel and black structure, firm on
Mahogany plinth. Nails varnished with
Chanel shocking! Ears jewelled: light hand
Tipped with dorcas' silver thimble tracing thin
Aertex edge: trimmings, and metal buttons

Stitched by hand. Slim needle and strong sharp
Thread. Coats' cotton-twist No. 48. Excelling always as
Soldier shirt finished floated down to earth.
But cold at night. We wrapt our own mystery
Around us; trailed in cerulean mosquito nets

As kale canopy lifted from cooler zones below.
Pack of stars in full cry icing the heavens
As we were compelled to descend. *Disendowed*,
By the State. By will of those hankering
After pig standards of gold. The fall was heavy,

Too sudden for our laughter so that we
Took it with us; dragged it slowly down through
Waled skylanes. Shocked Capricorn and Cancer who
Winked to control us like Belisha beacons.
Tacked out of our course into opaline dusk.

A huge silence ashiver. Huge Witness dwells.
In Celestial Study to right and left lucid
Eyes pay tribute, angel secretaries with
Paper wings – and paper so scarce – dyed mauve-scarlet
With chemical rings; speech blue behind aniline minds.

Away from this. Flattery. God-Hypocrisy.
Not even a whisper escaped our lips as we
Continued in sharp descent, like old minesweepers

Creaking through boisterous storms, *our own God
Within us.* Down into xerophilous air clarion snow

Percolating, oölite flakes warm as
Owl tufts or deciduous leaves. Falling on
Flesh with the lightness of moths. Without breath
Or bell of joy lurched slipped-slid into icy
Vacuums. Fell out of frozen cylinders. Flew

Earthwards like arctic terns the spangled
Mirrors still on our wings. Colder. Continuous as *newsreel,*
Quadrillion cells spotting the air, stinging
The face like a swarm of bees. Lower. A vitreous green
Paperweight – the sky is greenglaze with snow flying

Upwards zionwards. Such iconic sky bears promise.
Dredging slowly down, veiling shield of sky hard.
Cold. Austere. Tumbled over each other lurched
Into the dark penumbra: then, through a
Rift as suddenly, the solid stone of earth

Rushed up; hit us hotly as household iron.
Over this maimed cadaverous globe, the wind
Had streaked each ridge with piercing prongs
Of a curry comb, leaving here and there
A thin sheet of aluminium which shone from out

Of the Earth's crust. Over set currents
Of ice, emerald streams and blue electric lakes
Worked simultaneously to purify the
World… down driving down… following the thin
Strokes of mapping pens stretching page of

Music over vast terrain. This, and stronger
Network of rails: pylons and steel installations
The only landmarks of our territory...
Down, to this bleak telegraphic planet and its solid
Pyramids of canvas. Down, gunner and black

Madonna with heart of tin; surrounded
By fluttering greed of ravens, their
Beaks of bone breaking up the wounds of winter;
Croak; a mad voice sunk down a sink. The attendant
Curlews at the forage edge wearing moth-eaten

Shawls; shagreen legs brittle as ember twigs.
Pipe plaintive descants that sharpen the shale.
From ascending stirrups steps to the sun, down,
Dragged-down we descended the slimerot ladders,
Rats withdrawing each foot: rust worn where other

Boots had rung. To the Bay known before,
The warm and stagnant air raising wellshafts
Of putrid flesh sunk deep in desert sands. Stepped out onto
Blue blaze of snow. Barbed wire. No man of bone.
A placard to the right which concerned us:

Mental Home For Poets. He alone on this
Isotonic plain: against a jingle of Generals
And Cabinet Directors determined
A stand. Declared a Faith. Entered 'Foreign
Field' like a Plantagenet King: his spirit

Gorsefierce: hands like perfect quatrains.
Green spindle tears seep out of closed lids...
Mourn murmuring... remembering my brother.

His Cathedral mind in Bedlam. Sign and
Lettering-black grail of quavering curves.

Distrained... mallowfrail... turned to where.
But *today which is tomorrow.*

Salt spring from frosted sea filters palea light
Raising tangerine and hard line of rind on the
Astringent sky. Catoptric on waterice he of deep love
Frees dragon from the glacier glade
Sights death fading into chilblain ears.

NOTES

[by Lynette Roberts]

INSCRIPTION

Hast thou heard what Avaon sung,
The son of Taliesin of just lay?
The cheek will not conceal the anguish of the heart.

A crow sang a fable on the top
Of an oak, above the junction of two rivers.
Understanding is more powerful than strength.

Make the best on all occasions
Of what you already possess:
Better than nothing is the shelter of a rush.

CATTWG THE WISE SANG IT (5TH
CENTURY)

Part I

And they were all amazed, and were in doubt, saying one to
another, What meaneth this?

Others mocking, said, These men are full of new wine.

ACTS II, CHAPTER II

Quotation: from the Bible of William Morgan, the Bishop
of St Asaph's translation 1588: later amended and revised
by Richard Parry and John Davies, 1620. Here the English

translation is incorrect as the original Greek word implies sweet wine. John Kitto, DD, FSA, has pointed this out. The Welsh rendering is *Gwin* (the G a mutation), *win* meaning wine, *melus*: sweet.

Saint Cadoc: saint of the fifth century. Spelt in many ways including *Cattwg* (see Inscription, p. [112]). His festival is commemorated in early spring. To him are attributed many miracles, triads, and fables. The last being incorrect, as they belong to a Cadoc of a later period. He is one of the too many Cambro-British Saints (we gave some to Ireland!), Bernacus (Bernach), Beuno, Cadoc, Carantocus (Carannog), David (Dewi), Gundleus (Cynlais), Iltutus (Illtyd), Kebius (Cybi), Paternus (Padarn), and Winifred (Gwenfrewi), see *Lives of Cambro-British Saints* in translation from Ancient Welsh and Latin MSS in the British Museum, by the Rev. W.J. Rees, MA, FSA and the more recent translation by the Rev. A.W. Wade Evans.

Homeric hills: Geraldus Cambrensis wrote in 1180 in his *Itinerary Through Wales*: 'Maenor Pyrr... that is, the Mansions of Pyrrus, who also possessed the Island of Chaldey, which the Welsh call Inys Pyrr, or the Island of Pyrrus... distant about three miles from Pembroch.' There are historians who believe the Trojans came and settled on this coast. In years to come archaeologists may discover both the Temples and City as Sir Arthur Evans and Schliemann discovered Knossos and Troy – by studying the legends in the locality.

Woolglints: I had the image of iridescent bits of dust which float about in the sunbeams like pieces of flock. As the estuary is covered with sheep, and the atmosphere I wanted to create, a supernatural one, I felt that there was bound to be some density – a stifling quality in the air. I therefore imagined these woolglints, which were bound to float about from the backs of the sheep, and the minute weeds – almost-green invisible cells – hovering over the quagmires.

Ligustrum: botanical name for privet. One of the sacred trees mentioned in Taliesin's *Battle of the Trees*, see reference in *The White Goddess* by Robert Graves. Ash and lilac also belong to the Oleaceae family.

Orcadian birds: whimbrel: *Numenius phaepus phaepus* (Linn.), small curlew which arrives on our shore with the third stream of migration from the Shetlands and Orkneys, and is usually seen in early spring.

Cattraeth: 'The *Gododdin*, the subject of which is the disastrous battle of Cattraeth, contains upwards of nine hundred lines, and is the oldest Welsh poem extant, it was written in the earlier part of the sixth century.' Of the three hundred who took part, only three returned. Aneirin who wrote this Ancient Epic was one of the survivors.

Father of Denbigh Rock, Mother of Pembroke Stream: Roberts of Ruthin (i.e. Great-grandfather John Roberts of Bryn Mawr, one of the founders of the London Missionary Society): Garbutt ap Williams of Pembroke. My parents.

Stonehenge Blue: Sir Cyril Fox (director of the National Museum of Wales), when lecturing on 'Beaker Man in Wales and Wilts 1900 BC', said: 'The circle of blue stones at Stonehenge was of stone hewn and carried from the Precelly Mountain in Pembrokeshire, but no factual evidence had been produced as to why Precelly stone had been taken to Wiltshire'… he suggested that it might have been because it was a Holy Mountain.

Gypsy slit on ears: three notches cut by the gypsies on the ear with a wooden knife to prevent rickets.

Red Book of Hergest: one of 'The Four Ancient Books of Wales' in the library of Jesus College, Oxford, MSS of Ancient Welsh prose and poetry. Many of the authors still remain unknown. The 'play' here, is on the scribes who have tampered with the MSS in the thirteenth century, and the poet Iolo Morganwg in particular, who forged numerous parchment poems.

Pull down the flag: the Welsh flag was torn down by English soldiers who were drafted to a Welsh regiment. East Coast, March 1941.

Coracle: coracles are still used on the Towy and Teivy. 'Two men work together and take the river, one rowing and steering with one hand, and holds with his other hand one end of the long net; the other end being grasped by the second coracle man, and together they sweep the river for salmon and sewin.' They have their own dialect *'Gwar bach y gored.'* *Gored* means a weir for taking fish, and is a very early Welsh word, found in one of the poems in the MS 'Black Book of Carmarthen', *c.* 1159. 'The word coracle is probably derived from the Celtic word *Corawg*, which signifies ship.' From 'Geraldus Cambrensis', written in 1180: 'The boats are made of twigs, not oblong nor pointed, but almost round, covered within and without with raw hides. Today they are covered with Calico. The fishermen carry these boats on their shoulders; on which occasion that famous dealer in fables, Bleddercus, who lived a little before our time, thus mysteriously said, "There is amongst us a people who, when they go out in search of prey, carry their horses on their backs to the place of plunder." Unfortunately they were used three days ago to transport stolen butter across the river.' This event was printed in the *Carmarthen Journal* with exclamation marks! See also an article in *The Field*, January 6th, 1945, by the Author.

Torque: from Llywarch Hen, sixth century. (Translation H.I. Bell)

> Four and twenty sons were mine,
> Golden-torqued, princes of the host.

From Aneirin's sixth-century 'Gododdin' (translation Ernest Rhys): 'A brilliant spirited melody it is ours to sing – to tell how Cynon came, and at his coming the beaks of the grey eagles were sated by his hand. Of all the wearers of the gold torques, who went to Cattraeth, there was not one better than Cynon.'

From Geraldus Cambrensis: 'Moreover I must not be silent concerning the Collar (*torques*) which they call St Canauc's (AD 492); for it is most like to gold in weight, nature, and colour; it is in four pieces wrought round, joined together artificially, and clefted as it were in the middle, with a dog's head, the teeth standing upward; it is esteemed by the inhabitants so powerful a relic, that no man dares swear falsely when it is laid upon him.'

From Sir John Lloyd, MA, D.Litt, FBA Historian: 'A thick golden chain worn as a necklet by Princes and persons of nobility.'

In 1692 one of these chains was found near Harlech; it weighed eight ounces and measured four feet in length.

Semitic wings: not enough is said of the active part Jews took in this war. It is for this reason and no other, that I refer to a plane piloted by Jews.

Part II

Thou summer, father of delight,
With thy dense spray and thickets deep;
Gemmed monarch, with thy rapturous light,
Rousing thy subject glens from sleep,
Proud has thy march of triumph been,
Thou prophet, prince of forest green...

THE SWAN

Fair swan, the lake you ride
Like white-robed abbot in your pride;
Round-foot bird of the drifted snow,
Like heavenly visitant you show...
Pure white through the wild waves shown;
In shirt as bright as crystal stone
And doublet all of lilies made
And flowered waistcoat you're arrayed,
With jacket wove of the wild white rose;
And your gown like honeysuckle shows.
Radiant you all fowls among,
White-cloaked bird of heaven's throng.

DAFYDD AP GWILYM (c. 1325–85)

Quotation: the first part of the above translation (i.e. 'Praise to Summer') is by A.J. Johnes. The second part (i.e. 'The Swan') by H. Idris Bell. These I believe to be the best representative translation of each poem. To shew the misinterpretation under which an original poem goes, I will quote the first two lines of Dafydd's other translators to 'Praise to Summer'. A.P. Graves:

> Summer, father of fulness,
> Green-tangled, flower-spangled brakes;

David Bell:

> The father of loud ardency;
> The father of the wildwood canopy;

W.J. Gruffydd, Ernest Rhys, Nigel Heseltine, George Borrow have also contributed different translations to this poem. A rough and literal translation given to me by Keidrych Rhys would be:

> You the Summer, father of potency,
> Sire of the covered intoxicated tree-tops.

Myddfai Hills: on the roads from Llandovery over the Carmarthen Vans lies Myddfai and the lake from which the mother of the physicians is supposed to have returned. The physicians not only attended the Royal Prince of Wales in the thirteenth century, but handed down the famous book and talent from father to son 'for more than two thousand years' according to legend. '*How to be Merry*, If you would at all times be merry, eat saffron in meat or drink, and you will never be sad. But, beware of eating over much, lest you should die of excessive joy.' '*Recipe for Sore Eyes*, Take red roses, wild celery vervain, red fennell, maidenhair, house leek, celandine, and wild thyme, wash them clean and macerate in white wine for a day and a night, then distil from a brass pot. The first water you get will be like silver, this will be useful for any affection of the eye and for a stye.'

Seiriol: two monks that met at the well of Clorach, Llandyfrydog. Cybi had the morning sun in his face as he approached the well, so his face soon darkened; while Seiriol, coming from the other direction, had the sun on his back… and was pale… always. *Seiriol Wyn*, Seiriol the white, or pale. *Cybi Felyn*, Cybi the yellow, or sunburnt. Matthew Arnold wrote a poem about these two and mixed up the colours!

Tin-blower: a sheet of zinc to which is added a handle by the blacksmith. When the fires lose heart the blower is hung up by a piece of wire to narrow and intensify the draught. The rattle and ugliness of the tin is very irritating.

Ffyn-on-ol-Bri: LCC spring surrounded by barbed wire six hundred yards from the village. The only well that *does not* dry up; is not discoloured; and contains brown worms. This is the only supply of fresh drinking water for the village.

Part III

Consider your ways. Ye have sown much, and bring in little; ye eat, but ye have not enough; ye drink, but ye are not filled with drink; ye clothe you, but there is none warm; and he that earneth wages earneth to put it into a bag of holes.

Thus saith the Lord of Hosts; Consider your ways.

THE MESSAGE OF HAGGAI. CHAPTER I

Defending the Navy: on the Island of South Ronaldsay, 1941, the RA batteries defended the Navy when the *Prince of Wales* and other battleships lay in home waters. For this defence the RA received a special divisional sign. In spite of this scraps were frequent between the two services so that a distinction had to be made: the army attending the only pub at one hour and the navy at another.

Swansea raid: February 19th, 20th, 21st, 1941, when several members of the N.F.S. of Birmingham said the intensity of the raid was worse than their own Midland tragedy. The severest hardship was: no room for Welsh evacuees. In our village we had accommodated forty-five from east London, so that we were compelled to refuse children whose parents we knew.

Warden of the Marches: the Norman lords who took Wales piecemeal and divided it up into fretsaw boundaries. Each territory was governed by its own administration and jurisdiction, and controlled by an English King who was a Marcher Lord himself over larger domains.

Bézique: from the game of cards with two packs, 'probably from Spanish *besico*, little kiss, an allusion to the meeting of the Queen and Knave, an important feature in the game'. Table of Bézique scores: Marriage (King and Queen of any suit) declared, 20 points; Royal Marriage (King and Queen of trumps) declared, 40 points; Bézique (Queen of Spades and Knave of Diamonds) declared, 40 points. These are a few examples of the score to show that the arrangement of the cards is based on early everyday life. The symbol came to my mind as a good representative of soldiers longing for their home: and the pattern of soldiers themselves playing with cards at odd snatches of the day.

Pricket: the candle pricket, sharp metallic point on which candles are stuck.

Rhizome cat: the reference to a cat is linked with those mentioned at the beginning of Part II: *'On seafield pools shivering with watercats.'*

I used rhizome because it is an underground root just as this wild cat is of an underground root and lives in the undergrowth. I also had an image of a yellow striped cat: and rhizome is used throughout the country for yellow dyes. There is also something about the jungle in the sound and spelling of the word rhizome. Wild cats are still found in Wales.

Part IV

THE CRY OF THE MADONNA

The same your patience unfailing,
The same your cross and your cry,
Mary, mother of Nazareth
And Mary of Llanybri

DYFNALLT

Quotation: the above translation is from one of Dyfnallt's poems 'Cri Madonna'. He is one of our poets and a leading Nonconformist minister. I should like to point out here, that I have intentionally used Welsh quotations as this helps to give the conscious compact and culture of another nation. The village of Llanybri, around which this poem is set, is Welsh speaking. Most of the people, *with the exception of the older generation*, can also speak English; either better than we can, or with a strange imagery and intonation found in common with all peasants of the soil. I have *never* heard a Welshman say, 'Indeed to goodness,' etc., or any of the jargon which is broadcast or printed as such… and will have more to say on this subject on another occasion.

Incomputable finance: during this war the Government allowed apes at the Zoo thirty shillings per week for their food, while soldiers' wives received seventeen shillings and sixpence per week to cover food, rent, clothing, and the security and protection of a child.

Barddoniaeth: Welsh: poetry, verse.

Blue crayoned: a line of knotted string covered with miscellaneous notes: 'For Higgs & Porters try 00 Downing Street.' – 'I won't be more than five minutes John Evans' – 'Still carrying on Riggs and Rogues Ltd.' These, and tragic words interspersed, clipped on with safety-pins, wire, hairpins: or emergency signs chalked up with blue crayons on cracked and broken pavements; and behind this rain-washed line of dripping notes – a cloud of dust – SPACE – and wideways stretch of sheltered rubble.

Easter Cuts [sic]: huge mathematical heads and shoulders which grate against the fierce storms of the tropics; and puzzle us still whether they stand outside the British Museum or on the bleak plains of Easter Island. *A Prismatic Art*, each feature cut, alters in expression with the movement of the sun, so that he is grinning under the evening light, may sneer before the rising of the sharp dawn.

Part V

I heard the voice of the fourth beast say, Come and see.
    And I looked and beheld a pale horse: and his name that sat on him was Death, and Hell followed with him.
    And power was given unto them over the fourth part

of the earth. To kill with sword, and with hunger, and with death, and with the beasts of the earth.

And when he had opened the fifth seal, I saw under the altar the souls of them that were slain for the word of God, and for the testimony which they held.

And they cried with a loud voice saying, 'How long O Lord, holy and true, dost thou not judge and avenge our blood on them that dwell on the earth?'

And white robes were given unto everyone of them.

REVELATION. CHAPTER VI

Caribbean Crane: the poet Hart Crane 'who made a perfect dive' off the SS *Orizaba*, and was drowned in the Caribbean on 26th April 1932.

Catena: born Biagio, *c*. 1470–1531. A Venetian pupil from Bellini's Bottega. His painting in the National Gallery, 'Saint Jerome in his Study', resembles my own convent upbringing, so that I connect him with the fragrance of beeswax – peace – serene pervading warmth of the southern air.

Reed collar: used in this village on an occasional horse. The collar is made of woven reeds and has no outer leather cover: the shade is olive-green: neatness and firmness of craftsmanship something which we have carelessly lost. I have also seen one plaited in straw.

White starling: January 1943, there was a column in the *Western Mail* by an ornithologist saying that a white starling had been seen flying over Carmarthen. The starling has appeared in Welsh mythology more than once: and was 'dispatch rider' for Branwen when it flew and took her message from Ireland to

Wales, so that she might be delivered of her unhappiness and *hiraeth* for Wales.

Calder: Alexander Calder.

Gorsefierce: Leguminosae: Ulex and Genista both words of Celtic origin. The gorse is to be found in early Triads and Welsh literature of the sixth century: a favourite flower with King Alfred and the Anglo-Saxons: and worn later as a cognisance by the Plantagenet kings. In the language of flowers gorse symbolizes anger. A resisting spirit throughout the severest weather, when a sheet of piercing yellow covers the hills blossoming in this valley: November, December, January and February.

Plantagenet King: Lordship of Commote Penrhyn, owned by Edward I, Prince of Wales, during the Hundred Years' War and which consisted of a pasture and grange surrounding the present villages of Llanybri and Llanstephan: Edward, the Prince of Wales, at the same time also owned a larger portion of the Duchy of Cornwall.

UNCOLLECTED AND UNPUBLISHED POEMS

TO A WELSH WOMAN

In her eyes,
The warm pools of sorrow
The wombed look of beasts
The beaten quiver.
Hair, straighter than a gypsy's
Skin cool and light
Hands crossed... of the soil.
White strength gathered in corners
Clenched those hands found bruised threadbare
Willed through cam burdens held up against her
And dispatched them to the sun.
Gentle as stardust and as little known
She strained to the Future always remote
Faded the image at too early a date
Blurred – now pale –
Lone cymry.

Published in *The Welsh Review*, 1, 6, July 1939.

SONG OF PRAISE

I have seen the finger of God
Pale whirling with fury
Pointing the sea.
I have seen the same biblical finger
Draw water to columns
Sterner than He,
Not pagan-fluted
Or Rome's cardinal order
But vaporous smote hollow
A supernatural reed.
I have seen light birds sailing
A ploughed field in wine
Whose ribs expose grave treasures
Inca's gilt-edged mine,
Bats' skins sin-eyed woven
The long-nosed god of rain
I have seen these things and known them
The moth wings to my Light.
I have seen the mountain of pumas
Harbour a blue-white horse.
The tinsel-rain on dog's coat
Zebra shoes at night
Bruised eyes and locusts
Dull powered air
I have seen these things now free them
To Eternity in my Height.

Published in *The Welsh Review*, 2, 3, October 1939.

POEM

In steel white land far distant near snow shivers out bead
    sequins glare
Violent torrents thread-like glass pierce needle air bounce
    and curse
Screeching wind full flaying prey distorts the vision sweeps
    faith away
Hideous, torturous, ice to Creation, this terror fight self
    protect hasten
Or lonely stretched on blue-blade beds the green woad will
    hover weed out design
But come stern storm, hail 'Wuthering Heights' do what you
    will. I need fear no more
For my house is clothed in Scarlet.
Scarlet my household, Scarlet my mind, spiced herbed and
    cherished, all alcoves wine
Laughter in corners, winks on air chasing shadows on ceiling
    bruins in lair.
Plush lacquered incense, open flowers on wall, frothed milk
    bread and honey to overcome falls
So come myth children, no longer fear, the winter is impo-
    tent under my care
For my house is clothed in Scarlet.

Published in *Wales*, 11, 1939/40.

ENGLYN

Where poverty strikes pavement – there is found
     No cripple like contentment
Which stultifies all statement
Of bright thought from the brain's tent.

Published in *Modern Welsh Poetry* (London: Faber, 1944).

GREEN MADRIGAL [I]

Peace, my stranger is a tree
Growing naturally through all its
Discomforts, trials and emergencies
Of growth.
It is green and resolved
It breathes with anguish
Yet it releases peace, peace of mind
Growth, movement.
It walks this greening sweetness
Throughout all the earth,
Where sky and sun tender its habits
As I would yours.

Published in *Poetry* (London), 4, 14, 1948.

TRANSGRESSION

At first God wanted just himself.
And this huge output of light whirled in horror
Throughout the heavens with nothing very much to do.
Knowing evil and good he was bored.
Knowing life he was really fed up,
So he set up like an artist to fulfil his daily needs,
And wandered from the first day and entered the second.

This was the layering of the mists.
And God not seeing what was under his foot
Called this the second day.

The third day God saw what was emerging beneath him.
The green mist and undulation of land and water:
Its modulated rhythm and irritability of split forms
Spitting up from the earth's face massed fronds
And circular prisms of light.
These he watched, startled, until there evolved
The springing active branches of varied leaves,
Plants, shrubs and trees. A dishevelled array;
A residue of years impelling change of growth.
The reptiles unknown to him but already in birth
Peered at his curiosity and their own under a
Blanching light. The mammals also secure on
The tree of life and hidden by its enormous branches of
Passing mystery, clutched the young to their breasts.

On the fourth day the stars appeared in stern formation
But were obscured by the sun's warrior rays.
The evening of the fourth day found them poxed.

They shone with anger rather than with grace
And fulfilled no heavenly place.
The moon yielded a false light and all things
Living swayed with uneasiness and took
Note of each other... interchanging and companionable...
The secret of life stirred in their blood.
And this the serpent termed fear. And he was right,
For God disappeared that night into the mist.

By the fifth day God returned to travail and
Travelled with rage over his whole continent
His potent wrath aroused birds of splendid hue and pattern
Whirls of magical and myriad moths, flocks of all
Shocked shapes and colour, all whirling, half-flying
Rumbling above the earth, rising surprised at the sight of
His terror. Then having risen once they subsided in mist.
Now let man arise.
And he came with his green shell of a body with tender
Hue out of the greening mist.
The light of God warmed and floodlit his powerless frame
And dissolved his paralytic fear and mission of no sense.
He came forward stretching for guidance.
God weakened by certain loss of his creative flame
Isolated this creature...
Who soon became truculent with too much light.

Eve arose indignant at his side. She was not created.
Life compelled her forward. She held no scruples
And immediately sought the forbidden tree.
For this written evidence and graft of truth
We can be truly grateful.
Now at the end of this sixth day God having
Set his bait, fell away under his immortal palms
To quibble with his conscience. The garden was too large to
Till, and he had not given them their freedom.

The cows Eve said were the only bit of sense.

So God mused on the seventh day and lazed among the hills,
And Eve spying him out asleep against the hedge
Shouted, and knew herself to be a shrew.
This she said and meant it for thousands of years after.
'Boss, this is a man's game, it is the religion of man
Just who created woman... and where do we come in...
The seventh day is lousy it is our worst ever.'

Published in *Wales*, 30, November 1948.

THE HYPNOTIST (WELSH ENGLYN)

A fox stared and outstared me – in a wood;
   In a mood of false glee
I mocked his audacity,
Now he haunts me near that tree.

Published in *Poetry* (Chicago), 81, 3, 1952.

LOVE IS AN OUTLAW

Love is an outlaw that cannot be held
Within the small confines and laws of man:
Rather it will turn, as a planet can,
Man upside down, like a first line fabled
In a notebook lightly pencilled upon
To change his sense of direction. Dimpled
Wisely like an unbridled child, love is pebbled
With smooth water and myths: a glazed swan
Shadowed in reeds: a ray of light waylaid
On swiftly moving motes. Wholesome love attends
Its own shape, warm and shining. The man who tends
The herds and street lights symbols of its trade:
It is a pacing Genesis on two legs,
Dispossessing man who unapparelled begs.

Published in *Poetry* (Chicago), 81, 3, 1952.

THESE WORDS I WRITE ON CRINKLED TIN

To the green wood where I found my love:
To the green wood where I held my love:
To the green wood now my love is gone.

I follow death that stands on my breath;
My heart cut out by the timeless scythe,
All grievous foliage stifling and still,
I carve two marks on the bark's rough edge
To convince my grief he came here once,
Whose spirit shivers the poplar tree.

To the green wood where the woodcock flies:
To the green wood where the nightjar hides:
To the green wood with red eyes of a dove.

The young jays springing and curious,
Who peck eyes from the lamb's sweet face,
Resemble too well my heartless step;
For he loves me and I love another,
I love another yet he still loves me,
He loves me still yet I love another.

To the green wood where the green air fades;
To the green wood fluid with icy shades:
To the green wood afraid I follow fast

Past Syrian Juniper and tall grass;
Hanging with dark secrets the Brewer's spruce:
The pond that drew the young child in:
Among darkening leaves, a nightingale
Sobbing in the sunniest season,

'My love, my love, do I love the other?'

To the green wood where I found my love:
To the green wood where I held my love:
To the green wood now my love is gone.

Published in *Poetry* (Chicago), 81, 3, 1952.

TWO WINE GLASSES

A pencil left in her sweet room,
If love is true then sing our tune,
Lovers always know their doom.

And his cool mind the pencils know,
And his pained eyes her hands attune,
Lovers glasses wine rimmed flow.

Two glasses share each smile and pun,
These favoured two none else would do,
Held a secret... death claimed one.

Amid the trees, and books on art,
In sun such greenwood songs grew blue,
Filtered through their drinking heart.

Now stiff in death like icing cake;
And green as moon the glasses hue;
Only one now drinks and waits;

But she who death has iced away
Soon breaks in glassy fragments two
Birds and flowers from out her spray.

A pencil left in her sweet tomb
If love is true then sing our tune,
Lovers always know their doom.

Published in *Poetry* (Chicago), 82, 6, 1953.

TY GWYN

A whirl of cobalt birds against
A cerulean sky, flashing light and seen
Through the rigid hand holding a vase
Of cornucopia grace.
Window, falling back like a concertina,
Mellow mild happiness.
A pink distempered warmth
A rainbow of books, only the day
Grey and dishevelled surrounds the village
Like straying hoofs.
A chart of bird songs, prints, and
Two china dogs shine wisely from the shelf.
The orange-scarlet brazier of coals,
Flickering flames mauve, red and green;
The crimson heart encircling my love
Photographed in the cabbage patch.

Published in *Poetry* (Chicago), 82, 6, 1953.

THE 'PELE' FETCHED IN

The 'pele' fetched in. Water
Cracked, broken and watered down
Carried into the home. Sticks
Chopped on the iron top yard,
Then suddenly the snow. The sky opened
And out of it shed, these floating flakes
Dazzling blinding all earth's features
Her smaller troubles and unfinished tasks
Covered by a huge silence.

'Pele' = mixture of coal dust, clay + water' [LR's note].

A SHOT RABBIT

Sitting in the emerald of twilight
And I its singular flaw,
Whose eyes like forgotten stars droop
Nebulously into distant light years.
Wishing the past as dark as night
And the future all light, clarity's rays.
Yet knowing obscurely
At some central motive of my being,
That all will arise, all turn,
Encircle me, as the light years have spun
Invisibly around their gravel point.

LLANSTEPHAN MADRIGAL

Through the trees... sea,
Down to the sea-lanes... sea,
Sea downs, down-stream,
Pools and prisms of water.
Black at its nightfall,
Wretched in its vapours,
White-pitched and
Pure in its daystream.

Sweet, meadowsweet air,
Quiet pastures sloping
Down, down to the sea,
Towards their own mirror
And sea, sea of perfection.

DISPLACED PERSONS

For seven days the dawn,
And on each day a fresh fold of sky
Until the fifth, when a thick glow
Spread like a heath fire, and the fields,
Farm and hedges lay beneath like a Welsh
Quilt frozen stiff upon the washing line.
Wailing, the birds, like no other day
Would come suddenly, fly away at the sight
Then flutter down from all sides,
All kinds together.

Neither from the frosted leaf nor from
The grey hard ground could they find
Relief. They were no longer birds but
Beings searching after food, spirits of flesh.
Peering at,– out of the trees.

[Handwritten comment by T.S. Eliot at the bottom of page:
'Rough. but interesting'.]

SAINT SWITHIN'S POOL

I'll not wash now Mam
The big red earth will
Rise in my face as I
Open the drill…
I'll wash tonight.
And he died and lay
In the drill and the big
Red earth covered his face;
And he said this Saint Swithin
Now I am dead I can have
My wash, and it rained this day,
Next, and every day since.

BRAZILIAN BLUE

If I could create one tree
And hang it in the sky
And spray it with the living
Gold of the sun, and hold
The natural pattern of its growth,
I would say that I had done
More than enough.

But observe when the sun
Has set against the black
Edge of the leaves,
How other leaves seem
To drift from one
Branch to another, or
Were they birds against
This darkwinged Brazilian sky?

Wings that edge the
São Paolo woods.
This flitting by,
This sudden appearance,
And inconsequence of time,
Is the moment I would
Hold before you;
Tomorrow evening it will
Have gone.

IT WAS NOT EASY

And as the log burnt up and bright
So we shared our simple pleasures;
And as the grate cooled and grew ashly
We fed at poverty's gate;
Suffering persecution and equal bars
Of discomfort. It was not easy.
It is not. In spite of the tempest raging
Over the planet's calm green face.

CHAPEL WRATH

Fields of camomile and clover
Wet and green as the lakes of Peru
Guarding Chapel deaths and their
Domineering graded stones padlocked
behind a spiked iron fence. The
Jealousies and jockeying for space,
Like chessmen where one move
Could shake the boards of death;
Where pawns can eliminate a queen,
Peasant, a squire's disgraceful scene.
The now sad plighted machine-lettered century
Leaving no culture of their own, but a
Metallic copy of their earlier neighbours,
Whose deep set letters on shoulders of slate
Announced their death with the pride
Of a spirited horse.

TRIALS AND TIRADES

Concrete slabs measured overnight into
A façade of walls. The top flat with its
New pane of vitamin glass, reflecting
A precipitous green of sky, of weird
Accumulator hue. No curtain out of
A square white room: but tree shadows tremulous
On ceiling. The parallel beams of sun
Shimmering with neon springs of air.
A chromium chair, and wider day of light;
A workshop from where ourselves we lean
Over sill and table: yet do remain surrounded
By boarding brothels: and through the lurid
Hours of dawn, face up to a firing squad
Who would not have us write and type
Not at that time of night!

ANGHARAD

Eyelashes like barley hairs,
Calm – sweet sighs
Absolving her angry
Interval like water
Overcasting fire. Shrill
Cries dissolving. Gurgles
And blue pool eyed caves
Stretch like a sewin of tantrums
And rest under the water's wave.

PRYDEIN

Stern pattern cut.
A frosty child
Writhing with seasoned tooth
Purple headed and radiating
Rays of piercing pity, –
Poison and fissure distress.

OUT OF A SIXTH SENSE

Out of the hot womb into the cold night breeze,
Out of a synthesis of mist and winter pain,
Dark green ivy on wet branched trees,
    Sprang to birth my son
    From his own mother
        Revealed
        Overjoyed
God's blessing from His mightiest word.

GREEN MADRIGAL [II]

Green gregarious green
Dredged into the very roots,
Lighting up a shine of green
Green light bathing the earth.

The whither-thither of splendid leaves
Rollicking in the spring of the sky:
The wind breathes the branches apart,
To the core of its heartwood
And resilient rays.

Dark-glowering leaf pattern,
A spread of flaming black
Radiates at the tip of each blade,
Fixes an impregnable pattern
Of stoic growth of purpose,
In such a purposeless world.

PREMONITION

When fold of iron blue and
Rolls of sparse corotesque grass
Recede further and further away
Leaving a multitude of space
Taking as you go
The salutation from my side
I imperceptibly accept the pale
Night and its immense face
In which to hide my frozen fear.

MOCKERY

If you have your heart in a thing
Work or person and this is mocked at,
Then this is death.

It is a crack in the heart
That saps your pulse away
Into a damp pattern.

That flattens the mind
Like mountain ash against the sky
With frost crouched close at its heel.

RED MULLET

Very strange is this fish and gift,
Instinctively it has a myth;
Caves of Poseidon watch it drift
Towards Medusa's opal plinth,
Orphic chants on pink scaled nights
Resemble well my lover's rites.

THE TAVERN

With eyes like tired skies and shifting explosion
Of nerves; these saints of Bloomsbury, blue bulls
And poodle men, sniff out their congested haunts,
Shelve, or move on a drink scrounge to a plaid green pub.
Sneer over plastic tables at the empty glass;
Drink – in caustic celebrities to upbraid them –
When their own minds warn them of defeat –
That 'they are as phoney as a porterhouse steak'
Then to return in rubbled muddle, with flashing
Ties and black picoted nails; round and out
Into the bleak night of streets; down coffered cellars:
To peony papered walls: broken beds: chip and bacon whores.

THE TEMPLE ROAD

There was a carpenter at my door,
And the smell and sound of the paint blew into
My nostrils and ears, and gathered
My thoughts, as I looked out of the window
With my hands warm among the washing socks
To the wet earth sodden with too much water
And the green plants persisting
Among the cavernous ruins.
And this I remembered.
It was a long time ago and they were
Of mellow brick. The books charred and torn
Falling out of their structure.
Such is the justice of man that he will
Appal at such destruction; yet for the same feat,
Go with heroic strides to have his own breast
Plated with tinkling medals.
Under this Sacred Temple,
Inner Temple and London's Shrine, such
A week's devastation melted half the
Block with the fury of rising flame-throwers.
Then to Pimlico where I took the bus…
I found warm flesh charred…
It was a long time ago,
And there at the same time a family
Unknown gave me an egg from their only hen
And an armful of mauve lilac:
They promised me as well some Iris roots,
'They'd send to Wales', they said.
I ate the egg. Destroyed my soul,
For such an immense tragedy can not withold a soul.
But I did not receive the Iris roots.

THE GREBE

To pine, moan, grieve, to hone,
But this is not my world
There is no sunshine.
Grey grebes break in the sky
Trailing a line of fire,
Leaving a thread of red silk
Like a newborn wound:
They fall despairing into
The soil, and unlike us,
Hide among the bogs.
The flash of poachers, their
Carrion ways against the bank;
Heap of feathered mass:
And wild eyed shame.

He alone could get me out of this
But he neither knows nor cares
After Hell there is a full stop.

The storm in my brain its
High tensional rays,
The sickness in my soul
And the growl and biting grit
That sets me back
Each moment forward I want to fly
Forward on the wake of some aerial device.
Where every moment is fresh
A flower or bird not seen.

To some trespassed spot
Of rippling streams, good natured
Enchantment, ease, and plentiful rest,
Where there is no access to these painful and

Immediate idiosyncrasies:
Where peace is formal, wholesome and pure.
And I would not call this escape
Nor would I call this inaction;
But a source from where all
Growth and activity could reside,
Could breed and acquire
A new note and thought,
Conspire with him whom I have recently admonished,
A new foregathering of Spring.

THE FIFTH PILLAR OF SONG

Because you produced the birth of sound within me
Because you pierced me with your personality
I strive to reach you O people of Cambria
For I have something to say:
With corbeau hue in the spirit of a bird
I have sharpened my beak on the blue vein of rocks
These the oldest strata to your age.
Like a cynometer I have measured blue sea and sky
Seen the cycle of vision with Branwen's eye
Learnt the song from Rhiannon's wood.
O people of Cambria listen
For I have something to say.
Silurian age gave silurian fish saurian-mouthed
A surrealist world half creatures of sea and land
My company for thousands of years.
Out of this arose the Cimmerian age
Cave dwellers of cavernous birth
The cambutta and campastoral life
Dragons, long staffed Bards and Kings.
O people of Cambria listen
For I have something to say.
With wandering wings and a restless spirit
I flew in search of light in warmer climes
To find leguminous plants, camels, and cambric
All connected with the Greek cycle of K.
Cyperous pools strengthened my way
With music more liquid than dew.
There I found a Phoenecian fleet
Of colours that stretched all seas.

O people of Cambria listen
For I have something to say.
I followed these ships in a circular flight
To Islands as distant as Java, Penang, Bali,
And the purple Isles of Pliny.
With hardship and toil a hard storm
Scattered my glazed plumage with stones
Camstones from the astronomical skies of Sirius
That bleached my green feathers for life.
Scarlet sails shaded with the salts great sea
The ship deep waisted, splashed with Cyprian wine and silk.
The Luds warriors from north eastern Crete
Pulling their way, and the ships of Tarish
All guided to your shore by the
Stern face of the stars.
For the richness of your soil.
O people of Cambria listen
For I have something to say.
All this occurred before the birth of Rome.
Came fleets also – sounds from Indian seas
From the opposite direction
Thus completing the cycle of K.
So from this circular flight of a bird
A circle of sound is traced
The greek letter of K has resolved itself into C.
K is your letter and K the key to your tongue.
K stands in its migration more mystical than 7
Go back to the stars and soil
And great will be your reward.

BRUSKA'S SONG

I own,
Broken-down cars, doll-houses and pies
These the spice of the day.
I use,
Freedom and fearlessness hand in hand
To frighten gowned tutors away.
Hands crashed on piano and paint
The type-writer too carries my weight.
Flying tremendous
Throughout the hours,
I follow my fancy if fresh bread allows.
Exercise *never*! –
Except singing and swinging
To balance the hours into endless winking.

PENDINE

Where leaves grow out of tree trunks
And light of the sea is erased
By the moon's blanched rays
Into a sombre task of a grey
Serenity. The dolorous hills
With their cumbersome outcrop
Of green, hold my locked head
This evening as I grieve
Uphill through the rain.
My slow feet quite detached
From the full measure of my
Ponderous brain weighted with
So much sorrow on its bodiless carriage.

RELEASE

I spent my days in passage ways,
Groping in the dark. Lost in a maze
Of doors. And though I went through
Each one there was, they always led to places I knew.
Hearing only my futile walk.
For I knew of the way to the castle moat,
And where I could find a rowing boat.
Then one day there appeared a door,
Where there'd been nothing at all before.
And as I knew that it might
Lead to light, I tried, and I was right.

So now I enjoy the light of the sun,
As much, and more, than anyone.

DOWNBEAT

Sitting surrounded by wasps,
My only view in this lovely
And sad caravan
Are the graves and tombs filling
Each window pane ·
Clustering up the sweet earth.
And towards the front, –
For that is the side and back view only, –
They are at this moment
Building by degrees
From a five tiered cartload
Sheaves of barley into a
Platform of dry trash:
This I understand to keep it dry
For I have never seen this done before.
So the rats will come and their omens
But with them with more hop and joy
Fearless birds of splendid plumage.

FURTHER UNCOLLECTED AND
UNPUBLISHED POEMS

BLUE SEA SLATE GREY SHADOWS

Blue sea slate grey shadows
Stretching a mackerel pattern for hollow men.
Slugged ships slate grey cannoned
Pointing a loaded battle at hollow men.
Steel wires slate grey knotted
Confusing plan and purpose of hollow men.
Flat hills slate grey papered
Stencilling news and doom of hollow men.
All this seen in the lower altitude
Obstruction to the view.

At the higher altitudes there are kites scarlet and white,
A maypole sheltering light children
With a spectrum interweaving delight.
Dog-tails wagging, full faces drawing the sun
To laughter mud pies and flowers
Macadamized roads clear ahead.
Sun-birds heighten the sky sending high notes flying
To the gentler voices of soil
The long-toed Mole's deep chuckling
The jewelled toad's proud gurk.

Published in *Fantasy*, 6, 3, 1939.

UNIVERSAL SORROW, SLEDGEHAMMER TO THE BRAIN

Universal sorrow, sledgehammer to the brain
Pins the needle to a smile
Challenges the Future with ominous spade
Imagination grave.
A treadled pattern down the mind
Squinting sight, knotting way.
No longer sun-held but a grief steel-charged
The Cyclops of today.

Published in *Fantasy*, 6, 3, 1939; *Now*, 2, June–July 1940
(with the title 'Dirge').

POEM WITHOUT NOTES

A high light and the Moon is mine
No other wires can touch the board
Only a Poet's pen.
This contour I hold symbolic to Eternity
A prism in the spectrum
The result of few.
Facets are worthless for they are only flips
Far better conundrums
Or rollicking Western beer.
Pubs cannot deny this
Nor can the high light return
For it is already obscure, a shadow

Or eyelash on the pillow.
Slim people and sticks are the landmark of this Era.
No heaped lumps or volcanic fury.
Precipitous jumps through the ceiling are nearer truth.
The Choir sings but the measure tends to sicken,
Even the cricket's ear turns grey
His plus four legs wilt, mottled on the wall.
The moaning procession leads across the Moon
Merging into space everything mumbles
into the drum – distance.

Published in *Wales*, 6/7, March 1939.

POEM

I see 2 ears and a tail;
looking closer at the design
I see
fur ermine, and 2 blancmange eyes
no
(polished rose quartz.)
The white form nibbles teethed leaves,
the white form twitches pink nose.
I poke with stick
the white form continues to nibble.
Peter the rabbit always hid behind the piano.
He came when he was called
Peter... Peter...

he did not come.
Puzzled
is it a statue?
Yak from Tibet – Unicorn – white polar bear
or my pale memory.

Published in *Life and Letters*, 22, 24, August 1939.

SONG

Bellowed clouds, caught across the sky
Hard blue sky of hollowed shading
Paling to a flat grey sea – tin-foiled
With no leading.
Of breadth wider than vision
Water greater than thirst
Sound immeasurable.
Ships shark-shaped, reflect liquid pride
And move with even pace.
One breaks the page
Slowly glides with time's tide
A furnace of the sea.
Through an indigo creek
A weathered boat moans
And sweeps the silent deep
The sea dappled, lightens the burden
With rays hung down from a tent filtered sky
The bellowed clouds flung free.

Published in *Fantasy*, 6, 4, 1940.

THAT TOY-MANNERED CENTURY

far away above the ruffles,
sifting through the snuff
and 18c. mouche moues,
floats a cat's cradle
pricking notes of petit-point design
a clockwork box; that ends where it begins
tinkling notes shaped like early neumes
mincing minuets and minikin bows.
needle notes from nowhere
from the teapot? statue? came
the musical box of moments. gone.
needs winding doodle doo: –
ping wing ping
ti tiddle lee ping ti-o
ping wing ping
ting di-o
diddle lee ping di-o.

Published in *Fantasy*, 7, 1, 1941.

TO THE PRIEST OF THE MIDDLES
(CONCERNING THE NEW ORDER)

If there is to be freedom of mind and face,
If there is to be mind of different weight,
Then there can be no equality of race,
Neither of mind nor face; for the late
Mind might want what a quick mind could ban.
To give face and freedom to mass production
And cramp our mind to the dead-piece, can
Hardly mature equality of race, station
The heart socially. It would merely provoke
Late mind to mud and quick mind to silver:
Hard 'middles' is the answer: thus to invoke
I am content to stay a cottage harbinger
Content to express the fury of a kind
At this attack on the precincts of a mind.

Published in *Modern Welsh Poetry* (London: Faber, 1944).

AIRCRAFT IN FLIGHT

you sleek metallic machine
grazed with grail green sidings;
smooth jointed flight of chromium plated rivets
droning drowsy engines
through the fresh night breeze.
you monster of navigation
man's victory and defeat
with conflicting wings synchronise both ways twice
over a weird dawn
of your own making.
plotted with care through strutted glass
clouds wash the plane's wide wake
diminishing man's small world and worry of weld
to face a larger god
of light, sun of man.

Published in *Wales*, 26, Summer 1947.

PAULINUS

He descends as I touch his death,
His day stone of immemorial flight,
From a sixth century rising into the next
Where David's typeface dissolves into space
With strides of barbarous hexameters.

This Saint whose cromlech remains,
Whose burial height grieves in straightened stone,
Stands, in a dingy corner of a museum's frayed side
Neglected by man. As the bald-brained councillors
Neglect man, who flit through its impersonal ruins.
Paulinus, whose greenstone filled the lives of men
Is rent in three. As clover seeks his path;
A bird his rock; cattle their standing stone;
Dwellers who till, sow, reap, and live by labour,
Who placed yoke on shoulder, raised water from River Tâf,
Their holy hands carrying stones for this Scribe
Paulinus, a founder of Ty Gwyn… who remains…
And this I table as I touch your stone of death.

Published in *Wales*, 30, November 1948.

FARM CAT

You magnificent jet white cat,
Statue out of a mantel shelf
Sitting upright indifferent
To the crimes of war.
Until a sudden change
Softens your innermost eye
Turns head and feathered
Fur into a cloud of
Mist as elusive as your
Mantel stance or a cruel
Hedgerow prowl.

Published in *Western Mail & South Wales News*,
23 February 1949.

THE GREAT DISTURBER

Imperative mood
Green willingness to spread shade
Submerge and dissolve into primaeval glade
Such an enchantment held
With an iron grip as rainwater in a tank,
Mullein with their clipped buds protecting
A stirring-riot of touch;
Plaintive light seeking for darkness, for release,
As in the primaeval fall.

As potent as corn
As sacred as intangible as the wind winnowing the corn,
The steer rushing through its roots,
The steer is in the corn. Whose spectral white
Tense as bean-flower infuses the sight and air
With its fragrant breath and solitary pace.
He, of the lean lip and sharp acquaintance
Of shy and sallow grace sits at table-talk
Yet he is not there.

This our single meeting
Whose huge and shadowy image
Projects above all streets, paraffin lamps, hills, trains,
Reaching far up into the mind and strains it wildly
Into open spaces of pleasure and pain;
So are we by this disturber of love liberated
On to the bewitched shores of mankind;
And whether we are chilled or comforted
May we be part of.

Such a thing is it
Drawing of sun through the bones, that it flies
This disarray of estrangement into the air
Engages the ear, voice, curves around trees – the tree –
Hovers in the sky, clings to our sleeves and hair
So that we are not solitary neither are we free.
Yet he is not there who was across the street a while ago
And we stand unresolved
A bare branch in spring.

Published in *Life and Letters*, 60, 139, March 1949.

THE ORANGE CHARGER

My sacred charge
On you will I spring
All joy and tenderness,
Whose song falls into the air
Like a shower of dew,
So pure, so fresh, it
Each time is heard.
Who sings late in the mornings,
Or in some strange way
When no other bird sings,
So that your voice is signalled out
For its willing ease to please.
When rain is drawn from the sky,
Days of it...
And I sit all day at that window
This day and next...

Watching that rain,
Then sharply on my senses
As a ray of light were it
To descend on me
Falls your sweet notes on me.
You small orange charger
Are no common bird,
And I place you here
Among the earlier birds of myth
As a single fortune which has been
Handed down to us,
Who loves to migrate
And not to migrate,
Or sits with wistful isolation
In the perennial springs of the Azores.
You, who are the bird
Of the warm steaming soil,
Of the scent of the rain,
Of quiet temperate days;
From your orange breast
A sweeter cadence was never heard.

Published in *Life and Letters*, 60, 139, March 1949;
PN Review, 40, 2, November–December 2013.

DEATH THAT MONSTER

Death that monster that takes us unawares
Whose sleep is as naked as the golden collar
Cowers lest the sky should fall on his back
And diminish his agricultural hoard.

He is the haughty warrior defiant of all mankind;
He is in particular the Keltic god
With all the spiral trappings of our race:
The embossed gold studded beneath the soil,

Emblazoner, and cause of its split spoil.
The armoured trumpeter who diminishes all flesh,
Whose urgent missile and invisible flight
Points with a sickle horn at his various deeds:

The unbending grass now grazed by the cows,
Chapel and Church, playground to death's cause.
I call to death, his tenebrous voice that incites us
To invent, cling to superstition; who in loss

Leads us dingily through paths of release.
Who steps like sullen summer over the tusked terrain
From sign of Pisces to the Water-Carrier's glade:
And here death waited. Watched at the spring's source.

'And water-carrier I am' shouted the woman
As she downed the hill to fill her last can;
'That's him who shoves up our eyes and sweeps us
Into the hall of rocks... his watery foul box...

Pushing us back into hills of moving green...

Why stare through the leaves?' she muttered pouring
Water to her cattle. 'And resurrection?' wailed
The woman now down on her knees as she caught

A glimpse of death chained to a yew. 'Resurrection'
He replied, like hot breath rising from a ten-cent store,
'Is what you leave behind'.

Published in *Poetry London*, 4, 16, September 1949.

ENCROACHMENT

A black and fatal emptiness fills me this night
As I urge my work forward,
To conceal the weathered gaze
This coming mist and immovable flight of birds
That wail at the lovers going.
Such sudden departure I had never guessed,
Such a living death so fatal
To my own frail heart and fate.
O Grave Owners. O Encrusted Rocks,
Marble-veined and set with hard and singular sorrow,
Such crystallized misfortune I cannot hold
Whose constellation has lost its magnitude star
And well-known revolving pattern.

Published in *Life and Letters*, 63, 147, November 1949.

LET THE MAN OF DARKNESS OUT

Let the man of darkness out
That he may be free
Calm his face
And lighten his burden
From obscurity into light.

Let him like a tree at night
Grotesque and obscured by
Uncontrollable branches
Merge imperceptibly
Into light.

Take shape out of hedgerow
Clear definite shape
With every idea of creation
Penetrated revealed and known,
Concentrated on His work, on Him,
His illuminating resurrection.

Whether tree, bird or pasture
They carry His name,
And no Book nor human reason
Need cover His mind or seek their own.
The manifestation is here.
Victory over degree,
Man's livery of things unseen.

Published in *The Penguin New Writing*, 39
(London: Penguin, 1950).

OUT OF THE PAW OF NIGHT

Out of the paw of night
And out of my sodden self
A cry like the whining of the wind:
A filter of salt covers my eyes
Banks of sand rise in my throat
On hearing the foul news of his death.
Death so finite; so unacceptable.
I would use grief to some purpose
Allow it to harness my will
And strengthen my undermined health,
I would turn grief into victory
Black into white.
I would, I said to myself
Become twice as strong,
Twice set on my objective
Along the black road of life.
And then at the turn of the road
Caught sight of a tremulous pool
Towards which a fisherman might creep
With folded breath and much reverence.
Then downcast, without reserve
My will broke as the pool stretched
Into the memory of him who loved
Such coveted brooks.
My sorrow burst forth like a stream
And over the sharp boulders
Rushed unheeding along.
My resolve had been forgotten
Laid waste in the powerful
Currents of this wretched tide.

My tears stiffened and turned to glass
And my son said 'Don't cry you can have
Father Christmas.' I turned.
I felt sour within.
So, my beloved Father, the blight that rested
On your heart like the marked pestilence on an
Autumn leaf, caved in. And I received tidings
Of your dispersal into dust in an Argentine cable:
'*Passed away*'. But never passed for me
Who holds you in the very fibres of my being
Who will live as long as I live –
As all people live who are dead
In the breasts and minds of others –
Such is their resurrection:
And of these, the Saints wear the longest life:
The devil the most erratic, since he fluctuates
Within the frailty of man's estate
Whether he is absorbed in their nature,
Or scattered in fragments on the planet's rockface.
So death goes forward into the mind of men:
Death reinforces life: Death boldly held
Is rebirth of life. To succumb
Is to find grief foundered: loss ill-used:
Worse, it is an insult to the noble mind dispersed.

Published in *Poetry London*, 5, 21, February 1951.

WHOSE HAND I HAVE NEVER TOUCHED
To Norman Lewis

You Zeus, god, whose hand I have never touched
Whose back is turned ever towards me,
Who knows restraint but not restriction
Moderation but not meanness, shifting
Like lightning through space, seeking
Purification and its meteor death,
For whose encounter I have long waited,
And cast alone soliloquise with soft
Double pupilled eyes that raise in store
Some feline happiness, O Ravisher,
Turn to this your black dove and summer vice,
For after the battle and tribulation
There will remain only you upon the field
And your car that always passes by.

Published in *World Review*, October 1951; *Poetry Wales*, 19, 2, 1983.

SPRING

Spring rules the world with open wing
And leaves that sing vibrate the air
With birds so rare that man should fling
His stress of being aside to bear
The greater joy of King of Spring.

As from a lawn the ring dove flies
With soft silk sighs greets Capricorn
Her breast the dawn with ruby eyes,
Stirs sound. Arise sun's May day born
While wood larks charm the petalled skies.

When streams seep out of hidden stone
And beelike drone and celandine
With crystal shine and undertone
Of yellow zone so well combine
To serve Spring's Equinox well known,

Then through the hedge with outgrown pace
He trails green traces on horns of light
The farm bull white of sacred race
With bindweed lace and aconite
Recalls a rite of age-long grace:

Disturbs the trout's rock-pooled display
And roundelay of gorselit birds;
As gay as words they fly with May
And stir the day's white blossomed curds
Then out to fields their nests survey.

You these observe: then migrants come:
With wingbeat drumming, geese, cuckoo,
Warblers too, swifts scissored hum
The frolicsome dogs, sheep and ewe:
See round this valley strife is dumb.

For in this valley Artemis walks
With Sparrow, Hawks, and Spring-like Dove,
She fills the grove with rain that talks
And greens the stalks of birch above
Attend these leaves: The Queen of Spring.

Published in *Quarto*, 4, Winter 1951; *Poetry* (Chicago), 82,
6, September 1953; *PN Review*, 40,
2, November–December 2013.

THE AUTUMN MAENAD

Like a breast of bird held out in space,
Feathers richly marked to mirror leaves,
Autumn leans her veiled and brittle face,
             An old strumpet at ease.

Trails a mist to earth and grieves for grace,
Neither birds nor bees embrace her trees,
Hills recede, these myths her life retrace,
             Of that old maenad tease.

Bird of Paradise and man's solace,
Bleached and auburn hair her spirit weaves,
Known to all she stands and takes her place,
             A pheasant rich to please.

Published in *New Statesman and Nation*, 43, 1088,
January 1952.

This the legend like lake mist curling,
Round the barren heights of Hell,
Swamping man with bitter agony,
To the heel of Sawdde's pebbled shore,
The Lady of the Lake.

This the recurring theme and pattern,
As love and death descends upon our will,
She whose taste for individual freedom,
Divided her from others, and came,
Upon that Black Hill, yours:

Gave him, hand, love, and life.
Showed wit at a funeral: foresight at a wedding:
An acquired taste for rural bread:
And no love for locks or bolts:
His sweet demon lover.

Now as the monstrous season turns,
Thins the buttermilk of days,
Scouring his heart, and her mind:
At her command over the rippled lake,
At the third blow, turned,

Called her young heifer of flour white hide,
Bid her black bull calf 'Prydein come'.
All three dissolved into the wavering haze,
To her Living Grave and Lake of Birth,
Like midges in the air.

Like midges in the evening light
They stung and blocked his path;
He sent her combs for her sunflower hair
From his journey somewhere to new pasture:
Eyes watered like the sun.

Her flesh cooled like the evening pool,
Willows fell red on her shores,
Swallows stirred her gravel face,
Transcribed every act,
Fish fled from her side.

Published in *Departure*, 1, 1, [1952]; *PN Review*, 40,
2, November–December 2013.

CIRCE: THE FALCON
To be sung to a traditional ballad tune

I wish I was a bird again,
To fill his sight with golden eyes,
To draw him out into the Bay
And be his falcon for a day.

I wish to circle his dark form,
As love, invisibly go by,
Fly in, around his savage rocks
That hide our timbered nest and flocks.

I wish to free his mind of fear,
Float bells and shells upon the air,
To see his boat rejoice with spray
And hear him sing to clouds that stray.

But I am just an old grey crone,
Whose feathers are but dusty bone,
He's gone away far out of sight
And left me in the Bay's bleak light.

Published in *New Statesman and Nation*, 45, 1142,
January 1953; *Poetry Wales*, 34, 2, October 1998.

WINTER WALK

She left the hut and bright log fire at noon
And walked outside on crisp white winter snow
To find the iced slopes shadowed like the moon,
The wild wood desolate and bare below;
The red trees wet, adrift with icy flow,
The evergreens with glassy needled leaves;
A bloodstone veined red and white this view weaves.

But lifted off the path like crystal spheres
There lay cut prints of glinting stylized forms
Of birds not seen, large sparkling twig-like spears,
And squirrel pricks where fox's paw transforms
White single roses out of petalled storms;
While keltic scrolls transcribe where birds had been:
Then stamped in ice another track was seen.

A slight right turn of foot. She sensed him there,
Tree like with raincoat shouldered, fine large looks,
A four-armed god. From this sweet honeyed snare
She turned, upspraying, Marsh Tits, Finch, and Rooks,
Through brushwood hills, seeing by frosted brooks
His footprints: these she retraced like a bride
With loaves and wood returned to his keen side.

Published in *Poetry* (Chicago), 85, 1, October 1954.

NO WALKING PATH THROUGH FLAME

Now that all birds and flowers have sunk into the earth,
And I am left a solitary light on this aged and darkened world,
I feel all the past to be trivial compared to this, my most grievous woe.
No flame, no walking path through flame could affect my chilled flesh.
I am dead as no human being knows death.
I walk living, but can neither perish nor fall.
Such my Beloved is my dispirited being at your strange behaviour:
That you should tie up your own life for honour without love
When it can bring no happiness to either
But stretch you over grave bogs and wild mere, into the cold night air.

Published in *Poetry Wales*, 34, 2, October 1998.

SATANIC AQUARELLE

Owing allegiance to none,
I have taken this first step
And made fate my own.
To stand and study the play of words
Rising and falling like a tidal wave.
And I will definitely make clearings
Extensive clearings to find the light
The inner light of my own voice.
The sweet prism of all things
Seen with my own three eyes...
Mark how I break up the sentence
Reject familiar words, to bend and curb
The rhythm which I wish to convey
See how I persevere like this cow,
Who lies folded on the grass
And chews her own cud.
While from my caravan's calendar I see
Through Spring, Summer, Autumn, Winter
Her maturity digested, and the peace
Which reigns over her noble horns.

Published in *Poetry Wales*, 34, 2, October 1998.

A LETTER TO THE DEAD

(A lost poem in memory of Dylan Thomas)

To you Dylan with my own voice I pay tribute
With as natural a grace as though you were near,
Remembering in a dark night, your hand in mine
When you told me to think of myself, to go abroad
And over the bounds with my poetry: to care not a fig
Pig or jig for anyone, for it was Rabelais all the way, or
Then drew out the lines, the sonorous images
Of my own work that pleased your heart and eye:

> ...light birds sailing
> A ploughed field in wine
> Whose ribs expose grave treasures
> Inca's gilt-edged mine,
> Bats' skins sin-eyed woven
> The long-nosed god of rain...

So many years ago, the poem I would forget.
How many years was this?
Then followed the war, correspondence between us;
And you became best man at the 'Show'
Which turned out to be, not exactly happy but worthwhile,
And your head was flooded with the wedded words
Of pomp, fruit and carnal rectitude,
Caitlin patient, gentle, smiling at your side.
We have your signature to this, and photo in the Western Mail.
And we crossed the Estuary and visited or stayed at your domain,
Sending messages ahead with the ferryman, ringing his bell
To carry us on his back and row us in his cormorant boat,
While we, the lesser ones in the humble dwelling
Paying three and six a week to your four-storied house

Invited you, or unexpectedly found you both
Wandering in the neighbouring fields or lifting the iron gate.
Drinking and drinking, I have never done so much drinking,
And declared I would never do it again.
But you and he and they and she would insist,
And at it again, in order to discuss, listen,
Or conjure a word from you, and up with the glass again.
But what mattered: or what was remembered:
Cherished just then: the reading of those Anglo-Saxon poems
Which I gave you, 'the first time you had seen them' you said,
Riddles on our lives: the half-written poem, the concentration
And discipline of your behaviour to your so eloquent a craft:
Or walking up to me, your mind tight with the unsprung words,
Was I the 'Bird Woman' then? 'What bird is that?' you would say,
'And that? And that?' impetuously as they trilled and winged away
Sound and feather out of sight. It was on a cliff overlooking
Your Boathouse remember? Whimbrel, sandpiper and curlew I replied
And marvelled that you did not know. '*I want to know about birds?*'
Was your repeated reply. Then rising out of that flowing Bay
Seven years later, the birds yours, were lifted on to the page,
Recreated, made new, with us for ever.
Then in a span of time... not seeing... in the years of grief,
Until my caravan pitched in the graveyard
Where your body now lies, stood for as long as Eternity,
Or so it seemed to me then. The spirits in it rising
Over my distress and stress of doom.
At such unexpected moments we met,
In ship's pub and sea pubs drinking, and at it again
If only to be alive with you, was there no end to this?
Drinking and drinking, for I hated the damn stuff,
Until the evil spell cast upon me drove us apart
I to another region away from the duck green forests
Darkened by cormorants. To the metropolis of London.

There already a legend, your name was spilled about in the air
And your voice cast over the waves, the ninth wave
Charged with Mabinogion magic, or heard from a box
Reverberating that atomic symphony of Cain.
This, then, was our last meeting in the wings
Behind the bare auditorium hall
Where you and Edith stood alone.
Then when I did turn up that second time,
It was to arrive too late, too late for life
At the Churchyard Gates, passing up, through the down-going
Dying faces, up to your ever living form. Alone
At the grave, dug so many feet deep, by the gravedigger
Known to us both, the Laugharne owl staring from the yew.
You staring. And O I must tell you he had a hard time picking
At those rocks. The stone face refused to yield
To give her young Bard so soon a bed.
I saw Louis in the shade as his tears fell.
And past them all as they gathered round the pub
This time I had no need to drink against my will
For your company was everywhere. Out on the cliff edge I walked
Overlooking the Bay, its mudsilt, greying water-dunes and birds
Quietly stopping at the Boathouse, thinking to call.
What distance, since the others did not remove us,
Holds us together? What bird or bind of word
Substance of sound or rhythmic flow?
Could you, if you wished, now cold as a stream,
Warm my keen pen as it wanders afar
Out into the crystal air to charge those hypocrites
Who would acknowledge you with the mockery of your own voice
Snatch at your images, instead of their own
The rhymesters and feathered curs.
                                        If the air above Dylan,
If the air above had ears, and could hear my request,

Would it caress your head, that for me, so personally
Brought a standstill to my heart. I would say Amen on this;
Or write Lynette to end the page. But continuous as the thought
I write for you Dylan evermore.

Published in *PN Review*, 41, 2, November–December 2014.

A TRUE INTERNATIONAL

Like shining grass hard and clear
Grief shines again throughout the air,
Released as light the grave dust falls,
And cumbersome flesh no longer mourns;
Man dissolves into spiritual form,
Without bone or blood he takes new lease,
Travels everywhere the planets cool face;
An international of abstract grace.

ANANDROUS FLIGHT

Such a shower of peace crosses my brow
And soothes my steep and sensuous heart
With the freshening lift of these leaves
And newly washed hair waved everywhere.
As the oriole eye turns down in the sky
Leaving the white fleck of a hymen moon
My mind is lifted under this lowering bird sun
Like some dusky brown butterfly,
That Painted Lady or Brazilian Blue
Who carelessly balances on the shining sand
Throwing her wings open and shut
In promise of some antennae flight
Alone and above a tropical summer.

BLUES WITH A RUMBA BACKGROUND

He's got the China doll Blues,
He's stiff and frozen out.

He takes in her heart
That knew the red doves dart
Now it lies like a tout apart.

He takes in her hands
That moved castles of sand
Now sees them coarse as stubble lands.

He takes in her eyes
That harvested their lives
Now they're squinting china eyes.

He's iced he doesn't know it
It's plain to see
She's but a China doll
He's mean to me
He doesn't love me don't you see.

But the China doll she blazes
Her desires like rockets roaring
Her hair electric flames rising
Her eyes two neons flashing
Her hands are beating
Time against her
She is so hot. He is so cold.

For he's got the China doll Blues
He's stiff and frozen out.

DEDICATED TO 'BRUSKA'

Artificial flowers
Wax tinsel and paint
In a white storied flat 68
Gut-oiled rose
Sage rose
And single white rose all whitewashed
Scattered with sea-sequins by my cool hand.

Under the spell of snow and frost
I follow the silver ribbons of railway lines
The tinsel track of snails.

(Single white rose.)

Collecting these strips
I lighten the flowers
Artificial Flowers for festive days.

(Sage rose.)

The air I breathe and the song I sing
Weave a tissue for their birth
With the sea-frost to prime their design.

(Gut-oiled rose.)

All these have passed through my hands
Except the single white rose
Made from blue-white snow.
This I have kept

A sculptured form
Of alabaster weight
For the festive day, the sealing day,
When sin-born flowers trade the sky.

DORIAN MODE

Rest O my people for this is Zeus
Whose flaming mind and shimmering raiment
Orders upon you a shower of gold,
And through your shelled lids
A stratosphere of vermillion
Pierced alternately with his violet rays
His undying and healing persistence,
Who like the veins on some leafy hedge
Radiates before us his forked pattern
His magnetic hold, through his heart,
Through his warmth, on these his frosted beings.

EASTER MADRIGAL

And with the power that a flushed rose
Draws blushes from a young lover's face
So would I draw you pale to my side,
Where I lie petalled with soft desire.
Shot, and red shadowed with love's sharp pain.
And as the dunnock's grey beak of thorn
Sings mournfully of your frozen fate
So would I kiss the wry mouth of death
And with the power that a flushed rose
Draws blushes from a young lover's face
Restore life into your crimson cheek?

EISTEDDFOD

The mist in cunning ways is bold and blind
It hides the blast and myths so cold in mind
Surveys the shape and spreads it for mankind
With quiet persuasion around us winds a sometime
Cow, white as lime and sacred to man's find.

The horns dissolve and herds of men appear
With Gorsedd shirts each male a lake of fear,
To maid's set runes they strive to write in beer
Dead odes the Greeks would gladly spear, nor scan
The script, but ban as based on Englishman's slim gear.

The theme as dead. The mist arose. The oaks

Sodden as homesteads: the lopped Groves by folks
Destroyed. A well remains inside these oaks
Wet as 'Exiles'. Today the mocking Bard smokes and smoulders,
Then upstream shoulders canned words with garbled strokes.

Let him then rail, at the poet who with no income or care
Sleeps in the same shirt. Exclaim if he dare
The dissonant word the Anglo-Welsh. His first and rare:
For this we bless our chaired Bard's despair – for the scowl
Against the growl, of a full-blooded Welsh mare.

ETERNAL LOVE

Trellised grapes on warm south walls,
Sodden rose on dying stem,
Such a view toward the garden;
A rose leaf tremor on a thread.

Bare arm cool on dark verandah,
Hand raised shading eyes from sun,
Stands, with distance coaxed around her:
I wondered when I saw her there.

Chained Molossus barked and thought he,
Flashing down his iron run
Saw a shade of someone enter;
These fidgets set our nerves on edge.

Sunset hair brushed gay with birds,
Clinging skirt and shoes worn high,
Lover's knot ties this white blouse
So choice and stored away in years.

Never had she worn such garments
Dressed in tenderness and vapour
Lost, I tried to solve her patience,
To this she never would reply.

Damask rose on swirling lace
Gossamer breasts yielding as doves;
Folding back her years, she hovered,
To cup her chin on pensive hands.

Five hours fixed on black scrolled gate
Eyes, they never ceased to gaze,
Ballad day through crippled shades
Confused now fades in disarray.

Coaxing as I kept on spying
Held magnetic to her side,
Wine nor speech would never reach her,
And only once did she reply.

Fluttering in her violet mind,
Bats flew near as she replied
'Someone not seen... (for a long time?)
I am... expecting... someone...'

Veiling blue seeming myth
Cannot stay or stray overlong.
Together rest and peace, and wind
Around the valley glades.
Park grace could never be told
That the mist which of old
Trailed to the Bay. Grey dishevelled
Trelled hiding in caves, finding
Sprinkets of gold green, filaments
Winding from the bright gay sun.
To behold on winter's day
A spring light over the countryside
A cow through grisailles of hay;
Mist glittering with damp undergrowth
And sparkling streams.

Tune
Grail away Borage
Flat hover of kestrels,
Ruin groans out of day
Stains wideworn windows.
Dredge flowers on fields
Lime buds on lane,
Grail away Borage
Float on you kestrels.
Strain sun to a colour
Shed blue on calico,
Run green into ventricles
By chequered brooks

Plovers' eggs.
Bee drone on borage
Blue light a lighter sky
Ruin grows out of day
Strides on twigs
A snail's radiance.

Pipe against the sky
Blue rinse your teaming mind
Spring, blow piper,
Shed sorrow from your princely chest.

Pipe against the sun
In amazing wonder skip joy, and sing,
In lime lanes spring flowers
Joy and merriment of growth

Corymbs of sun
Sprinkle and span the hedge
Drive through the crackling branches
Wake. Pipe against the sky.

Cool
and calculating
(2,160 miles in diameter.)
I rotate every 29 days.
Do you hear Pagan Earth?
and you, you blurred bitched poets?
Cleanse your sight;
for I am neither mysterious nor inconstant
you perceive me too vaguely
in your fuddled way.

      (Emotional Earth,)
      Centralise, and accept
      clear perception
      With a secret to your ear.
      ('ROGUES both, each other's deceiver
      Reflecting other Light
      Like God's prophets.')
      Assuming strange personalities
      Green and blue
      With bleak rays
      Bleak ways – Moon – Earth.

'To eliminate mystery of Halos
The fiery and watery rings.'
Moses the cause of one
The Lady of the Fountain the other.
They migrate here full 238,000 miles
Once every 13 Light years.
(Small Moon scandal)
The rest of the time

Moses combs his beard
And the Lady of the Fountain
Drowns herself in Welsh sorrow.

You weep green tears Pagan Earth
I see your contour streaked with red.
I Moon, cool – and calculating
With my Magnetic Light
Will cleanse your
£.S.D. World.
¾ d.

HE DID NOT KNOW I COULD BE GAY

He did not know I could be gay,
And rich in such a careless way,
As treetops in a swaying wood,
With flights like squirrels after food,
And dressed in gorgeous blossomed mood
With lacquered beaks on nails so fair;
He did not know I could be gay,
A butterfly of lips that dare,
And rich in such a careless way,
To kiss the falcon in the air,
With barley plumes wreathed in the hair:
But gayer still my heart is May
And light as featherdown Rose Bay
He did not know I could be gay,
And rich in such a careless way.

I'm only a
child' of twilight
race' to gather blue
moss' to gather white
grace' to see the world
toss' with – rhythm.
Pagan rhythm sifting through the
air' pagan rhythm distant feet.
Pagan rhythm swinging largely
to' demolish even beat,
I'm now a
child' of blue-white
hue' to pierce dim
light' to select sharp
rays' to convey the
mood' in – rhythm.
Pagan rhythm coursing through the
veins' pagan rhythm catching fast.
Pagan rhythm drumming synco
pated' flashing past.
I'm at last a
child' of Transit
Era' to these the
measure' of my full
weight' with –
Rhythm' rhythm' sounded sleep in the
soil'
Of rhythm' rhythm' born.

IN THE GREEN GLADE OF AN AFTERNOON

In the green glade of an afternoon
Reeded grasses flowering like snow:

the dark pull of the earth raises such storms
Of emerald air around her course.

In the green glade of an afternoon
Mars felt his face to be out of tune:

Found riches on the planet's wet face
Reflecting grass reeds and aftermaths.

Peace joined their circuit a blue sash of sky
Swathed them in content as in peace they lie:

The Evergreen Chronicles of Time.

LULLABY

Sweet on my dear
Wood larks do sing
Clear as the wet spring that shines.

Soft on his head
Air with the sun
Spreads on the blind one that cries.

For lost to his mother who
Walks on the streets, for the
Pleasure of men who poison her keep.

Sleep my own dear
Wood larks do sing
Clear as the wet spring that shines.

Soon death breaks his shadow to
Lighten her woe, releases
Her mind to the sun and the air.

Sweet on my dear
Wood larks do sing
Clear as the wet spring that shines.

Mother the air
Mother the sun
Spreads on the blind one that smiles.

Take comfort my birdling, the
Grimace of sin, led a
Blind face to sing with the faith of a bird.

Sweet on my dear
Wood larks do sing
Clear as the wet spring that shines.

NIGHTJAR'S CHATTER

What has become of the Age of Reason
That the same adventure can be acclaimed
Both with contempt and heroic treason:
That from a village drawer a poet disclaimed
His paper-poems and gathered them bound,
For the Salvage Man on his weekly round.
That for this queer deed a busy Britain turned
At such a Great and Heroic Gesture
While few apart turned in their minds and spurned
The action, the misapplied adventure.

NINE BELLS

The air has carried the ring of the bell forward
Ringing cold and crisp in the frost night air
The church-owls grey as stone stand huddled on the larches.
The yew berries fall red: leaves scattering orange
Up and around the caravan window, somewhere and about
A dog howls in an iron trap caught in an underworld vice

More fiercely the dog star casts a tear of shining light
Down pricks her rigid retinue that stride over the fireless hill
Steers round, breaks hedges; sensing movement and blood
Cats alone curve by the hearth with an indifferent poise.

OH MAX

Oh Max you are more beautiful than the Moon
And I know your desire
It is, to be as full as the moon.
But I will keep your secret
If only you tell me where you got those bruin ears
The sun-faded coat with its deep blue shadows
And your two honey eyes,
Max turn, for I am speaking to you.

Oh Max you are more beautiful than the Moon
And I know your desire,
It is to bite the teasing boy's leg.
I will let you do this thing
If only you tell me where you got that ape scratch
The pale cross on your chest and wise biblical look
And your furrowed brow.
Max attend, for I am speaking to you.

Oh Max you are more beautiful than the Moon
And I know your desire,
You have fled from Jonquile and his charming games
And now you miss his ways.
I will fetch him to you

If only you tell me the tale of Elisha and the bears
Of the prophet's loyalty and magical cloak,
And the two she-bears.
Max speak, for I am listening to you.

(Barks)   Bears, Brown Bears, Syrian Bears
(growls)   They all trample round in the brain.
                 Bones, Brown Bones, Syrian Bones
                 The children Elisha trained.
                 These my ancestors
                 Bears, Brown Bears, Syrian Bears
(sneezes)   The twin 2 she-bears
                 And for their dead I wear the cross.
(dreaming)   Eyes honey, my people straining
                 At a syrup image before their sight.
(Scratching)   The monkey trick, from Ravines of Hermon
                 Where agile beasts scratched with might.
                 Elisha enlightened taught us wisdom
                 Hence the well creased brown
                 'That masters personified in mantles
                 The power that commanded deeds.'
(in deep thought) ...
                 Thus you child my mantled mistress
                 And I your handsome Brown Bear.

Oh Max you are more beautiful than the Moon
                 My Guardian Angel and My Pride.

                 Bones, Brown Bones, Madeiran Bones
                 Swift by my flight.

SOLOMON'S SEAL

Slipping through the sap-green ravines
with shy-eyed flowers.
Tracking along railway cogs
eating rose petals
Where wayside boy presented sugar cane
   for my stray steps.
Reaching mountain of Cabra with open view
   fresh air, moist.
Imagination fled to
'Hide and Seek' blossoms
Solomon's seal
Moments gone to
Song.

SONNET: ON THE BLACK OUT

There is a quiet soft night that comes to us
Now and then with a leap year's sly warning
A night that is smothered black; a tomb's fawning
That stifles all sound with a padded hush
Guided by zebra-shapes stretching half luminous
Along cold grey roads. The 'Masked' now pawing
For greater Light, with activity thawing
The steel silence that hangs lugubrious
Like a snore over nature's blue bed. DEFEND
Some say with sweeping haste, flash, search the skies
With crab-like walk. Prick out the leprosy

From alcoholic wings and once more DEFEND
The Empire Home. From what? War! Yes! then rise
To the crash of reality, to things that be.

THE BLACK COLLARED DOVE

In flies the black collared dove,
Winging in from the Korean shores:
Proo-proo oo-pru he coos.

In flies this solitary dove,
And all he finds as he nears the coast
Is dark water hiding life and land:
Proo-proo oo-pru he sobs.

The hawthorn is sunk on the Lincolnshire marsh,
Yet he calls for his mate in vain;
He waits as others share his grief
With feathered instinct continues his strain:
Proo-proo oo-pru he calls.

THE WARRIOR AND THE HARLOT

In the cold shade of a black wood,
And far from men of fate,
There drifts a sea green warrior
Shining in Etruscan plate.

And crouching on his golden mesh
There drum a nightjar's wings;
The bird sits on his metal neck,
And churrs of dusk-like things.

His kneecap creaks, his visor closed,
Legends around him reign,
He lifts his head for scent and sound,
And then champs on again.

He waits for her, he loves and knows,
And through this tree and that,
Barred very close through the dark pine wood
He proves an acrobat.

That she will die, without his myths,
Of Unicorn, Hawk, and Roe;
That he will die, without her world,
Of weird uranium woe.

Five birds with their transparent wings,
Five suns through petals seen,
Five years since they had met and loved,
Seemed years to them between.

Then suddenly a cheap perfume
Arrests his easy pace;
She waits for him, she loves and knows,
Each line carved on his face.

She drew him on, she drew her skirt
Up to her lovely knees,
She wore the same red garters edged
With sequins like the seas.

She tried to push his visor up
And coaxed him with her touch;
She spoke of scarlet corsets
That he had favoured much.

Outside her vortex world maintains
A 'disastrous polished dance';
The slow synthetic sly machine
Revolves as in a trance.

Drawn to his lore and liquid mind,
Her loose breasts raised, her mouth, and sin
All stretched for recognition,
The sky whipped thin as tin.

His head now bent, she grovelled close
To feel his sun-pierced looks;
Her boldly painted eyes all life
That dimmed the sparkling brooks.

He placed one arm around her waist,
He drew his visor down,
And then her face, her face it seemed,
All blotched just like a clown.

Her screams they filled the darkened wood,
Cut by the light's saw edge,
Her knight was blind, he had no sight,
Such was the sacrilege.

THE WITNESSES

Now that I am no more
And the dark passage of time
Has swept away the visage of my face
I am, in the sighing of the trees
And upswept gales to heaven,
A shrill light
Fretted with growling clouds
Which lie quiet against the sombre hill-line
The stars spinning around my skull
Fill me with dizzy thoughts
This grave evening,
Where alone, outcast, and foreboding,
Let down, I see that truth
Is a palsy. That justice does not exist,
But depends erratically
On the yes and no of the Welsh people:
The witnesses. These witnesses of my life,
Their indecisiveness: their going back
On their word destroyed my faith in them.
All that is left is but a husk,
A grail light fretting among the clouds,
O grave dwellers comfort me,
Let thy spirit fortify my soul

For I am as flesh dissolved
And no longer of this earth.
And the one I loved
Is like the dark spirit of a tree
Who wanders through the tall grass of tombs
He broods, stands sentinel over my vanished body.
The silhouette of houses the cut
Into the sky, are, as is my heart
This frail and enormous heart,
Uprooted and recorded against the earth's feature.

TRANSCENDENTAL DOMAIN

The first bird sings like no other,
Its loud wail coarsens the ear of man,
The sadness prolongs his breath
And shakes his dubious belief.
The first bird's utterance is all woe,
Water railing white, and strained of all blood.

The first flower is yellow.
Spring's royal colour;
It has mild petals and no central portion;
It is a flower on its own stalk and owns no pasture.
For this flower of the sun. For this flower
I would give the centre of the world.

The first tree is in shape as no other,
It calls for tenderness, and has in the ease of its
Branches light which transmits from its radiant growth.

It holds the pale green thread which enfolds all sweetcorn,
The cradled care of a first reluctant birth.
It is all covered with a rich fruit of no special design.
It is the tree of light and also the tree of life.

The first beast arose from the dead,
It fed us with grace and taught us
Servitude... his and her name...
Bison, buffaloes, and all cattle broke from his bonds.
He is a sacred symbol of patience, endurance, and
Because of this is a real force of wisdom.
By this beast we are marked down
In our respect for his pleasure.

SACRED WHITE CATTLE

Who gleam through the woods as white as owls,
So still a herd do they remain,
That winged with rare Ionian grace,
They dip their horns to the moon's cold face.

Electric tension; scent of man
Sends them charging into caves
Where forebears lay on rock and ice,
Huge fossil bones on stalagmite.

From pillared stones to sacred rites
In Groves dark as their black-blue eyes
With silk white flanks of Mabinogion grace
How they drift with dairy-like faces

To and from the lake, The Lady
Close by their side. Drowsy and dreaming,
Drawn by her under the Lake.
Their eyes pooled with new-formed myths.

They were, they said, all born of woman,
Like the proud white bull of Connaught,
With calves hidden and fed at night
From black udders shiny and warm.

Their crescent horns tipped with black;
The forelegs where they kneel, black;
Their ears listening for her voice, black;
And folded hoofs, black. Now out, dripping,

Today towards Pwyll's Hunting Woods,
Dalkeith and Gisburne, Chartley, Dinevor,
There hidden among green flowery branches
Sacred; white, with distinctive pride,

They hold the gaze of all mythology.

ALONE

Alone
And as the mind whirls encircling
Thoughts spinning round and round the room
And you think you have got something
Some idea caught,
You find uncircling round and round
That it is your sense torn over
Some desolate place, space,
Footsteps or distant barks
Of strange dogs which the night air carries
And travels through your mind.
The silence pricks out the notes
Of some misguided event
And you are lost on a round thought
Back, round and round to where you belong
In the jive world of today.

We are here; and I am dead at last,
My furious body has committed suicide;
Here is the long pier, telescoping up the past
To where the souls of those who died
Before me tried to go. I must ride
Along my honest heart; and ride fast
If I intend to reach the end of time
Where no-one dwells.
              I have not yet passed
The cross of love where all must stop. I would
That I had, and I was really dead.
And still I can't forget my horse's proud
Memorial swagger; but if I could,
My journey's end would lie very near. And ahead
Would be an open road.

INVOCATION

O dust, O molecules, pinned down around
The planet's wet face, catching the early rays
Of dawn that drift up from the ocean's curdled
Wash, seeping through shades into secretive shallows,
Onto the mirrored sea breathless as death.
The spiritual mind breathing all present.
See how the boat of fire appears mysteriously
Out of its watered grave. With Love's growing force
The unknown rower holds the spell... stealthily...
Silently, the incoming tide rises proudly
Like a well-loved breast. The pearly vapours lighting
Up each leaf, pricking out the varied patterns
Starkly defined, until warmth stirs the wing
Of birds, as they open their eyes clear as seashells
And sing to the Magenta Disc of Day. O bring me
My heart. Bring it as a field of buttercups.
O let them blaze forth glistening as finite suns.
Let my tears crystallise among you in praise
Of the cosmic source exploding into a rainbow
Of coloured brilliants that fall sparkling, wet
On to the flowering grass, through Jay blue
And woodpeckers darting from the trees, through pink-pink
Of the chaffinch, chiff-chaff, woodlark and dove.
All quivering, scintillating, rinsing petal, bud and wing:
O lovers of death leave your sorrow. See
The naked plant unchanged, as I, now out of
My flesh, a spirited voice of the dawn, find
Rebirth in the Manifestation of Light.

THERE IS NO OTHER TIME THAN THIS

There is no other time than this
When all the creatures leapt their skin
To find controlled the music thus: –
A word, spoken edgeways from the dusk.
'Soon there will be no shadows all a quaking light
To will all those who fared away a curious punkah rest,
Denying none, accepting all,
I'll frighten the day cower the night
With a wonder controlled by one.'
A shining Light fused through my own
And I alone attend.

AND THEY HAD FOR THEIR GRAVE PLAGUE BONES GROUND TO DUST

Clotted blood – excrement – gutters wet and red.
eyes on boots, and blouses filled with flesh:
the headless man ran down the street,
and brains fell like ribbons from the
woman's head. those who were 'shocked'
stood in pools of blood… unearthed cries
continued as pick entered warm flesh.

These things happened and continue to happen
I tell you now only some of it.

There was a tunnel not far from here
stuffed with lime-ridden men. They died
wounded and foaming. Others drowned
in their own water and filth – a sewer
had been pierced. From the stagnation
surging over their heads, release them.
From the futility and comedy of war,
stiffen our sight that we may adjust
ourselves to this terrible truth:
(the universal truth suffered by all at war).
Against the farcical rendering of
'few casualties… little damage done'?
                My God.
Take us through to the clean dawn
To the cold sheet and sky:
That we may start with crisp green thoughts
Close to the universal mind of man.
That we may rise like a blue
Flame on ice. With a cool glow in our minds
But revolutionary aflame.

AS YOU WERE

Driven back to this home,
Driven back against the ghastly consequence of time
To a shattered visage – his – so erring
With inconsequential rot.
Where loyalty does not begin
Since it is a misguided virtue
Covering what should not exist,
This foul and feathered air seeps with nostalgia
And the classical beauty of his features
Lie – seeped again as his – in sentimental hate,
Soaked in Celtic atmosphere and
Unwanted sodden violence.
I would have some clarity on this dearth of behaviour,
Some clarity, from this claustrophobic cause,
Some penetrating ray of microscopic intensity
On so cruel a pattern.

FIELDFARE

The sky that blues like wholesome bream
Heart my shadow quavers downstream
All clouds that spiral high and bare
Tears in scales of blue to birds where,
My wings in flocks unknown do dream
Break a spell in consternation.

I WILL HAVE NONE OF IT

'I will have none of it,' he cried
As I found Christ tame and nervous among the hills
Sheltering his uneasy body
Under the splendours of His Heavenly Sky;
Couched among His stables
And earlier friends of before,
The cows, sheep, and farmer's rural expenditure.

He went, this farmer, for a walk, and during its
Splendid rush of wind and sweeping blue skies
And refreshed by this glistening splendour,
He remembered God. He remembered with contempt
How they rushed to his Father in sorrow.
He walked hurriedly with this Praise
To push open the door.
But the door was closed, the Church against
His Praise.
And this was not the first
Withheld by man from the Head of God.
On the second occasion they said
When he rebelled:
'O but you must ask the vicar for the key'.
And the vicar said, 'I think Miss Williams
the cleaner has the key'.
And Miss Williams who was milking the cows
Said: 'No, I can't think where it is
Have you tried Lewis up the hill?'
So Praise became wretched.
The clergy exist between man and God;
And Christ's disciples lock his Temple door

The churches are distempered and battened
The Vicarage distempered and cemented;
While below them in a wild and blind state
Two-roomed cottages stand sodden and condemned.
18-inch windows hold the diseased souls of men,
Bedrooms meaning lofts, some six feet by five
These have warped boards that disintegrate their feet,
For they in the shallows are not
Seen by the frockcoated men.
So the church embraces the Atom
Shakes a blessing over its apocalyptical defeat
And explodes the Myth of Christ.

'I will have none of it', He cried
And wept from His Great Green Heart.

MYSTICISM

Mysticism is the opposite
To that which is portrayed;
It is the closer and warm
Perception of humanity
Towards external objects
Whether alive or dead.
And it gives in that main radiance,
Like herrings freshly caught, fish

On a dark kitchen table,
Light, its own light,
Which like phosphorescence
Travels along the wake of the soul
Radiating a clear vision.
In its defined state a scientific
Pattern: not wet, cosy, vague,
Foggy, nor obscure, but
A light which cannot be put out
In its true existence.

ODE IN MARCH

O Aspen leaf! I cannot follow your March movements,
Nor the budding cell of your myriad moods.
I am haunted by your sad tiredness, and
The force of your nature still eludes
Me. Your low lovely whisper drags once more
My heart to its original sorrow.
Fascinated by your acrostic drag, I enter
The madness of tomorrow.

But yours is the mystery of a March morning;
When you are many; then I am few.
When the day fades, you are older than time;
But nocturnally you grow new.

PROGRESSIVE MAN

(4:5: shift.)

Gay in chalk stripes
With nicotine hand
This working man
With plateware astray
Longs in drab flat
For bathroom and land
For his progressive mind.

But soon he found
Grey with knuckle dust
Boots for vision
Food on trolley tray
Plank for his bed
Bray factory on trust
For his progressive kind.

So he grows green
With the scarlet beans
At the sill edge
For 'widow of peace'
Takes public baths
According to means
For his progressive mind.

SHOULD THESE WORDS NOT SHINE

Should these words not shine, blame me,
The day clears everything, engages
Wondrously all manner of wonders, clears leaf,
Stem, soul, and seasoned tooth, rinses
Trees splashing the sky with freshening
Drops of rain. A radiant shower and large
Passing cloud is the grief of man's mastery
Its very tentacles rake out the heart.
This part of me blame; if clouds of obscurity
Arise: to relent is not sufficient: to admit is all.

TEA LEAVES

Someone they tell me has brought
This long etiolated man on his
Lying stretcher, and have left him wet
In the church aisle,
Waiting to give him
Name, history, and fate.

I would if I dare,
Enter this church,
Peer at his Pendine face
With bold courage and despair;
Then kneel for that prayer
Which was never said.

With my third eye
I saw all this happen before,
I saw his tall collapsed figure
His pale sickness
Intense worry over
Some military pact.

So that I knew when he came
Here at my gate
That it was him
And I sensed in that moment
As they walked up that hill
Through the graveyard tombstones
And battleground of my caravan
Lifting the sea sodden mass
Navy blue and bruised,
That these four policemen
And the Black Maria
Had a fearful burden to bear.

THE TABLET OF APHRODITE

For the flesh,
Death is night without day.
For the mind,
Death is day without night.
Death is full stop in space
Releasing a charged mind
Springing white
On fresh pasture of air

That sieves and gathers
Towards the touch of love
Where all wisdom is held.

THE WHITE HEART

Will he I wonder return from Saigon?
From the yellow swamps and cool leather hills,
Will he, O Love of my heart,
Return with the green April rills of rain?
Who works now with Emperor against communist bandits
Caught in the indigo throngs of peril.
Dark is the hour, O my heart, where I see:
'Full beneath an early moon, his face, O and his
Deep eyes, furtive under the whip of pain, -
Yellow and scarlet are the guards about him; -
Yet he will out, as with such reasonable force,
He always will. Out of the stretch of wire,
Out of the seasons torrential rain... on to
The mechanised road, erased bazaars, on to the aeroplane
    tarmac
Of China...' O my Beloved, I command,
Send word of your return.

TINAMOU

Do you remember Sansevieria, Tinamou?
In the fazendas of Brazil?
Where Marouska and I wandered
Through the Quintas at our will.
None to disturb or hinder
As we lay gently still
Scheming child's fancy
The elusive Future to fulfil.
Shy goldfish passed us by
Slotted to their green canopy,
Wild parakeets measured the sky
An emerald cloud to blacker field.
Everything pulsed with even beat
To a tension strained with breathless weight
Until a bird screeched
The mocking Lachesia –
Creatures darted in and out
White-eyed, legless, helpless cessed
For they *alone* 'possessed' –
Knew the hearing of this bird
Meant that Fate held us by.

APPENDIX

RADIO TALK ON SOUTH AMERICAN POEMS

EL DORADO 1953

PATAGONIA (ARTICLE PUBLISHED IN *WALES,*
SUMMER 1945)

One of the earliest memories I have of my childhood was to wander out of the gate and stare at the South American pampas. The quiet grey grass stretched over to the horizon where a plantation of sugar cane and maize drew a thread of bright green along its edge. A bison wandered over the plains and nothing more. Near the house lived an old woman who earned her living by making mud bricks. My father, who was in charge of the Mechita railway junction, and always rode back and fro to work on horseback, scolded me one day for straying on the plains. Then the bison disappeared.

It was when I wrote the rondel 'Blood and Scarlet Thorns', which was published in my first book of *Poems* in 1944, that I used these early images for the birth of Christ. I shall now read you the poem:

> Who bends the plain to waist of night
> And stems the bird to tree of flight,
> Who stretches leagues to see a bone
> Of bison cast as proud as stone,
> Who lengthens maize and sweeps the light
> Of grenadine right out of sight;
> It is the hard and monstrous plight
> Of weeping birth this citron dawn,
> This citron dawn,
> A heart breaks through the ice of night
> Who is, and bursts a paper kite
> That sails the day into a dome
> Of joy, and tears, and monotone,
> This day maintained: a child was born,
> A child was born.

The New World with its strange subtlety absorbed me with its vivid impressions, the spinning windmills irrigating the *quintas*, and as the corrugated containers filled with water, I bathed in them within shadow of the peach trees. A favourite haunt of mine was the patio kitchen, filled with creollos and flies with the smell of the carbon fire and oil, where I would wait until I had sucked the very sweet *maté amargo* out of their *bombillas* as they passed the gourd round. We ate frogs and wild birds and the first view I had of a large spider lifting the roof of his house in the mud and slamming it back, I shall never forget. The small pueta where people lived with their horses tethered to the wooden post outside their shacks, their songs, knife-fights, guitars, the dark shadows the peons cast as they gamble behind clouds of dust as the horse race took place. They were and still are the root culture of the Argentine soil. So when the thatched roofs were torn down and corrugated roofs placed in their stead and values were placed on the wrong issues, I rebelled and wrote to establish belief in these people in my poem called 'The New World'. Here it is:

Memory widens our senses, folds them open:
Ancient seas slip back like iguanas and reveal
Plains of space, free, sky-free, lifting a green tree
                    on to a great plain.

Heard legend whistling through the waiting jabirú,
Knew the two-fold saying spinning before their eyes
Breaking life like superstition, they too
                    might become half-crazed.

Staring sitting under the shade of Ombú tree,
Living from the dust: kettles simmer on sticks,
Maté strengthens their day's work like dew
                    on hot dry grass.

So the people baking too close fulfilled time,
Mud became brick walls and the legend flared high,
Shadows broke, flames frowned and bent the sky
                              proclaiming Indian omens.

Roofs fell clattering in on man and child,
Black framed their faces, from fire not from sun:
While before them land divided announcing
                              stake peggers' loud claim.

Death ate their hearts like locusts over a croaking plain,
Tears fell red as fireflies on the rising dust;
Barbed wire fenced them in or fenced them out,
                              these outcasts of the land.

So the people fled unwanted further on into the land,
On to the Plain of White Ashes where thorns spread
Like the wreath of Christ. Further out on to
                              the Ancient Sea of Rhea.

Ombú turned hollow as it stood alone:
Spiders lifted the lids of their homes and slammed them back
Sorrow set the plovers screaming at the falling
                              hoofs and feet:

Cinchas bound their eaten hearts: leather sealed their lips;
Ponchos warmed their pumpkin pride: as insects floated,
As windmills grew. Ventevéo! Ventevéo! And further they
                              strove, the harder not to be seen.

Lost now. No sound or care can revive their ways:
La Plata gambles on their courage, spends too flip-
pantly,
Mocks beauty from the shading tree, mounts a corru-
gated roof
over their cultured hut.

This reminds me that an editor asked if I couldn't change 'corrugated roof over their cultured hut', it was so ugly. He did not see that that was the purpose of the whole poem. The *estancias* were being sold or mortgaged and the money drifted into the Casinos at La Plata. The peon or gaucho and the land were left in despair.

During holidays from the Convent of the Sacred Heart in Buenos Aires I often went on my father's yacht on the River Plate. He had such a fever for boats and sailing throughout his life that I even remember his building a boat and its hull, which hung like a skeleton mammal in one of the Mechita stables. And this was far from water on the plains. So I watched this River Plate as it lapped past reflecting the blue sky, the oranges blown into the water, wild sylvan grass and its own warm fawn colour, and I wrote this song for the River Plate:

The pampas are for ever returning
The orange river pounding the sea,
From a high dry plain with a tint of tea
La Plata spreads, and churns drowning
The dust from the charcas murmuring
At the bare roots of the Ombú tree:
The pampas are for ever returning
Bright green birds into a piranha sea.
Over spare-dust and barbed wire slowly
Cattle die from thirst wounds, returning
Like maté ships shivering, bringing

No sound but white bones back to me:
The pampas are for ever returning
Bad bones and dust into an angry sea.

Other holidays were spent at the foot of the Andes on the Chilean lakes. At Traful there was just the one house and on a distant hill a white horse, whose owner would appear once or twice a year to change maize for leather-work he had made. No one knew his language. A *guarani* sang as she washed at the open tub, a wild fox tame at her side. Mrs Dawson had tamed it, and her husband was out shooting pumas, the children riding barefoot and bareback throughout sandstone gorge. We raced after the wild animals and threw *bolas*. But I rode with a sheepskin and could not throw the *bola* well. They caught their game. Then into an Inca burial, where a skeleton was found lying upside down, handmade gold jewels and trinkets. Mrs Dawson had them on her mantelpiece. So I wanted to know more about Peru and the Incas. Certain phrases of theirs inspired me, such as lion grass, the mountain where the sun was tied up, the eyebrow of the mountain. The word 'Traful', where we played, apparently meant 'lake of pools'. And these later grew into a poem with the Inca title 'Xaquixaguana' meaning 'the Valley of Beauty'. In this I tried to create the whole quality of that race:

In the lake of pools
Where icebergs stand firm on the ground,
And refrain to move for beauty of their image,
Five Temples lie wounded on their sides
Each plundered and more progressive than the last.
I speak of the one with the grey-crusted sleepers
Sitting in the splint-blue cave.
Especially he, of the up-side-down burial
With arrows set like buhls in the rib of the wreck:

Who was this white man of Peru?
And what flat burial did he deserve
To stir their sandstone agave? To face emerald sky
And snarling rocks where the sun's tied up:
Lying stiff among gold filaments and animate clay
Snouting Azrael forms and intricate beads:
Those Huacas spread and exposed under cacti water-
    beds,
Green as tunas, weathered with poisoned alizarin
    darts
Who was this man who stole their store of gold?
Who found down here down Pilcomayo way,
Near lion grass and glass birds sailing the lake,
Who was he, that lies buried at the Haravec's feet
Aggrieved by this ice and basaltic sheet?

During the interval that my father was General
Manager for the Buenos Aires Western Railway and was
contemplating buying an *estancia* in Mar del Plata, I sent
him a sonnet supporting his opinion of administration
and the beliefs which he held. And beside him throughout
this period was the office boy who first helped him at
the Mechita Junction. He was now his private secretary.
I said in this poem to my father in 1939, which I called
'Argentine Railways':

> To you who walked so proudly down the line,
> Promoting men from engine plates, skilled
> Workers from the sheds: the Board soon killed
> The cut you had to socialise the 'decline'.
>
> You, who planned man's bonus among the
>   whine
> And shrill of people on the go; filled

The sleeper's clock with admiration; drilled
Time in travelling into a close combine

But now I prefer to think of you set back
Upon the land, with eucalyptus trees
Shading corral from dust; plan as you please

The round hill into a wholesome farm. 'Their'
    lack
To accept your methods receive with ease,
For they will come to that in the end or 'freeze'.

For the British born in the Argentine there are many sea
voyages, and in one of these ten trips I particularly remember
having the director's coach set down to us in order that we
might go up the one cable railway to São Paulo. During the
war, from a Welsh village these nostalgic *saudaded* came back
to me and I write this poem 'Royal Mail':

I would see again São Paulo:
The coffee coloured house with its tarmac roof
And spray of tangerine berries.
I would again climb the mountain cable
And see Pernambuco with its dark polished table,
The brilliance of its sky piercing through the trees
Like so much Byzantine glass or clear Grecian frieze.
As we stumble higher, strolling gourds and air-plants
Spring from muscoid branch to barnacle wire:
I would see old man should it come my way,
The mahogany pyramids of burnished berries, gay
With surf-like attitudes of men sitting around
In crisp white suits, starch to the ground.
The peacock struts and nets mimicrying butterflies,
And the fazenda shop clinking like ice in an enamel
    jug

As you open the door. The stench of wine-wood,
Saw-dust, maize flour, pimentos, and basket of birds,
With the ear-tipped 'Molto bien signorit', and the
     hot mood
Blazing from the drooping noon. Outside sweating
     gourds
Dripping rind and peel; yet inside cool as lemon,
Orange, avocado pear.
While in this damp and stony stare of a village
Such images are unknown:
So would I think upon these things,
In the event that someday I shall return to my native
     surf
And feel again the urgency of soil.

And then on these same journeys almost as soon as the
ship had dropped anchor off the Cape Verde Islands, Las
Palmas, Madeira, a great sweep of hundreds of boats frail
as matchsticks, overloaded with lace trinkets and shawls,
and up these men would scramble and without pause for
the eye to rest, in a flash the long stretch of the main decks
were transformed into gorgeous bargaining bazaars. The gulls
screaming and gliding overhead the farewells. Here then is the
'Seagull' poem:

> Seagulls' easy glide
> Drifting fearlessly as voyagers' tears:
> Quay and ship move as imperceptively,
> Without knowing we weep.
>
> Cry gulls who recall
> An ocean of uncertainty;
> Greed of rowing men
> Mere flies at the ship's sides.

Last bargains roped and reached:
And as imperceptively regretted,
Tears of fury and stupidity
Reel down the runnels of those cheeks.

And then after a long interval, as I drew upon the rich store
which this lovely country had given me, I wondered if I might
not write a long ballad, an autobiography of my early childhood.
Then I again rebelled. There were too many books, poems, etc.
of childhood memories. I resolved then to write about a true
[story] which had occurred on the pampas, in surroundings
which I knew. Mr Cadvan Hughes had sent me many letters
about [an] expedition his father-in-law had made into Indian
territory. And as this had been conveyed to him personally, while
Mr Evans was living, I choose this theme. And so the Ballad
of 'El Dorado' was born. In it of course I used many of my
own memories, as a background, or reconstruction of the
event. For instance, a habit we have on the pampas when out
riding of continually tightening or loosening up the *cincha*, the
belt which holds down the sheepskin, the leather stirrups, the
hooded ones that I had seen and the looped leather stirrups
which I had used. The quality of the thistles which they used
for fuel and making rennet, their hollowness and crack, seeing
iguanas as they flashed past from before the horses' hoofs, the
legends, the racoon that I found on my dressing table, and
who later was found curled up in sleep in my bed, the nutrias
in hundreds, and flight, colour and song of the myriad birds,
these I wanted to recreate. And so from the journey out of four
companions, the Indian massacre of three and solitary return
of Evans to his Patagonian soil, there remained for his comfort
the pampa lullaby, one that the great naturalist W.H. Hudson
quotes as being two centuries old. The same lullaby which my
mother in Mechita sang to me and is recorded here at the
end of this ballad, which was broadcast in the early months

of this year, and from which I will only read a few stanzas of
the setting out, and a few stanzas of the return of Evans alone:

> Up then leapt the leader Evans
> On his favourite spirited steed,
> High and proud on his mounted pack
> A pioneer in the lead.
>
> A pull on the cinch and Davies was up
> On Zaino with new head gear,
> The raw hide bridle upon his horse
> Incenses him to rear.
>
> They would ride they said for gold, Hughes
> Evans, Davies and Parry,
> To mountains unseen, and unknown places,
> For its hidden in dust or scree.
>
> The bells rang as the mare set off
> With tropilla of packs and hide,
> Thirty horses followed her pace,
> The wilder one tied to her side.
>
> They moved dark forms from out the corral,
> Creating light on their way:
> Quiet and silent as gauchos ride,
> Who leave at break of day.
>
> A creak of leather fills the air
> And rhythm of their hoofs,
> The lights soon twinkle in distant huts
> From holes in iron roofs.

The siskins upside down on thistles,
The migrants yellow and blue,
The scarlet cardinals, humming birds
All shimmer as South Seas do.

In space like this possessed by birds,
The Indians cut a stalk,
And piping still transform these birds
And make the cuena talk.

And then Evans with the solitary return journey, riding for days over the desert and unknown lands until he reaches his native river:

Down towards the Chubut River
Past the Iamacan,
Evans sought the Indian trail
Like the fox of man.

It all was known and sweet to him,
He spun through pampa blasts
As it flickered high around his horse
Like a sea of tossing masts.

Then slower as he journeyed on,
With sad reflection back,
No friends, and no madrina bells,
No flourish of hoofs on the track.

The Chajá cried into the night,
A wagon rumbled high
With twenty horses leading abreast:
Wistaria spread in the sky.

As dawn arose, the Settlement,
So quietly it would seem,
No herd, or dogs had turned their head,
It might have never been.

A child had scampered out of bed
Curled in the Patio sun,
With corn cob hair and racoon bear,
She sang this song to her son.
'A ro ro mi niño,
A ro ro mi sol
A ro ro pedazo
De mi corazon.'

EL DORADO

Introduction: a ballad partly based on the true story of John Daniel Evans as related to his son-in-law Mr T. Hughes Cadvan in 1936. The expedition took place in Patagonia in 1883. (The Welsh, having landed in Chubut to found their Colony in 1865.) An introduction of Argentine music is suggested, but this must have a strong Inca flavour, as the Indians of that time predominated on the plain. Such music which contains the cuena or pincullo, drum with the metallic cord attached to it, and Indian guitar. This is made from the armadillo shell, is high in pitch and very clear. (The author has such records in her possession.)

CAST

The narrator
John Evans
Davis
Hughes
Parry
[Indians]

[I]   Up then leapt the leader Evans
                 On his favourite spirited steed,
                 High and proud on his mounted pack
                 A pioneer in the lead.

                 A pull on the cinch and Davies was up
                 On Zaino with new head gear,
                 The raw hide bridle upon his horse
                 Incenses him to rear.

They would ride they said for gold,
    Hughes
Evans, Davies and Parry,
To mountains unseen, and unknown
    places,
For its hidden in dust or scree.

The bells rang as the mare set off
With tropilla of packs and hide,
Thirty horses followed her pace,
The wilder one tied to her side.

They moved, dark forms from out the
    corral,
Creating light on their way:
Quiet and silent as gauchos ride,
Who leave at break of day.

A creak of leather fills the air
And rhythm of their hoofs,
The lights soon twinkle in distant huts
From holes in iron roofs.

The more they rode, each hut fell back,
Until with leagues apart,
The last mud hut with pelt hide roof
Stood high as the wheel of a cart.

Stealthy they rode, the cattle turned,
The hens flew down from trees
And squawked as ugly mongrels bayed
Stabbing the sinister eaves.

A ranchero stared. The plains received
Strange waves and spells of fear
As these young riders galloped past
To find their way now clear.

Dawn on the
plains.

In darkened light the scrub bush swayed
Further than they could see,
Cold waves of air rustled the stalks
As water through stones of the sea.

The steam arose from the horses' backs
And mingled with the plains;
The mist flowed; the sun soon glowed;
The gauchos drew in their reins.

Faint bird notes

Each bush of thorn on fire, each bird
Far wilder than they'd been,
Each stone vibrating singing sweetly
All nature in song and seen.

In this new spirited air flashing,
The cold night air creeps back,
As plovers and plovers rise calling
New wings in lilac and black.

The siskins upside down on thistles,
The migrants yellow and blue,

Indian cuena music is
heard in background,
merging into sound of
hoofs

The scarlet cardinals, humming birds
All shimmer as South Seas do.

In space like this possessed by birds,
The Indians cut a stalk,
And piping still transform these birds
And make the cuena talk.

Six more leagues they'd make a halt
So eager were they to ride;
The madrina's bell sweet to their ears
As the birds that flew at her side.

The horses were wild and hard to handle
For some were still untame;
Though branded clearly: they bucked freely:
To throw the packs their aim.

Evans:

'*But this was better*', Evans said,
To console himself and friend,

Evans:

'*These beasts caught in the wild state
Fend for themselves, and tend*

*If the rein is slack to dodge and guide
Us over snake, iguana;
Or avoid the holes of vizcacha burrows:
Sense water from afar.*'

And as he spoke, the horse then shied;
He patted the silken neck.

Evans:

'*Now take this beast with white star head
So dark with this white fleck.*

*Mendoza, when he sailed, he left
Twelve horses on our shore;
The herd then spread throughout the land
And raised our rich folklore.*

*And such a one is this, my steed;
The Indians fear the mark.
'El Malacara', bad face, they say,*

And turn morose, or embark

On Spanish Conquests of their land:
On bad or pioneer strangers:
Falkner, Musters, Hudson, Darwin
Whose virtues stick like burs.

But one tall tribe was good to us
And fought all other tribes;
On our behalf taught us to hunt
And fed us without bribes.

They trusted us on Chubut soil,
Brought ponchos, fur, and hide.
And sold us horses in sixty-five,
The Chief sought us with pride.'

[III]   When nine days passed they knew no land
But only as it wound,
The Chubut River with crystal quartz
That shines up from the ground.

It lit their drying faces. That night
Parry dismounted first;
He hobbled the mare and freed the horses,
Untying the packs as he cursed

Parry::   And chattered, *'The fire was hard to light.'*
They cut dried meat and drank
Hughes: Some maté. Hughes then shouted, *'Tie*
A horse to some branched bank

Or bunch of pampas. With no food
The mare may stray tonight.'
The River shone and rippled clearly
Pearly through the night.

Cry of geese
heard.

The plain soon dipped towards the dawn:
A wolf had chewed the tether,
And stood to watch as they in vain
Sought horse and broken leather.

They searched for prints, uprooted grass,
A stone knocked out of place;
Then hours later found the rift
The mare had made their base.

Parry::

'But Hughes will make another thong
Or halter of raw hide.'
He looked the gaucho in 'wide-awake' hat,
And lived that life as 'guide'.

The rest wore tattered hats, tied scarves,
Old ponchos on their back,
Mugs and knives at their waist, bomba-
    chas,
Boots and shoes of sack.

Davies:
Mocking Indians' gold
stirrups.
Hughes:
Mocks back, offering
inferior thonged and
hooded leather stirrups
of the country.

'And make a pair of stirrups', said Davies
'Each gold for either side!'
'You'll get looped pelts or hooded hide
Iron spurs thrown in beside!'

IV
Music of
the plains.

Three hundred miles they kept the
    course;
And hunted daily for food:
They'd use the lasso, bola, or gun,
Repair them while it brewed.

And where the Chubut joined the
    Lepá
And green willows unfold;
To rest their mounts was their desire,
And sift the beds for gold.

Among the tall red canyon heights
In the Andes iced domain,
They queried cattle's four feet horns
That drift near guns to aim.

In whining and in searing winds
They sieved the River bed,
With quilt that shone like gold on
    their faces,
The gold-dust flushing them red;

Hiding the grains in their boots –
    what's that? –
A thunder of hooves stiffened
And shook the earth, as they leapt to
    their mounts
To round up and defend

Their troupe from a wild horses' stam-
    pede.
For they might attempt to draw off

With caresses and neighing our thirty head:
We circled our troupe to push off

The endless hooves that passed for an hour
By yelling and whirling lassoes.
The piebalds, black picasso with white
Legs and face, roan blues,

The yellow horse with the black stripe,
The spotted and strawberry roans,
The splashed horses, the good cruzado.

Parry: 'Such a mixed group atones

*For the fear once they are passed. And that white
Horse with the black mane
Ears, fetlock, muzzle, and tail,
Is surely a Dynevor strain,*

One of the breed of the Sacred White?'
The trees now buzzed with gnats,
The madrina's bell tinkled again
And evening released the bats.

Rejoiced they stood around the fire
And fed it with dry stalks;
While Davies sat on a bullock's skull
And started on one of his talks:

Davies: '*Not long ago when we lived in caves,
And Indian stood bare…
From nowhere… My father spoke:
The Chief stood back with care.*

Suddenly the Indian's wife bent down,
And with thorn and thread as sinew,
Without a word Father's trousers tacked
And repaired the tear as new.

Look over!' The dust rose red and high,
They all looked, sheepdog,
Horses, *'If dust would only settle*
Instead of this red fog.'

They saw. Now plovers rising up,
And crying birds; guanacos

Evans: Leaping with lowered necks; *'Two Indians!'*
Parry: Evans: *'Arucanians?'* *'Foes!'*

They came, and bareback fast with spears
Both lit with brilliant feathers,
With copper shields and glittering beads,
And gold and silver leathers.

What shine of rich stirrup silver!
With gold drops on their rein.
The Indians grinned for they knew these men
They had traded with them for grain.

Indians   *'Had they not met at Trelew once?*
Low and slow of   *What are you doing? Why?*
speech   *Where are we going? Why not home?*
     This Indian land. Why?'

We shared the rhea that they had caught,
They swung their bolas with skill
The lead and thongs had tied the legs,
They drank the blood with will.

We shared the night, and when dogs strayed,
They stood on their horses saying:

Indians
'Why don't you visit our Sunica Chief
In his 'toldo' camp laying

A hundred miles to west.' Persuaded,
At sunrise two of us rode;
Hughes and Evans with two Indian guides
Not to disturb their code.

Evans: *'O ghost of Martin Fierro aid us.'*
For unknown to the four
The Government soldiers had camped near
And broken Indian law.

Suspicion grew, and Evans turned,
Back to Lepá with Hughes:
Evans: *'We'd better turn as fast as we can*
It's the Canyon Carbon we'll choose.'

The Tehuelche Indians think we're spies:
Or have seen us sift for gold.
We'll cross north of the Chubut River
And leave these veins of gold.'

Overawed with rocks of wrath
The blood tint shadowed with vultures,
We soon were filled with fear and foreboding
Of Indian scalps and tortures.

With no shoes, the hoofs were bleeding,
Parry and Hughes collapsed.
They took fresh mounts and strapped the men
With cinch and hide to the packs

And drove them forward with the mare
Taking the stony route,
To leave no trace and ride through streams
Not to disturb a root.

So they entered the Canyon Carbon,
And rested dog and mount,
Cutting sharp flints from out of the hoofs,
Helping the sick dismount,

Passing the maté gourd on its round,
Nervous, too weak to eat;
Hanging harness and skins on poplars;
No rest for days, dead beat.

They spoke of home, Trelew, Rawson:

Hughes: *'They're gathering fuel stalks*
              With sheepskin gloves to avoid the thorns.'
Davies: *'The shrilling wind through the hawks*
Quietly and with emotion
Hughes: *'Wonder how my 'china' is?'*   (joking, 'china' means
Evans: *'The corn with bad harvest*   Spanish girl)
              And all that irrigation we did.'
Parry: *'The mare won't sleep or rest*

              One ear forward and one ear back
              She knows an Indian death.'

Hughes:	'What's that?' 'To one man dead they kill
Parry:	'Fifty living horses... death

Is *Alhuemapu. Around the square grave,*
Standing dead on their legs,
They wait to carry their skeleton riders
To heaven on stilted pegs.'

Quickly, *Davies:*	'Loók at this skéleton with an árrow in his ríb!'
Slowly, *Evans:*	'The Malónes were a terrible race.

They killed at sight, but here we're safe'
Under the Évil Spírit's rockfáce.'

[V]   They dozed, and at dawn were hungry, but
                 moved –
             They packed away their guns
             And set off towards the Vale of Kel Kein.
             The sheepdog turns and runs

             As Evans, set on his favourite steed
             Raced to get fresh food.
             He returned with cavies tied to his horse
             And knew the food was...

             A piercing yell! The Indians' War Cry! –
             Spears and bodies jerked high,
             As they leapt to their mounts unseen till now
             In pampas grass or sky.

             A flurry of frenzied beasts shot out,

Evans:
Here speaks in action
and in galloping away
from the Indians and
attacked by them as
he speaks, he can only
get quick glimpses
of his friends. The
speech though still in
lines of 4 and 3 feet is
therefore disjointed.

And clouds of dust. *'We were stunned!*
Our horses leapt in terror they were through
The tropilla on top of us, stunned, –

With hardly a glance – Parry seated
With a spear in his side – at the rear
Young Davies falling a lance splintered
*   through*
His neck... I pushed the spear

And down... just in time, the Indians missed
Hughes? at that moment the point
Of a lance, cut my arm and I spurred
And lashed the horse... the joint

Read with *speed*
and *smoothly* but
a c c e n t u a t i n g
change of 4–3 feet
line from iambic
to anapest

..−| ..−|..−|..−
..−| ..−|..−|..−

..−| ..−|..−|..−
..−| ..−|..−|..−

Of my arm held.' A powerful plunge,
Eyes out, the terrified steed
He then bolted, to the hills, to the peak,
    with the Indians
Pursuing, with neck breaking speed,

And the tossing, of his mane, and the
    foam, as it floated,
As they raced, to the chasm, only proved,
That he flew, with a speed, that he could,
    not exceed,
Even so, Evans lashed, as he moved,

For a húndred yards ahéad, the dárk gorge
    gróws,
The precipice expands,
The horse flying leapt into the air…
    apart…
They landed on trembling sands.

Then mounted again without looking
    round;
Climbing with loosening pack,
As lóoser rócks fell dówn on them
The Indians halted. Turned back.

Read with pronounced
trotting rhythm, 4 and
3 feet lines of trochees Their yells echoed, but they would not
    jump:
Two times, three times, four and
Evans let his horse now trot, and
Owl flew in his lap, and

−.| −.| −.| −.
−.| −.| −.|
−.| −.| −.| −.
−.| −.| −.|

Swível-ling her head she hoot-ed
Stumbling horse, but Ev-ans
Noth-ing no-ticed, on he rode, the horse
    did
Trot with two winged orphans

To a saline lake the black silt cracked,
The water powdered white;
Through vampire flies, and stench and
    slime,
To air so fresh and light

That held caranchos and vultures circling
Pin pointed to their prey,
Above this Valley of Kel Klein
Now five salt miles away.

Evans: *'Bydd myrdd o ryfeddodau'*   (This was the actual
hymn which was
sung in the Valley.)

O mutilated beyond all rage:
His three friends dead, and the sight
And lament of their dogs graying the air
With necks stretched out to night.

His noble steed drooped. The sedge
Half buried in sand, cut
His hoofs while salt lay raw on the
    wounds
He'd climb and take the rut

Towards the marsh to water his beast
Before the desert plains.
A cloud of crimson wings arose
The flamingoes flushed up rains

And sprays of water over the two; –
Tired and solemn with pain.
The green shadow caught in the leaves
Ease the throbbing brain

As it shuttles out vision after vision, taut
From the haunted mind;
His friends neglected by him, yet close,
As orange fruit to rind;

Evans: *With what térror they hád fled as 'dóves*
                before háwks'.

Read with sense A fox lifted his head
of peace.   To swallow evening water the peace
            vibrating
        As other beasts were led

To lift their muzzles, masks and beaks
To some unknown grace
Or favoured god: Evans prayed:
Held a marsh birds face –

Evans:

'*Chorlito*' warm to his hard cracked skin.
The wild bird circled his sobs,
And flew in brilliant clouds of rainbows
Above the palpitating throbs

Of his heart pulsing like a lizard
On the flowering banks of the lake.
That night, the horse's back was raw:
Into the middle of this lake

He threw the recado-saddle, it sank
Like the Golden Statue of Peru
He greased the forelocks and mounted on sheep-
    skin
Coaxed the bleeding hoofs through

The twenty miles of waterless land.
He took the stiff route
Avoiding the trail: then dismounted and walked:
And after a compass dispute

With stars, lead El Malacara
Towards the Iamacan:
So high: so dry: so lonely: that a Spirit
Gripped his will and he ran

With madness over the plain seeing
High hipped sloths and curs
That blot out his brain, blackness

Swirls forward and unfurls

A South West Wind as it rushes
    driving
Before it screeching birds
Caught up faster than sound driven
From miles around, the lake birds,

The herds hit by the hail, the horse,
Evans beside it, fell,
They clung as one drowning, the
    rising sand
Hid them like a spell.

Then found them at sunrise like a
    thirsty boulder
Set in the sand. For miles
And miles wounded and dead now
    lay
In desolate sandbaked piles.

VI

Bones of Toxodons bleaching the sky,
Exposed by drifts of sand,
Stratas of quartz and fossils brought
The eight footed horse to hand.

Pumas, rheas, armadillos hit
By hail as large as eggs
By the atomic hand of God, lacerat-
ed,
Groaning with broken legs.

He stumbled out to get away,
He saw fresh grass, a green spread

Through the haze of his eyes, green
    water,
But the parroquets lay dead:

Their wings scattered green all over the
    plain.
He tugged and pulled at his horse:
For miles he faltered bent like a hag
His twenty years bent to the course.

The horse as though their fate were
    known,
Pressed on, his tongue now hanging
And swollen, sucking the dry stones for
    moisture,
Limps white-eyed to the spring.

The canyon grew higher and redder as
    they neared,
A rider stood still on the ridge:
Evans laughed but made no sound;
Evans watched that ridge.

And watched that rider. Should he move
Evans – would – not show?
The rider from the Welsh Colony
Watched in the valley below.

A team of guanacos. He saw Evans.
He trembled at the tale.
Muttered between sips of water:
He trembled at the tale,

And wail of absence of all. He took
El Malacara; gave Evans
His mount and favoured his return to
    Trelew;
He'd wait for the wagon vans.

Down towards the Chubut River
Past the Iamacan,
Evans sought the Indian trail
Like the fox of man.

It all was known and sweet to him,
He spun through pampa blasts
As it flickered high around his horse
Like a sea of tossing masts.

Then slower as he journeyed on,
With sad reflection back,
No friends, and no madrina bells,
No flourish of hoofs on the track.

The Chajá cried into the night,
A wagon rumbled high
With twenty horses leading abreast:
Wistaria spread in the sky.

As dawn arose, the Settlement,
So quietly it would seem,
No herd, or dogs had turned their head,
It might have never been.

A child had scampered out of bed
Curled in the Patio sun,
With corn cob hair and racoon bear,
She sang this song to her son.
>   '*A ro ro mi niño,*
>   *A ro ro mi sol*
>   *A ro ro pedazo*
>   *De mi corazon.*'

From the early maps cut out in wood to those engraved and shining in their original glaze, we are able to trace the first shapes and histories of Patagonia by such distinguished cartographers as Ptolemy, W. Blaeu, and J. Jansson. During this period men of letters also contributed to this early form of documentation, and among them were Sir Walter Ralegh, Sir John Davis, Sir Francis Drake, and Michael Drayton. A.F. Tschiffely in *This Way Southward** suggests that Fernão de Magalhaes may have obtained the idea of a sea passage existing between the Pacific and Atlantic Ocean by an early map which was issued in Portugal some years before he made the Strait discovery; and it was this tract of land, named after him as Tierra Magellan, that now exists as Patagonia. Today as we look at these maps, what do we find? Tribal men riding bareback or on saddles of extravagant height; Indians facing and going in no particular direction; sleeping in woven cloths slung to trees; or crouched in groups around a sheep gently cooking over the quiet embers. Monsters and beasts of the sea leer and prowl out of their shaded haunts; the scaled and heavy sea beasts drag their heavy crested tails through the hot dry sand; while the high-hipped Toxodons stand awkwardly out of the sea. Fish fly like birds over the surface of the Ocean. The ship *Vittoria* harbours triumphantly among the curving scrolls of the cartouche, and the men on this ship, once awake in their time, took back to their families the legends of ostriches, gold-dust, and hardy creollo sheep.

This afternoon, when I had finished reading *This Way Southward*, which is a description of a tour made by a Mr Tschiffely around and into the interior of Patagonia and extending as far south as Tierra del Fuego, I was very much aware of this primitive and magical force of life still existing,

---

* *This Way Southward* by A.F. Tschiffely. Hodder & Stoughton, Ltd. 10/6 [LR]

besides having my own memories of this strange and illusive land. I remembered as well, how W.H. Hudson had called this region his *Parish of Selborne* and his description of the creollo sheep; Mr Tschiffely's references to the long bones of Toxodons found in the sand; the woven cloths and guanaco furs pieced together by various Indians; the chapters on the various Tribes he encountered, and with the exception of one misunderstanding, the Indians' devotion to the Welsh. This incident, and many others of the great hardships which are still endured by such persons as E. Lucas Bridges of Rio Baker, who in our lifetime was forced to suck putrid hide and eat the half-digested food from a guanaco's stomach, links up with similar hardships which Fernão de Magalhaes had to resort to when he practically starved to death. The author's best descriptions and sympathy are with these early Tribes and pioneers; and this is only natural considering that he is, in a sense, a pioneer himself. He writes briefly but well, of the faith shown between the early Welsh Settlers and the preconceived dreaded savage Indians. A number of wild-looking Tehuelche Indians suddenly arrive at the Colony; one of the settlers describes this incident to Mr Tschiffely, and the author writes: 'He was standing talking to a wild-looking Indian, when to his surprise, one of the Indian women knelt down beside the Welshman to mend his trousers which were torn at the bottom where he had caught them in a bush. Without saying a word, the Indian woman produced a needle, made out of a long thorn, threaded it with some finely cut ostrich sinew, and neatly mended the tear.'

This act of humility, and the other of faith when the Indians brought the Welsh Colonists a guanaco to cook for them and said they would return to eat it towards the end of a few days; and that it was cooked, and they did return to eat it, shows how well both sides trusted each other. Of the one misunderstanding: this tragedy upset the Indian Chief so much when he heard about it, that he went in person to apologise to the Welsh members of the Chubut Valley. When Mr Tschiffely wrote about this incident, which to me has all the epic simplicity and intangible wonder of Ibsen's great plays, the Welshman who had experienced this miracle was still alive. He, and three other settlers, disheartened by a bad harvest, set out to find some gold-dust, and their direction took them towards the foot of the Andes where at that time, Indians were being badly attacked by Argentine soldiers. The Indians met these Welshmen and questioned their direction. They became suspicious, as the Welshmen, unknown to themselves were heading for the soldiers' camp. They therefore asked the Welshmen, who had never covered this territory before, to return and speak with their Chief. This the settlers promised to do, but on the following day, thinking they were left alone, they suddenly decided to continue as quickly as possible in their original direction. The Indians, suspicious and skulking behind bushes, had seen them: 'To their horror, the four Welshmen realised that they were being pursued; worse still, that they were cornered at the bend of the river, where deep precipices barred their flight. A number of yelling Indians were rapidly catching up with the terrified fugitives, three of whom were horribly slain. In his terror, John D. Evans, who was in front, riding a swift mustang, made straight for the precipice, across which his gallant animal, obviously realising the danger, made a tremendous leap, thus saving his master's life, for no Indian had the courage to follow this desperate course.' Towards the end of his tour, Mr Tschiffely one day entered Trevelin on a Sunday when everybody was at Chapel. On their return from the service, he met Mr Evans who took him out 'to a shady glade where he halted in front of a big rock on which was carved:

AQUI YACEN LOS RESTOS DE MI CABALLO EL MALACARA
QUE ME SALVO LA VIDA EN ET ATAQUE DE LOS INDIOS EN
EL VALLE DE LOS MARTIRES EL 4.3.84 AL REGRESARME
DE LA CORDILLERA. R.I.P. JOHN D. EVANS.

(Here lie the remains of my horse 'Whiteblaze', who
saved my life during the attack of the Indians in the
Valley of the Martyrs, on the 4th of March, 1884, as
I was returning from the Cordillera.)'

These accounts of hard and wild life, together with the
mystery of much of the unexplored territory in Patagonia,
are not sufficient in themselves to represent the modern
conditions which exist today, if we are to know the Welsh
Colony in its true perspective. We need more sincere travellers
like Mr Tschiffely, besides the interpretation and sensibility
which distinguished writers, artists and poets could contribute.
A more comprehensive and up-to-date index of its natural
history is also required. For instance, I have often wondered
whether the colder regions of Patagonia ever had butterflies.
Then, there is the more progressive side of the Welsh Settlers
themselves. The fact that they overcame, and are overcoming,
the great shortage of water. How through their tenacious spirit
and persistence, over half a million acres of desert land were
put under cultivation. How much of the valley – growing part
fruit and corn – came into existence by the scientific irrigation
system cut out by some of the early Welsh Settlers. Patagonia
is no longer a backward sheep-rearing concern isolated from
the outside world. They have the oil-field industry, chilled
meat factories, fruit, wool, and wheat exports. There are the
new methods of collecting water. Santa Cruz has water laid on,
and Deseado; others are to follow. Sole reliance of depending
on rain water is quickly disappearing, which is more than we
can say of our lethargic methods of water collecting in the

various rural villages of Wales. The vast low-lying tract of land in Patagonia has lent itself to flying, and many airlines run regularly so many times a week as far South as Tierra del Fuego. In this way both Argentine governed and private planes belonging to families and firms help to make this part of the world, not the most isolated, but the most up-to-date in transport. There could be much improvement in this field; and perhaps after the war, more transport with cargo will be carried by air in this way, overcoming the shortage of ships for export and the lack of good roads. The immediate petrol and tyre shortage will probably be restored at the end of the year. The Welsh people not only have contact with their wireless sets, but often make frequent visits to Buenos Aires. They also have 'their own unofficial Parliament where important matters are discussed'. And these in Welsh. In fact, the Welsh language does not seem to be dying out as quickly as the English press is inclined to think. The same mistake is made with regard to the Welsh-speaking peoples in Wales. The language which is dying out in the Welsh Colonies both in the Chubut Valley and in the Settlement Colonia 16 de Octubre, is no other than the English language. I wish to make this clear, as Mr Tschiffely has been misquoted on this point. He writes: 'looking back, it seems incredible that I had to go all the way to Patagonia to learn a few words of Welsh.' The very fact that Eisteddfods are still held, shows that not only can many of its competitors express themselves in Welsh, whether in the plays, poetry, or choir singing; but that the audience to whom they speak, and the adjudicators themselves, must be fluent in their Cymric tongue. The last of these Eisteddfods was held at Trelew this year, when Evan Thomas of Gaimon, won the Bardic Chair.

I should like to think that today, when Wales seems oppressed partly through her own misdirection and partly through outside jurisdiction, she could turn and concentrate more on her Welsh Colony in Patagonia. This would help to extend her vision, which at the moment, through suffering has become too parochial. An exchange, I believe, on all matters, such as agriculture, political and cultural, would stimulate and help both Countries to develop. How do the sheep farms in both Countries compare? Are the owners of these camps interested in the new breeds of sheep? Have they yet found an animal which will live with a scanty water supply, produce strong wool and a good depth of flesh? Have they tried the Welsh Mountain Sheep recommended by Moses Griffith? What sort of year have they had with regard to the wool export? Fruit and corn harvest? What do they, the Welsh in Patagonia, know of the younger generation in Wales? Of the living young writers and painters? I should like to see what use the Welsh in Patagonia have made of their magnificent lakes; woven samples of the remaining Tribal Indian culture; attend lectures on Patagonia illustrated with film documentaries. See the actual botanical plants displayed, together with the birds, fossils, and original samples of the rock; to see their colour, texture, and mineralogy defined. See photo exhibitions exchanged between both Countries. The work of artists who have painted Patagonia. Their weaving. Leathercraft. Plan of airfields. Airports. Style of architecture. I should even like a weekly column on Patagonia in the Kemsley and Northcliffe Press which represent South Wales (the *Western Mail* and *South Wales Evening Post*). *Y Cymro* and *Y Faner* do occasionally publish news or letters from this Welsh Colony. But perhaps my interest in this matter is singular. For it pleases me very much, when I read in letters from relations that 'they came across a tame King Emperor Penguin, a highly intelligent bird which had started to get its colourful plumage, the bright yellow turning to orange around its supposed ears'; this creature had been kept as a pet in Tierra del Fuego, 'until he intended to wander off to the sea again.' Of the cocktail party which 'gathered at Rio Gallegos where in one evening 2,000 pesos were gathered for the British Red Cross, besides the auctioning of a trout which had been caught, for 117 pesos.' Of the terrible floods this year, that not only held up the fishing but cut the railway line to Zapala, bringing down sides of the hills in the Cordillera. 'The water was dark brown, which means no fishing in the Aluminé, but luckily the Quillan was clear so we were never without enough fish for the table.'

A.F. Tschiffely, in a Postscript, written some years after his Patagonian tour, speaks of his present occupation, which is lecturing for the British Council in Buenos Aires; may he, and other persons of distinction, who also have a first-hand knowledge of Patagonia, bring back that link which we have too easily lost; and help unite the Welsh people in these two Countries whose interest on both sides have fallen into such neglect.

Philip Gbeho's West African dance class in London, early 1950s, attended by Lynette Roberts and Robert Graves. Graves's children Juan and Lucia are in the foreground. Photograph reproduced by kind permission of William Graves.

EPILOGUE

Since Carcanet published Lynette Roberts's *Collected Poems* in 2005 we have discovered so much more about her significance to twentieth-century literature. Roberts's *Diaries, Letters and Recollections* followed in 2008, and for the first time her work was easily available, finding many new readers excited by the freshness of her vision and the distinctiveness of her voice.[1] Roberts was once again recognised as a deeply original poet writing about locality, war, love, culture and nature in surprisingly innovative ways. Her work is now widely celebrated, the subject of academic conferences, literary festivals, PhD theses, international press interest, and a dedicated collection of essays covering everything from her Elective Welsh identity to her late prose work *The Endeavour*.[2] Her poetry is now also regularly anthologised – for example in Meic Stephens's *Poetry 1900-2000*, and Carol Ann Duffy and Gillian Clarke's *The Map and the Clock*, the latter balancing the simplicity of Roberts's 'Poem from Llanybri' with the more radical voice of 'Poem (We must uprise O my people)'. James Keery's *Apocalypse*, a recent anthology of mid-twentieth century poetry, contains several Roberts poems alongside excerpts from *Gods with Stainless Ears*.[3] In 2009 the poet Owen Sheers chose Lynette Roberts to be a key subject of his BBC television series *A Poet's Guide to Britain*, devoting one of only six episodes entirely to her life and writing.

But there is still more of Roberts to be recovered, and this new edition of her collected poems is an important part of that work, adding a further twenty-five uncollected poems, and bringing together all her poems known to be previously published. In addition, forty poems are published here for the first time, edited from manuscripts and typescripts some eighty years after they were written, and thirty years after Roberts's death in 1995. This represents a significant expansion of the primary textual material of one the most exciting and important poets of the twentieth century, as we continue the process of reconstructing her textual life after her long neglect. Roberts changes our understanding of modernist writing itself, and this edition changes our understanding of Roberts.

Those writers whose reputation is established during their lifetime and who remain in the literary canon can nevertheless present a modern editor with many challenges, but textual scholarship tends to keep pace with their reputation. Since 1952, editors of T.S. Eliot have been guided down some well-worn grooves by different editions of Donald Gallup's *T.S. Eliot: A Bibliography*, which identifies and categorises Eliot's books, contributions to periodicals and miscellanea with loving detail. Editors of Robert Graves have turned to Fred Higginson's comprehensive bibliography since 1966. The job of editing a writer such as Roberts, who for so long fell off the literary radar, is differently challenging. Throughout their most creative periods as writers, Roberts and her husband Keidrych Rhys were living frequently itinerant lives through the chaos of war and its aftermath. The careful curation of their literary papers and reputations was never likely to be an immediate priority, and their restoration to a contemporary readership consequently involves a good deal of literary detective work, which can be exhilarating and frustrating by turns.

I came across many of the additional uncollected poems in this new edition whilst researching and editing Keidrych Rhys's *The Van Pool: Collected Poems* in libraries and archives across the world.[4] Rhys and Roberts inevitably occupied similar poetry circles in the 1930s and 40s, and much of their work appeared in the same small-press publications, where it lay largely unnoticed, for many years. When it comes to unpublished materials, the editorial challenges can be even greater. Many of Keidrych Rhys's later literary manuscripts are in the National Library of Wales, but a line of enquiry also led to a significant archive of hitherto unknown notebooks, papers and letters from the 1940s, deposited with the artist Stanley Lewis after Roberts and Rhys separated, and kept privately by the Lewis family ever since, along with a lost portrait of Rhys by Cedric Morris. Many of Roberts's manuscripts are somewhat easier to trace, thanks to their acquisition by the Harry Ransom Center, The University of Texas at Austin, but there is also a cache of Roberts's poems amongst

Robert Graves's papers in the archive of St John's College Oxford, and other manuscripts still in the private possession of Roberts's family. Much of this material is overlayered with annotations, some in Roberts's own hand, and others by Graves and Eliot. There are often several versions of texts, some clearly made at different periods of her life, and many emendations and variations to navigate. Whilst some poems are handily dated and located, others are impossible to pin down in chronology with any degree of certainty.

'A Letter to the Dead' is a poem very precisely dated 9.05pm, 12 February 1954, and lends its name to this new edition of Roberts's collected poems. It is a late epistolary elegy, inspired by the death of Dylan Thomas in November 1953, and recalling several different occasions and conversations from their long friendship. It was first published posthumously in *PN Review* in 2014, the centenary year of Thomas's birth, but written sixty years earlier, and is one of Roberts's last poems.[5] Its plainly conversational style is unlike much of her previous work, partly because of the epistolary form, although it is otherwise characteristic in its use of collage and its allusion to Welsh mythology. Roberts moved into a caravan in the Laugharne churchyard following her separation from Rhys in 1949, the same year that Dylan and Caitlin Thomas moved back to Laugharne and into the Boathouse, hence the poem's descriptions of their renewed sessions 'In ship's pub and sea pubs drinking, and at it again / If only to be alive with you'.

In the early 1950s, Roberts's career was opening in fresh directions as she negotiated new life and freedom after her divorce, and as Britain slowly emerged from post-war austerity. Faber published *Gods with Stainless Ears* in 1951, and in 1953 she secured a contract from the new and exciting publisher Peter Owen for her astonishing novel *The Endeavour*, based on Captain Cook's first voyage to the south Pacific Ocean, which was published in 1954. She gave poetry readings to various audiences, including in 1952 to the East End Music Association, Wadham College Oxford, and the Oxford University Poetry Society. She also took part in an initiative called 'Poetry and Plays in Pubs', sponsored by John Masefield and Dame Sybil Thorndike. There is a photograph of Roberts in a summer dress holding a brightly coloured scarf in one hand and a baby pet rabbit in the other, identified on the back as taken after her reading at Wadham College in Spring 1952. One productive outcome of the Oxford readings was her appearance in the brand-new *Departure: A Magazine of Literature and the Arts*, edited by John Adlard and Alan Brownjohn. Their very first editorial is instructive in identifying the changing literary landscape negotiated by Roberts and her contemporaries in the early 1950s:

> Next, we refuse to subscribe to the view that innovation in art is no longer valid. Much as we are bound to respect the increased awareness of literary tradition, and support the arduous demands of a new criticism, we at least will not suffer them to stifle experiment or write off whole reaches of literature for trifling reasons. And a disinterested academic approach to the function and forms of poetry ill-becomes a writer whose literary conscience tells him that he should like literature first.[6]

One page later their defence of the experimental against the tide of a growing conservatism in British poetry was manifest in the publication of Roberts's 'You within the Enchanted Circle', a poem inspired but not contained by the circumstances of her divorce from Rhys, and one which Brownjohn said he admired without ever fully grasping.[7] The poem is structured around a Welsh myth originating in the Carmarthenshire countryside where Rhys grew up. The myth of Llyn y Fan Fach is centred on the lake of that name, and a fairy lady who emerges from the water and appears before a local farmer, who falls in love with her. He hopes to win her over with his baking, and on the third occasion when he takes her perfectly baked bread, she agrees to marry him. Her father gives her a dowry of miraculous cattle, but with the warning that should the farmer strike her three times, she will return to the lake. Their life together is fruitful, but on three occasions he strikes her, first with a tap from a pair of gloves, then at a wedding (for crying), and a funeral (for rejoicing), and she returns to the lake, taking her retinue of cattle, including a white bull and a little black calf already suspended on a meat hook, but leaving behind her children. In 1942 the myth was alluded to by Rhys in the name of his only collection of poems to appear in his lifetime: *The Van Pool and Other Poems*.[8] Ten years later Roberts takes the myth and makes it her own, as her two young children are transformed into the magical cattle accompanying her into the renewing 'Lake of Birth' itself:

> Now as the monstrous season turns,
> Thins the buttermilk of days,
> Scouring his heart, and her mind:
> At her command over the rippled lake,
> At the third blow, turned,
>
> Called her young heifer of flour white hide,
> Bid her black bull calf 'Prydein come'.
> All three dissolved into the wavering haze,
> To her Living Grave and Lake of Birth,
> Like midges in the air.

The close relationship between writing and the natural world for Roberts is evident in the detailed metamorphism of this and may other poems. Sixty years later Brownjohn vividly recalled a moment from Roberts's Oxford reading when she reflected on her process as a writer: 'She referred to the problem of getting caught with an idea for a poem and no means of writing it down ("nothing to write it *on*"); and she cited an instance of walking in a wood, having an idea, and writing words on a piece of bark from a tree, with a burnt stick'. He also recalled the small pet rabbit captured in the photograph escaping in an Oxford coffee house and being chased by undergraduates.[9] Roberts went home to tell her children she had lost the rabbit, which recalls one of the earliest poems collected here, published by the twenty-year old Roberts in *Life and Letters*, and another early addition to her poetic menagerie:

> Peter the rabbit always hid behind the piano.
> He came when he was called
> Peter... Peter...
> he did not come.

Roberts's menagerie frequently contains detailed observations of the particulars of her subjects, a deep concern for their ecology, and the Romantic potential for their figurative possibilities. Her diary entry for 6 February 1947 mentions her reading of David Lack's classic book on the robin in the context of the almost complete disappearance of the bird during the terribly cold winter that year:

> And it is my intention one day to write a poem on this masterful young creature. Not a 'garden spade' poem: but something which holds the whole measure of this bird. Of its migration, communal interest, clear personality and sweet voice which somehow seems to follow the rain so that its song contains the mingled freshness of the rain and clearness of the sun.[10]

The poem she wrote is collected here for the first time. 'The Orange Charger' describes the freedoms of the robin and its migratory patterns in contrast to the earthbound limitations of the lyrical voice, albeit that Roberts's youthful experience of life in Argentina and her own early migratory habits between continents allow her some identification with her subject. It is the robin:

> Who loves to migrate
> And not to migrate,
> Or sits with wistful isolation

In the perennial springs of the Azores.
You, who are the bird
Of the warm steaming soil,
Of the scent of the rain,
Of quiet temperate days;
From your orange breast
A sweeter cadence was never heard.

Whilst Roberts identifies with the geographical and spiritual freedoms of the robin, the music of the poem is relatively conservative and describes rather than reenacts the birdsong itself. Elsewhere, Roberts's developing later style sees a more frequent intensification of the musicality of her poems, at the same time as her syntax and vocabulary are clarifying from the wonderfully difficult constructions in *Gods with Stainless Ears*. In 'Spring', first published in Winter 1951, the music of the poem itself transforms into the sounds of Spring, as the season becomes a soaring bird alive with the intertwined music of birdsong and the restless harmonies of new leaves rustling in the breeze. Nearly every syllable resonates through alliterative, assonantal or rhyming patterns with another, in intense harmony and rhythm:

Spring rules the world with open wing
And leaves that sing vibrate the air
With birds so rare that man should fling
His stress of being aside to bear
The greater joy of King of Spring.

The story of the season is told through its bird life, from the 'roundelay of gorselit birds' to later arrivals: 'With wingbeat drumming, geese, cuckoo, / Warblers too, swifts scissored hum', and the poem begins with the King of Spring, and ends with the Queen of Spring, in the form of Artemis, taking his place.

In the previous Spring of 1950 Roberts wrote to Robert Graves about her explorations of music in relation to rhythm:

I am trying to get a Talking Drum – tom-tom or some tribal drum which has a *low sound*. This I want to use purely in relation to rhythm. I want a group of us to listen to the varied rhythms & each to place on paper their individual opinions.[11]

Roberts's daughter confirms that such a drum was found, and in late 1953 Roberts approached both Graves and T. S. Eliot asking them to be referees for a Leverhulme scholarship to study the relation between African music rhythms and Western poetry. In response Eliot wrote her a chiding paternalistic Christmas letter:

Certainly I will be one of your references for a Scholarship [...]. I hope that you succeed; but at the same time it strikes me that to try to live on one grant after another is a very precarious way of life, and that you will have to find a regular job in the end. It would be a good thing to learn short-hand and typing. But a job of some kind you must have, eventually.[12]

Roberts outlined the Leverhulme project in more detail to Robert Graves:

I put in for *poetry research* with an emphasis on rhythm in relation to social and national environment [...]. An example of what I mean is for instance the rumba and dance rhythms of today and how in studying African rhythms in order to get at the basic nucleus of these jazz rhythms, I found the true source and poetically unadulterated version of the present samba rhythms used in Brazil filtered into our own poetic metres.[13]

Whilst the Leverhulme application came to nothing, in the early 1950s Roberts did draw Robert Graves further into her study of music by taking him along with her to West African Dance classes in London, led by the Ghanian musician and musicologist Dr Philip Gbeho (who later wrote the Ghanaian national anthem). The occasion is captured in a previously unpublished photograph from Robert Graves's personal family collection, and Roberts's daughter recalls that Roberts also bought a 78-rpm record of Gbeho's music that she played constantly. The kind of experimental thinking about how jazz rhythms could translate into a poem is evident in texts like 'I'm only':

> I'm now a
> child' of blue-white
> hue' to pierce dim
> light' to select sharp
> rays' to convey the
> mood' in – rhythm.

The syncopations here are marked by the apostrophes to highlight the rhythmic emphasis of certain syllables over others. If this is a slightly crude experiment in the recreation of syncopated jazz rhythms, the poem 'Blues with a Rumba Background' is a much more involved and creative pastiche of its chosen musical genres:

> But the China doll she blazes
> Her desires like rockets roaring
> Her hair electric flames rising
> Her eyes two neons flashing
> Her hands are beating
> Time against her
> She is so hot. He is so cold.

The poem is possibly a distant riff on Isham Jones and Charles Newman's much covered hit from 1932 'The Wooden Soldier and the China Doll', but Roberts's imagery is contemporary with the United States's Viking space rocket programme of the early 1950s and gives us a kind of sci-fi Pygmalion dancing to the tune of fusion Latin American Blues and bewailing mismatched passions. It is a poem that plays a key role in Roberts's unpublished radio verse drama 'O Lovers of Death', which was another significant product of her career as a professional writer in the 1950s. 'O Lovers of Death' tells a disturbing story of familial jealousy, separation, broken betrothal and murder. A young radio officer has been on naval duties in the far East for three years, and on his return his ship is wrecked on the Anglesey coast near to his family home.[14] The young woman to whom he has been betrothed goes to find him, and we encounter them together talking in an Italian Fish and Chip shop, where 'the wireless plays the Blues "China Doll Blues" on and off throughout'.[15] He is traumatised and emotionally cold; she is heartbroken and leaves sobbing. The radio officer's father, a graveyard stonecutter, is mad with the jealous thought that the young girl will rob him once again of his son, and he plans to murder her as she walks through the graveyard. But in the dark he mistakenly kills his son instead. The young girl discovers the horrible murder, declares herself free, and faces the coming dawn whilst incanting the text of another poem published here for the first time, 'Invocation':

O bring me
My heart. Bring it as a field of buttercups.
O let them blaze forth glistening as finite suns.
Let my tears crystallise among you in praise
Of the cosmic source exploding into a rainbow
Of coloured brilliants that fall sparkling, wet
On to the flowering grass, through Jay blue
And woodpeckers darting from the trees, through pink-
pink

Of the chaffinch, chiff-chaff, woodlark and dove.
All quivering, scintillating, rinsing petal, bud and wing:
O lovers of death leave your sorrow.

'O Lovers of Death' was broadcast in December 1952 by the BBC on the British Home Service Welsh.[16] Roberts intended 'Blues with a Rumba Background' to be set to music and outlined a soundscape for the production in the stage directions and notes, flagging up her artistic well-connectedness in the process:

> No music accompaniment to the two songs in Part I). Only to the Blues. This should have a background of rumba rhythm surfaced by the slow wail of the Blues rhythm, both rhythms played at the same time. Preceding the Dawn Poem ['Invocation'] in part 5 a few chords of Britten's *Rape of Lucretia* […]; Holst's *Planets*; or selective sections from Bartok; or Sir William Walton's first movement violin concerto. The bird songs of chaffinch and chiff-chaff from Ludwig Koch's records, used towards the end of Dawn Poem. Daniel Jones (Welsh composer) who I know and arranged an audition with my uncle the late Sir Granville Bantock could compose this rumba rhythm superimposed over a Blues.[17]

Whether her lyric got the musical setting in the broadcast itself remains unknown.

A different kind of poetic musical experimentation from around the same time earned the displeasure of T.S. Eliot. 'The Warrior and the Harlot' is a pastiche in medieval ballad form and was one of two poems singled out for critical comment in Eliot's unpublished letter to Roberts of 27 May 1953 rejecting her collection 'The Fifth Pillar of Song' for publication by Faber. In a rare moment of directness, Eliot wrote:

The other poem which I think is definitely a failure, although I suspect that you think very highly of it yourself, is 'The Warrior and the Harlot'. You will find that on this I have made a number of pencilled comments. I am afraid I really think that this misses its effect by tumbling over into the absurd.[18]

Whilst Eliot marks up two stanzas as 'flat' and one merely 'silly', he reserves the rebuking comment 'ludicrous' for:

> She drew him on, she drew her skirt
> Up to her lovely knees,
> She wore the same red garters edged
> With sequins like the seas.

There's certainly ludic playfulness here, and perhaps too frank a description of female allure for Eliot's liking. Roberts felt stung into characteristic reply, and the manuscript also contains her defensive note:

> The knight here is symbolic of all mythology: the harlot is symbolic of the materialistic world. It was after reading W. P. Ker's chapters on ballads, in which he states all good ballads should have a second underlying structure quite apart from the narrative, that prompted me to use this formula. The ballad itself was directly inspired as a result of hearing about Mr Wyndham Lewis's grief. I read this ballad to him, and he loved it. It therefore, for me, served its purpose. It made him happy.[19]

Wyndham Lewis and Roberts corresponded from the late 1940s to the mid-1950s, they met on various occasions, and Lewis sketched her in 1948. His letters complain about his material circumstances:

How I surmount (partially) the difficulty is that I never leave Rotting Hill, never buy any Chateauneuf du Pape or Armagnac, never have my teeth attended to but just let them rot like everything around us, only eat food that is sent me from America, and of course my ration and any bananas I can ogle out of the greengrocer, never buy trousers to work in, never buy a shirt.[20]

Roberts sent him twelve large white eggs, her butter ration, a pair of gaucho trousers, and bought at least one of his paintings. She also sent him her poetry, about which he wrote: 'I felt myself like a bee, more and more ponderous with honey, moving from odd beautiful units of imagery to next unit, and so on and on - as if it were in a dark Conservatory'.[21] As a result of a brain tumour, Wyndham Lewis went completely blind in 1951, which is the grief that Roberts references in her note to the poem, and the reason her medieval Knight is sightless. One of the poem manuscripts is dated June 1951 at the caravan woods bird sanctuary, and another has a note in ink referencing Paolo Uccello's 'A Stag Hunt by Night' in the Ashmolean, indicating that both a natural and artistic wood inspired her poetic medievalism:

> Her screams they filled the darkened wood,
> Cut by the light's saw edge,
> Her knight was blind, he had no sight,
> Such was the sacrilege.

The new poems in this edition are wide-ranging in terms of geography, subject and style, and include some of the earliest and latest of her poetic output. Many share the subject matter with which we are now familiar: the attention to detail and wonder found in the natural world, the love and understanding of colour, the domestic and the cosmic, the tensions between deracinated freedom and the power of locality and community. There are poems looking back to her South American childhood and early adventurous travel such as 'Tinamou', further poems charting her experience of life and culture in war-torn rural Wales such as 'Death That Monster', and a later group of texts exploring major life events, including the elegy 'Out of the Paw of Night' on the death of her father in November 1949. In the ballad 'Eternal Love', also an elegy, she recalls early memories of childhood, and her mother, who died when she was thirteen. Other poems expand the menagerie further, including a group that are either about or allude to Welsh white cattle and their historical and mythical importance, including 'Sacred White Cattle' and 'Eisteddfod'. Here too Roberts did her research, eventually tracking down John Storer's classic book *The Wild White Cattle of Great Britain* despite the obstacles put in her way by libraries reluctant to lend it:

> I cannot receive it at the County Library even if it were transferred there as I cannot leave my 2 babies, one under 2 years of age and a son of 4 1/2 months so, humiliated, I had to write and beg from a stranger. A Major living miles away in Norfolk.[22]

Whilst these poems are written despite the straitened circumstances of motherhood in 1940s rural Wales, others reflect on a time earlier in her career when she had significantly more freedom. 'Dedicated to "Bruska"' recalls her work as a high-class self-employed florist working out of a flat in 68 Newman Street in the 1930s, and creating artificial flowers with the same loving detail as she reconstructs flora in her poetry:

> The air I breathe and the song I sing
> Weave a tissue for their birth
> With the sea-frost to prime their design.
>
> (Gut-oiled rose.)

In 'Winter Walk', a late poem, she reads the shapes of animal footprints on a palimpsest of snow-covered ground, and inscribes the fox as artist, who stamps a rose-shaped print into the snow and in so doing transforms the snowstorm that made it possible into white rose petals, evoking summer in the depths of winter, and perhaps with an echo of the legend of Olwen from the *Mabinogion*, and the white flowers that bloom in her footsteps:

> But lifted off the path like crystal spheres
> There lay cut prints of glinting stylized forms
> Of birds not seen, large sparkling twig-like spears,
> And squirrel pricks where fox's paw transforms
> White single roses out of petalled storms;

That intense fusion of nature, art, colour, shape and music is characteristic of Roberts's best poetry, and is also present in 'Experimental', where her skill as a visual artist and writer achieves a kind of perfect harmony. Even Eliot gets close to a compliment in an annotation to the manuscript, saying 'Nonsense but I like it':

> Grail away Borage
> Float on you kestrels.
> Strain sun to a colour
> Shed blue on calico,
> Run green into ventricles
> By chequered brooks
> Plovers' eggs.
> Bee drone on borage
> Blue light a lighter sky
> Ruin grows out of day
> Strides on twigs
> A snail's radiance.

For literary scholars, Roberts's writing has shifted the geography of modernism away from the metropolitan centre, and extends the chronological stretch of what is sometimes now referred to as late modernism beyond even the 1940s. Roberts's is an importantly female perspective in a previously male-dominated sphere, and as a Welsh writer hers is a newly-prominent voice in the reinvigorated interest in Welsh writing in English as a distinctly important field of literary and cultural studies. There's much more reconstruction still to do. Her first published novel *The Endeavour* has been out of print for over sixty years, and her first novel, 'Nesta', based on the life of the 12th century Princess Nest, has never been published, although we now know that the manuscript still exists.[23] Twenty years on from the first edition of her collected poems and it is still difficult to overstate the freshness and originality of her writing, and the distinctiveness of her voice and vision.

Charles Mundye, 2025.

NOTES TO EPILOGUE

1   Lynette Roberts, *Collected Poems*, ed. Patrick McGuinness (Manchester: Carcanet, 2005), and *Diaries, Letters and Recollections*, ed. Patrick McGuinness (Manchester: Carcanet, 2008).

2   See, for example, Siriol McAvoy, ed., *Locating Lynette Roberts* (Cardiff: University of Wales Press, 2019).

3   Meic Stephens, ed., *Poetry 1900–2000* (Cardigan: Parthian, 2007); Carol Ann Duffy and Gillian Clarke, eds., *The Map and the Clock: A Laureate's Choice of the Poetry of Britain and Ireland* (London: Faber, 2016); James Keery, ed., *Apocalypse: An Anthology* (Manchester: Carcanet, 2020).

4   Keidrych Rhys, *The Van Pool: Collected Poems*, ed. Charles Mundye (Bridgend: Seren, 2012).

5 For a more detailed reading of the poem, see Charles Mundye, 'Lynette Roberts and Dylan Thomas: Background to a Friendship', *PN Review*, 41, 2, 2014, 20–23.

6 John Adlard and Alan Brownjohn, 'Editorial', *Departure: A Magazine of Literature and the Arts*, 1,1, 1952, 1.

7 Personal communication from Alan Brownjohn, 10 July 2013.

8 Keidrych Rhys, *The Van Pool and Other Poems* (London: Routledge, 1942).

9 Personal communications from Alan Brownjohn, 10 and 22 July 2013.

10 *Diaries, Letters and Recollections*, p. 75.

11 Letter from Lynette Roberts to Robert Graves, 6 May 1950, 'The Correspondence between Lynette Roberts and Robert Graves', *Poetry Wales*,19, 2, 1983, 114.

12 Unpublished letter from T.S. Eliot to Lynette Roberts, 28 December 1953. A copy of the letter is among Lynette Roberts's family papers. The original is held in the Harry Ransom Center, University of Texas at Austin. Reproduced by permission of Faber and Faber on behalf of the Estate of T.S. Eliot.

13 Unpublished letter from Lynette Roberts to Robert Graves, 21 January 1954. Reproduced by permission of the President and Fellows of St John's College, Oxford, and the Estate of Lynette Roberts.

14 As a young woman in April 1939 Roberts had first-hand experience of shipwreck at Carmel Head, Anglesey, aboard the cruise liner *Hilary*. For an account of how Roberts entertained her fellow worried passengers, see Anon., 'Girls Stage Cabaret as Ship Grounds', *Daily Mail*, 10 April 1939, 9.

15 Lynette Roberts, 'O Lovers of Death'. Quotations are from the unpublished manuscript in the Lynette Roberts archive, Harry Ransom Center, University of Texas at Austin.

16 'Radio Odes, "O Lovers of Death"', by Lynette Roberts, was broadcast on 3 December 1952 by the British Home Service Welsh, 9.55 pm–10.20 pm. See *Radio Times*, 1516, 30 November–6 December 1952.

17 Roberts, 'O Lovers of Death', unpublished manuscript. Roberts was related to the British composer Sir Granville Bantock (1868–1946) and corresponded with him in the 1930s. The Welsh composer Daniel Jones (1912–1993) was also close friends with Dylan Thomas and composed music for *Under Milk Wood*.

18 Unpublished letter from T.S. Eliot to Lynette Roberts, 27 May 1953. A copy of the letter is among Lynette Roberts's family papers. The original is held in the Harry Ransom Center, University of Texas at Austin. Reproduced by permission of Faber and Faber on behalf of the Estate of T.S. Eliot.

19 Lynette Roberts, handwritten note on the unpublished manuscript of 'The Warrior and the Harlot'. Roberts is referring to W. P. Ker's *On the History of the Ballads 1100–1500* (London: OUP, [1910]).

20 Unpublished letter from Wyndham Lewis to Lynette Roberts, 26 July 1948. A copy of the letter is among Lynette Roberts's family papers. The original is held in the Harry Ransom Center, University of Texas at Austin.

21 Unpublished letter from Wyndham Lewis to Lynette Roberts, 20 September 1948.

22 *Diaries, Letters and Recollections*, p. 79.

23 Lynette Roberts, *The Endeavour: Captain Cook's First Voyage to Australia* (London: Peter Owen, 1954). The manuscript of 'Nesta' is in the Lynette Roberts archive in the Harry Ransom Center, University of Texas at Austin.

Poems

Poem from Llanybri

Lynette Roberts wrote this for fellow-poet Alun Lewis (1915–1944) as an invitation to Llanybri. At the time Lewis was in Longmoor, Hampshire, with the Royal Engineers. His response is the poem 'Peace' in *Raiders' Dawn* (1942). For an account of the friendship between Lewis and Roberts, see John Pikoulis, 'Lynette Roberts and Alun Lewis', *Poetry Wales*, 19/2 (1983), pp. 9–29. Tony Conran, in the same issue, writes that the poem 'combines centuries of tradition, a modern Welsh accent – "If you come my way that is" – a controlling urbanity and a singular freshness of description. [...] The poem is written within the convention of the guild of poets.' Conran, who met Roberts in 1953 when she was living in a caravan in Hertfordshire, recalls 'She once told me she only wrote it as a poetic exercise' (*Poetry Wales*, 19, 2, 1983, 132–3).

savori fach: Satureja montana, winter savory.
cawl: Welsh broth.
Cwmcelyn is the name of the bay below Llanybri facing Laugharne.

The Shadow Remains

In her diary entry for 4 August 1942, Roberts describes this as 'a good poem about my v. simple life'. The poem also alludes obliquely to her miscarriage, a subject more directly treated in 'Lamentation'.

Plasnewydd

Plasnewydd, meaning 'new hall' in Welsh, was the name of the childhood farm of Lynette Roberts's friend Rosie Davies, who features in several poems, as well as the prose piece 'Swansea

Raid'. The idioms and direct quotations in the poem are Rosie's, and in her diary entry for 17 June 1940 (headed 'The Fall of France'), Roberts notes a conversation with Rosie:

> 'Well, you see, it's like this, Mrs Rhys' ... and Rosie on one foot with her hand on her hip, she licks around her mouth, then begins talking again, and it is always the same, 'Well you see, it's like this, Mrs Rhys. I can't imagine the war or fighting at all, I've never travelled at all, only to go to Cardiff, so I can't imagine this war at all. She's very wrong mind you (meaning the WAR), and what I feel is they're all flesh and blood like you or I Mrs Rhys, arent they? If you were to be stabbed you would feel it just as much as they, wouldn't you? WAR there's no sense in it. We're simple people. We all get on. War there's no sense in it'.

In an entry for 2 September 1940, Roberts recalls: 'I wrote about Rosie and used her idioms in the poem called after her childhood farm "Plasnewydd".'

Pussy drwg: literally, 'naughty cat' in Welsh.

Hal-e-bant: West Wales Welsh for 'shoo' or 'get going'; literally, 'get him/it away'.

Fan Fach: 'Llyn y Fan Fach' is a lake in the Carmarthenshire vans, associated with a Welsh folk tale from the *Mabinogion*, 'The Physicians of Myddfai'. In the story, a widow of Blaensawdde sent her son to watch her cattle as they grazed near Llyn y Fan Fach. One day he saw a woman rise out of the lake, and fell in love with her. After courting the Lady of Fan Fach, the young man was told by her father that he must not strike her three times without cause, or she would disappear. Before disappearing back into the lake, the Lord of Fan Fach offered as his daughter's dowry as many animals as she could call in one breath. The couple went to live on a farm near Myddfai, lived happily and had three children. On three occasions, however, the husband tapped his wife on the shoulder, and on the third she summoned the descendants of the animals she had brought with her, and they all disappeared back into the lake. The three boys became healers, the 'physicians of Myddfai'.

Low Tide

Roberts's diary entry for 12 July 1940, 'Keidrych called up', reads:

> Rosie offered me her daughter, Iris, to sleep with me when Keidrych was 'called up'. This seems to be customary around here. Mrs Bollands, i.e. Sarah Ann, has also offered me her sister's love child who was six years old. But naturally I refused. [...] I stayed at home and wrote 'Low Tide'.

Raw Salt on Eye

In the summer of 1942 many of the villagers of Llanybri began to suspect Roberts of being a German spy. The episode is referred to in her diary entry for 4 August of that year:

> I feel wretchedly lonely. The village, most of them have turned on me and treat me as a spy. The malicious talk seeping in so far that it infilters the minds of the children and they throw stones at me. [...] So I wrote about the gossip and suffering in Raw Salt on Eye [...]

Amelia Phillips: one of the villagers whose idioms and sayings are recorded in *Village Dialect*.

Lamentation

This poem is about an air raid in which farm animals, including Rosie's cattle, were killed. Roberts makes the connection between them and her miscarried child, the 'death before birth', the 'emptiness of crib'. Among the most vivid entries in her diary is 'Air Crash' (the entry for 12 June 1942), in which she recalls her experiences of air raids in London, Dover and West Wales.

Broken Voices
In her own notes to this poem, Roberts explains her 'attempt to apply the strict metre form of the Welsh englyn to the English language'. The commonest form of the *englyn* is a quatrain form in which the lines have, respectively, ten, six, seven and seven syllables. The seventh syllable of the first line announces the rhyme, with which the last syllable of the next three lines rhyme. Roberts mentions Robert Graves as a poet drawn to the Welsh strict metre forms, and Graves's father, Alfred Perceval, had published *Welsh Poetry Old and New* in 1912. Another poet who experimented with such effects is Hopkins.

The *englynion* by R. Williams Parry quoted in Roberts's note to the poem translates as follows: 'Humble, warm-hearted Tom – who remains/ long in the sea:/ So cold is his death now/ Beneath the water's flow, beneath the salty wave.// Oh wondrous peaceful multitude – the dead/ And the seaweed mingled/ the parlours of pearls, the acres of fish/ Are the grave of brilliant learning.'

Earthbound
In her diary entry for 2 February 1941, Roberts describes talking with English evacuees who came to Llanybri. One of these, the diary records, helped her make the wreath mentioned in the poem.
greaving room: in Old English *greave* means 'thicket' or 'brushwood', 'twigs' or 'branches'.

Spring
aconite: a poisonous plant; deadly poison.
xerophyte fern: xerophyte plants are those adapted to live with limited water.

Rhode Island Red

Rhode Island Red: a breed of chicken.

Poem

This poem is part of the opening of the second section of *Gods with Stainless Ears*. In their correspondence about the book's publication, T.S. Eliot asked Roberts if she would consider including a section of her 'long poem' to make up the length – the manuscript of *Poems*, minus the few poems Eliot wanted omitted from the volume came to twenty-seven pages. In a letter of 24 November 1943, Eliot makes a tactful enquiry about Roberts's use of unusual words: 'The words *plimsole*, *cuprite*, *zebeline* and *neumes* seem to exist but I think that bringing them all into one short poem is a mistake'. In a letter written on Christmas Eve 1943, he tells her: 'I like your defence of your queer words [,] and now accept all of them, but I am still not happy about *zebeline*, which appears to be a Lewis Carroll invention'. 'Zebeline' becomes 'zebrine' here (meaning striped), but returns in *Gods with Stainless Ears*. See notes to Part II of *Gods*.

Curlew

In a diary entry for 15 July 1941, 'Bird Notes', Roberts refers to the curlew's 'grey shagreen of shark, small-netted, thin and firm'. In a letter to Robert Graves of 18 December 1944, Roberts answers his criticism of a phrase in the poem, 'shagreen bleat':

> I especially wanted to write well on the *curlew* & had admitted my failure to Eliot before publication. I think the idea is good & result quite appalling. I shall attempt this again but how I don't know. I *did* want to get the feeling of frustration in relation to the bird's imprisonment & lack of a wholesome environment *in*

relation to all peoples living in the world today. I tried to use the exact [qualities] of a curlew's call which so often breaks with those 4 shrill notes – – – –. Shagreen bleat is *bad* as you point out. I had in mind the shagreen quality of its legs, the greezing gooseflesh of its voice.

Moorhen

In the same diary entry, 15 July 1941, Roberts makes notes on 'today's moorhen':

> The dull slate ostrich texture of its breast feathers. The sheen of rust or parmoil lichen on its back – the brown yellow-gold of ginger nuts. The two scarlet garters above the shining and rather large-scaled legs whose vivid colouring was lime-green, as fresh as the inner barks of trees. Enamelled or lacquered beak, scarlet with a bright yellow or orange tip. Brown eyes with a red-purple sheen when caught in the sun's rays. With this bird you SKIN it, not feather it.

Crossed and Uncrossed

This poem refers to Roberts's visit, en route to visit Keidrych Rhys, to her friend Celia Buckmaster, in the recently bombed East End of London, in June 1942. (See also the poem 'The Temple Road', which recalls the same events.) In her diary she writes: 'I turned up while the Library and buildings were still smouldering and continued to burn for another five days. The Round Church wet and empty like a grotesque sea shell.' In her auto-biography she recalls:

> I was astonished to find the results of the raid were still pending after days. The firemen were pinned to the bleached bricks trying to put out the fires. The library books were in heaps on the ground. The Round Church had taken a direct hit. The coloured windows were blown

out and in brilliant pieces on the ground. Pegasus had
melted and fallen. There remained a plane tree, some lily
of the valley (*Poetry Wales*, 19, 2, 1983, 49).

The poem is also written out of another experience described in
the autobiography, in which a German plane dropped a bomb
on Yarmouth pier as Lynette and Keidrych were walking past.

The title 'Crossed and Uncrossed', according to Roberts,
refers 'to the ways of burial of the crusaders. Their shock
I point out in the poem causes the crusaders to uncross their
legs and through burning they turn into tang shapes' (ibid.).
Lamb's ghost: Charles Lamb, born in the Temple in 1775.
proud widow:. Celia Buckmaster's mother, mentioned in
Roberts's diary for her resourcefulness during and after the
raid.

Orarium

In a letter of December 1944, Graves wrote enthusiastically
about this poem, having just criticised, a paragraph before, her
overly 'modernish' approach in poems such as 'Cwmcelyn':

> What gets me most about the end of *Orarium* is its exact
> conformity with the most ancient poetic secrets of all,
> the ones that I am exploring in *The Roebuck in the Thicket*
> (now a much longer book than when you last saw it).
> The last three lines are the end-of-the-year calendar
> formula in all languages & literatures. The man of God
> *has* to have sorrell red hair to be authentic.

Quotes:
> Lynette Roberts is one of the few true poets now
> writing. Her best is the best: for example, the perfect
> close to *Orarium*.

Signed R.G.

(If you care to pass this onto Fabers.)

Roberts replied:

Concerning what you say about 'Orarium', the poem was written straight off – almost subconsciously; though that which I expressed in its final phase is something which I had accepted and believed it [sic] *intuitively*: not through my study of mythology or penetration into science. [...] The rhythm & syntax was influenced by a reading of Anglo-Saxon writings which I had been studying the previous week in order to try & find out which *were* the first Saxon rhythms to be used: that is Saxon as opposed to early Celtic schools.

Blood and Scarlet Thorns

This is the first of a series of poems about Argentina. In July 1941 Roberts wrote:

> I was lonely and homesick for the Argentine. I wrote a succession of my S. American poems: about the 'Pampas' 'The New World', about the Incas mountain grave, 'Xaquixaguana'; about my father, 'Argentine Railways'; about the 'River Plate'; about Mechita where I was born, 'Blood, Scarlet Thorns'; about the convent 'Canzone Benedicto'; about São Paulo Brazil which I called 'Royal Mail'. I had the strong desire to leave the village & go to S. America.

Rainshiver

In a diary entry for 23 June 1940, Roberts notes: 'I experimented with a poem on Rain by using all words which had long thin letters so that even the print of the page would look like thin lines of rain.'

The New World
Maté: a herbal tea drunk in South America.

Xaquixaguana
The title refers to a historic Incan site. The word means 'valley of beauty'.

buhls: buhl is ornamental inlaid patterning.
agave: a spiny cactus-like plant native to South America.
Azrael: the angel of death.
alizarin: the red pigment of the madder root.

Canzone Benedicto
caladium: a plant native to South America.
monandrian: 'monandria' in botanical terminology refers to plants with one stamen or male organ and hermaphrodite flowers.
boracic: like or derived from borax, the acid borate of sodium.
calandria: a South American mockingbird known for its distinctive song.

Cwmcelyn
See the notes to Part V of *Gods with Stainless Ears*.

Gods with Stainless Ears

The poem is dedicated to Edith Sitwell, with whom Roberts corresponded from the early 1940s to the mid-1950s. Sitwell praised *Poems* effusively, and was far less inclined to question and correct than Graves or Eliot. Her garrulous correspondence contains interesting comments on the poetry scene of the 1940s, and topical waspishness at the expense of, among others, Julian Symons, Laura Riding and Anne Ridler. Roberts wrote to ask if Sitwell would accept the dedication to *Gods*, and received a telegram:

Part I

The prose 'arguments' at the beginning of each section of *Gods with Stainless Ears* were added at the suggestion of T.S. Eliot.

Saint Cadoc's Day: 25 September, formerly 24 January. Saint Cadoc is the patron saint, among other ailments, of deafness.

vail: to bow or bend.

cyprine: blue vesuvianite.

Confervoid residue: *Conferva* are a type of green freshwater algae.

pridian: on the previous day.

John Roberts: the ferryman of Llansteffan, mentioned also in Roberts's short story 'Fisherman' in *Village Dialect*:

> John Roberts known for years in the village, and as much attached to them as they were to him, stood in front of us now in his rough Breton suiting; his burnished flesh glowing like coals of fire; trousers rolled up above his bare feet and knees. I wanted to ask if it were true that he had dropped two of his relatives into the river by the full curve of the moon. But I was scared: scared of his answer. For I depended on him, as did many others to be ferried entirely at his mercy over that particular estuary. And like them, had been thrown across his back, lifted over sand and rock, dropped in the boat and quietly rowed over a mirrored water of birds (p. 26).

1620B64: Keidrych Rhys's army number.

Maeterlinck blue: Maurice Maeterlinck (1862–1949) Symbolist playwright, poet and essayist, author of *Pelléas and Mélisande* and *The Blue Bird*.

'Evans Shop': this is the Welsh habit of joining a person's name to that of their trade or place of work. See, later, Jones 'Black Horse': the local pub landlord.

CERAUNIC CLOUDS: ceraunics is the branch of physics that deals with heat and electricity.

argyria: silver poisoning.

acetated minds: glass discs coated with cellulose acetate were used for direct recordings by means of a cutting stylus (as distinct from pressing); hence 'acetate recordings'. This fits with Roberts's reference to gramophones, recordings, film and newsreel.

xantheine: xanthene is a compound used to make fluorescent dyes.

pele: a mixture of coal dust, clay and water for burning in hearth fires; see the poem 'The "Pele" Fetched in'.

ambuscade: to lie in ambush; to conceal.

cark: to burden, or to be anxious.

chevron: the mark on the sleeve of an officer. *Chèvre* in French means 'goat' – hence the play in the next line on 'kid'.

callid Cymru: callid means 'crafty', 'cunning'.

Part II

The first part of this section appeared, in a slightly different version, as 'Poem' in *Poems*.

gault: gaults are beds of clay and marls between the upper and the lower greensand.

zebeline [zibeline]: a Slavic word for the fur of the sable, black.

neumes: in medieval music notation, neumes are signs representing certain melodic patterns, often indicating a single syllable sung to a cluster of notes. The notes on the stave were recorded at certain historical periods in quadrilateral shapes, hence their shape rhyme with slates and bird boxes. Compare with Ezra Pound in the *Pisan Cantos* transcribing the birds on telegraph wires as musical notes (Canto LXXXII).

hispid: rough, bristly.

pinnate: like a feather, having leaves or branches arranged on each side of a stalk.

frescade: a cool walk or alley.

fieldfare: a species of thrush.

cymes: a cyme is a flower cluster in which each growing point terminates in a flower.

chyles: chyle is white milky fluid produced in digestion.

MO: Medical Orderly.

zinnias: a zinnia is a plant of the Americas renowned for the beauty of its flowers.

deflexed: bent downwards.

XEBO 7011: Lynette Roberts's number during the war.

collyrium: eye wash.

'Cow and Gate' lorry: Cow and Gate are a firm of baby food manufacturers.

Part III

himmel hokushai: *himmel* means 'sky' in German; Hokusai was the eighteenth-century Japanese painter whose views of Mt Fuji became popular in Europe in the late nineteenth century.

febrifuge: anti-febrile, fever-soothing.

ciliated: fringed with cilia, or fine hairs.

chagrin: shagreen, an untanned leather; also a sort of silk.

paleozoic: dating from the most ancient times; Roberts will have also had in mind the specific sense of palaeozoic Cambrian rocks or strata, found in Wales. 'Cambria' is the Latinised derivative of Cymru, the Welsh for Wales.

Kuan glaze : a greenish-grey glaze with a crackle effect.

iridium: a white metal of the platinum group, resembling polished steel.

defledged: unable, or no longer able, to fly.

Freud, Norman Haire/ Or Stopes: Sigmund Freud; Norman Haire (1892–1952; an expert on sexual education) and Marie Stopes (1886–1958; feminist and family planning pioneer).

distrained: the verb has two senses: 'to compress' or 'grasp tightly', or 'to pull asunder'.

shine of celandine: the Lesser Celandine, a woodland plant with bright yellow flowers. See also Wordsworth's 'The Small Celandine'.

Part IV

In the original edition 'Part IV' was misprinted as 'Part VI'.

Epigraph: Dyfnallt was John Dyfnallt Owen, poet and Nonconformist minister (1873–1956). Dyfnallt wrote several poems about his harrowing experiences on active service in the First World War.

rimmeled: the reference is to the cosmetic brand Rimmel.

forcipated: delivered by forceps.

third magnitude: the brightness of stars is measured on a scale called magnitude. The scale works in reverse, so that the lower the number the brighter the star. A third magnitude star can be seen without optical instruments.

shrived: to shrive is to impose a penance; also to absolve.

grailed: to grail is to make slender; also a comb maker's file.

seels resinate woe: to seel is to stitch up the eyes of birds; figuratively, to make blind, hoodwink.

Grisaille: decorative painting in grey monotone to represent forms in relief.

tansy tears: tansy is a herbaceous plant with clusters of small yellow flowers.

Paillettes: bright metal or coloured foil; also a decorative spangle for a dress.

Part V

Cycloid: the curve traced in space by a point in the circumference of a circle as it moves along a straight line.

ichnolithic: ichnology is the science of studying fossil footprints.

anthracite: a kind of coal, brilliant black.

ichnographic: an ichnography is a ground plan of a building or a map of a place.

Chinese blocks of uranium: in the first version of this poem 'Cwmcelyn', Roberts has 'Chinese fields of tungsten'.

boracic: from borax, white salt crystal.

cyanite: an aluminium silicate, usually blue.

ketch: a two-masted boat.

kestral: kestrel (American spelling).

cade: a pet lamb, or an animal reared by hand as a pet.

Calder 'stills': the Alexander Calder (1898–1976) to whom Roberts refers in her notes was a contemporary American sculptor who built mobiles. One of the most famous of these was 'Animal Circus mobile'.

'Singer's' perfect model: a reference to the Singer sewing machine.

dorcas: in the Acts of the Apostles Dorcas is a maker of clothes; also a brand name for thimbles.

Aertex: a cotton material.

Waled: ribbed.

Belisha beacons: flashing lights at pedestrian crossings.

aniline: chemical dye.

xerophilous: able to survive with little water.

oölite: limestone composed of small rounded granules; roe-stone.

curry comb: a comb or metal instrument for grooming horses.

Isotonic: musical term meaning 'equal tones'.

palea: the *OED* defines the word as 'a chaff-like bract or scale; *esp.* the inner bracts enclosing the stamens and pistil in the flower of grasses; […] the scales on the stems of certain ferns; […] *ornith.* A wattle to dewlap.' Critics have been confused by this word, to the extent of speculating that it might be a typographical error. It seems more likely that it is intended, and intended to invoke the first, botanical, sense noted.

Catoptric: relating to mirrors or reflections.

Uncollected and Unpublished Poems

All but two of these poems ('Downbeat' and 'Release') form part of one or other of the typewritten manuscripts of unpublished poems. One of these typescripts is untitled and collects unpublished poems and 'El Dorado'; the other is entitled 'The Fifth Pillar of Song'. It contains approximately eighty pages of poems, of varying quality and states of completion.

The title page of the typescript reads: 'THE FIFTH PILLAR OF SONG BY LYNETTE ROBERTS', and contains a list of poems. At the top of the page Roberts has written 'The pencil notes in this MSS are by T.S. Eliot whom the poems were sent to for possible publication Summer 1951.' The typescript also contains numerous handwritten notes, explanations and alterations by Roberts herself. It is also in places mispaginated. The other typescript essentially replicates, in different order, the 'The Fifth Pillar of Song' typescript, but begins with 'El Dorado', and has ticks beside the titles of poems that had been published.

The uncollected poems are published here not as they are in the typescript, but as they appeared in the first publications noted below them in the text. The unpublished poems are taken from the typescript, with obvious errors corrected, but otherwise unaltered.

Song of Praise
According to her autobiography, Dylan Thomas had told Roberts that 'he wished he had written "the long nosed god of rain"' (*Poetry Wales*, 19, 2, 1983, 35).

Englyn
In the manuscript of 'The Fifth Pillar of Song' this is part of a four-stanza poem called 'Either Or'. Roberts kept the last stanza only.

Ty Gwyn
Ty Gwyn: 'White House' in Welsh; where Lynette and Keidrych lived during the war.

The 'Pele' Fetched in
In her diary entry for 15 January 1940, 'Making "Pele"', Roberts describes the process and draws a picture in the margin.

Displaced Persons
In her diary entry for 26 June 1940, Roberts describes the arrival of evacuees in the village, and mentions writing a poem 'about the "Displaced Persons" of Europe likening them to the birds without food and dying of starvation'.

Chapel Wrath
In her diary entry for 26 June 1948, Roberts describes visiting the graveyards and studying the lettering on the gravestones. 'The best cutting', she writes, 'were those on natural slate, where their stabbing was exceptionally deep, so that the letters stood quietly out in spite of the handicap of years and their dullness of colour.' Earlier she had found the chapel 'as both church and chapel always are… locked… locked against humanity'.

Trials and Tirades
The poem's original title was '13 Bergson Street: Trials and Tirades', altered by hand in the typescript.

Angharad
The name of Lynette and Keidrych's daughter, born in 1945.

Prydein
The name of Lynette and Keidrych's son, born in 1946.

The Temple Road
Originally called 'The Blow Lamp', this poem is suggested by the arrival of a carpenter (described in the diary entry for 6 March 1941), who uses his blowlamp to remove paint from the front door. The smell reminds Roberts of the aftermath of the bombing raid on the Temple Road and East End of London, described in another poem, 'Crossed and Uncrossed'.

The Fifth Pillar of Song
This was the title poem of the collection Eliot turned down.

corbeau: dark green; *corbeau* is French for 'raven'.
cynometer: an instrument for measuring the blueness of the sky.
Branwen: in the *Mabinogion*, the daughter of Llŷr and Penarddun; she married the Irish king Matholwch, but he banished her to the kitchen. She taught a starling to talk and sent him to tell her brother of her plight. War between Wales and Ireland followed.
Rhiannon: Rhiannon was the wife of Pwyll, King of Dyfed, and mother of Pryderi. In her first appearance she rides a magical horse. To her belong the birds of Rhiannon, who sang for those who returned from Ireland.
Cimmerian age: the age of darkness.
cambutta: a pastoral staff used in the ancient Celtic church.
cyperous: Cyperus is a species of aromatic marsh plant.

Bruska's Song
'Bruska' was the name of Roberts's flower-arranging business. See also Keidrych Rhys's poem, 'Ephemerae for Bruska', in *The Van Pool and Other Poems*. 'Bruska's Song' is not listed in the table of contents of 'The Fifth Pillar of Song', but its pagination makes clear that it was part of it. On the manuscript is written, and

deleted, 'Child's Song or Bruska's Song', and 'Dedicated to Posy, the Youngest'.

Pendine
Pendine Sands, a few miles from Laugharne and Llansteffan.

Release
This poem is not part of the manuscript of 'The Fifth Pillar of Song', and seems to have been written later. It is typed up on a sheet of paper with various fragments of other, also unfinished, poems.

Downbeat
In 1948–9, Roberts moved to a caravan in Laugharne, adjacent to the graveyard. She divorced Rhys the following year.

Further Uncollected And Unpublished Poems

Blue Sea Slate Grey Shadows
gurk: 'A belch' (*OED*).

Universal Sorrow, Sledgehammer to the Brain
The poem has the alternative title 'Dirge' in *Now*, 2 (June–July 1940), 7.

Poem without Notes
A manuscript has the alternative title 'Transition'.

Poem [I see 2 ears and a tail]
A manuscript has the alternative title 'For Posy and her Past Pet Peter', and a handwritten note: 'about my pet white rabbit'.

That Toy-Mannered Century
mouche: 'A small black patch worn on the face as an ornament or to conceal a blemish' (*OED*).

moues: moue is a 'pouting expression, often conveying (mock) annoyance or distaste' (*OED*).

petit-point: an embroidery stitch.

neumes: see notes to Part II of *Gods with Stainless Ears*.

minikin: 'A thin strand of catgut used for the treble strings of a lute or viol' (*OED*).

To The Priest of the Middles (Concerning The New Order)
In a letter to Robert Graves, 10 February 1944, Roberts writes: 'I see John Betjeman (the new 'Priest' of the middles) is making an effort. The Devonshire parsons of the nineteenth century have given him a tip. Did you see his poem in *Cornhill* or even his book reviews in the *Daily Express*. They (the Tory stooges) are going backwards to go forwards, because they have no courage, creative, or staying powers.' *Diaries, Letters and Recollections*, p. 172.

Aircraft in Flight
A manuscript dates the poem 10 August 1943.

Paulinus
A manuscript dates the poem summer 1948, Llanybri.

S. Baring-Gould identifies St Paulinus as born in Carmarthenshire in the late 5th Century, founder of 'a monastery in 480 at Tygwyn ar Dâf, or the White Habitation on the Teify', and as a teacher of St David. *The Lives of the Saints*, xvi (Edinburgh: John Grant, 1914), p. 311.

Three inscribed fragments of what is known as the Paulinus stone are in Carmarthen Museum.

Farm Cat
A manuscript indicates the poem was written at Tygwyn, Llanybri.

The Great Disturber
A manuscript dates the poem summer 1948, Llanybri.
Mullein: verbascum – a flowering plant native to Europe and Asia.
spectral white: another poem inspired by the Welsh white cattle.

The Orange Charger
A manuscript dates the poem summer 1948, Ivy Cottage, Llanybri.
Roberts's diary entry of 6 February 1947 records her reading David Lack's *Life of the Robin*, and her further reflections on poetry and ecology: 'It is my intention one day to write a poem on this masterful young creature. Not a 'garden spade' poem: but something which holds the whole measure of this bird. Of its migration, communal interest, clear personality and sweet voice which somehow seems to follow the rain so that its song contains the mingled freshness of the rain and clearness of the sun.' *Diaries, Letters and Recollections*, p. 75.

Death That Monster
Roberts's diary entry for 21 June 1940 records: 'Outside the village down a steep hill about 600 yards away there is a trickle of water, but we never had a pump except to look at! No remarks will be made about this; for those in a position to complain have their own private pumps and remain immune from discomfort. Though these last few days ... the third week without rain ... did threaten those further afield. So I wrote about meeting "'Death That Monster' down at the well" and was the questioning Water-Carrier.' *Diaries, Letters and Recollections*, p. 18.

Encroachment
A manuscript dates the poem 22 January 1949, Ivy Cottage, Llanybri.

Let The Man of Darkness Out
A manuscript dates the poem 1948, Ivy Cottage, Llanybri.

Out of the Paw of Night
A manuscript dates the poem 4 November 1949, Laugharne. Roberts's father Cecil Arthur Roberts died in Argentina on 3 November 1949. The following day Roberts wrote to Robert Graves from The Caravan, Laugharne: 'Robert, he's dead. My beloved father. And it is wretchedly so, since I had looked forward to seeing him after the divorce was through. I remember so well his tears when he kissed my goodbye 15 years ago and they surprised me. And death is finite; and to me so unacceptable. That "all flesh is grass" is no consolation. As for the resurrection it's just the churchmen's bait for the little fishes.' Father Christmas – in the same letter to Graves, Roberts writes: 'Prydein said "don't cry I'll be your daddy". I told Prydein that I preferred him as Prydein. That at 2 he was too young to be my father. He said "When I am a big boy I will be your daddy - don't cry" and when I rejected this, he said with mastery "then you can have Father Christmas"'. (This letter, unpublished in this form, is reproduced by permission of the President and Fellows of St John's College, Oxford, and the Estate of Lynette Roberts).

Whose Hand I Have Never Touched
A manuscript dates the poem 1949, Laugharne. Roberts sent this poem to Robert Graves along with a letter on 20 April 1950, saying 'I owe a great deal of the above poem to you Robert in the sense that I obtained the source material from your book *The White Goddess*'. 'The

Correspondence between Lynette Roberts and Robert Graves',
Poetry Wales,19, 2, 1983, 114.
To Norman Lewis: the British writer who was friends with
Roberts in the late 1940s and 1950s. See also 'The White Heart'.

Spring [Spring rules the world]
Farm bull white of sacred race: another poem inspired by the
Welsh white cattle.
Aconite: an early flowering plant in the buttercup family.
Artemis: daughter of Zeus, goddess of hunting, born in the
Spring and often worshipped in Spring festivals.

The Autumn Maenad
A manuscript dates the poem autumn 1950, Bell's Wood.

You within the Enchanted Circle
A manuscript dates the poem summer 1949, Laugharne.
On the manuscript of the poem that Roberts sent to Robert
Graves she added a pencil note: 'See T. Gwynn Thomas, *Welsh
Folklore and Folk-Custom*'. Thomas's book was published by
Methuen in 1930 and contains a description of the myth of
Llyn y Fan Fach, on which this poem is based.
Sawdde's pebbled shore: the river Sawdde runs close to
Bethlehem, Carmarthenshire, where Keidrych Rhys was born.
The river's source is Llyn y Fan Fach.
Her black bull calf 'Prydein come': Prydein is the name of
Roberts's son.

Circe: The Falcon
The given subtitle as later published in *Poetry Wales* follows the
'The Fifth Pillar of Song' manuscript rather than the original
publication: 'Circe: The Falcon *(To traditional air 'Died for
Love')*'.

Winter Walk
A manuscript dates the poem December 1950, Bell's Wood.

Satanic Aquarelle
Aquarelle: 'A kind of painting or illuminating with Chinese ink, and very thin, transparent water-colours; used to represent flowers, small landscapes, etc. Also, the design so produced' (*OED*).

A Letter to the Dead
This poem was first published in *PN Review* in Dylan Thomas's centenary year, edited and with an accompanying article by Charles Mundye, entitled 'Lynette Roberts and Dylan Thomas: Background to a Friendship'. *PN Review*, 41, 2 November– December 2014. Roberts was one of the many mourners at Thomas's funeral and burial at St Martin's Church, Laugharne, on 24 November 1953.
Light birds sailing – god of rain: lines from Roberts's poem 'Song of Praise'.
The 'Show': Roberts married Keidrych Rhys on 4 October 1939, with Thomas as Best Man.
Until my caravan pitched: when Roberts separated from Rhys in 1949, she moved into a caravan initially situated in the Laugharne churchyard where Thomas was subsequently buried.
Atomic symphony of Cain: Roberts describes a specific occasion in London for her final meeting with Thomas, at a concert performance of Humphrey Searle's setting to music of Edith Sitwell's poem 'The Shadow of Cain', for two speakers (on the night in question, Dylan Thomas and Edith Sitwell), male voice choir, and orchestra. It was performed at the Palace Theatre, London, on 16 November 1952.
I saw Louis in the shade: Louis MacNeice, a fellow mourner at Thomas's funeral.

Anandrous Flight
A manuscript dates the poem August 1949, the caravan, Laugharne.
Anandrous: etymologically meaning 'without males', and in botany, to describe a plant with no stamens.
oriole eye: an oriole is a songbird occasionally seen in Wales and the rest of Great Britain.
Painted Lady and Brazilian Blue: butterflies. See also Roberts's poem 'Brazilian Blue'.

Blues with a Rumba Background
The poem is included as a text in 'O Lovers of Death', Roberts's unpublished radio drama.

Dedicated to 'Bruska'
White storied flat 68: in the 1930s Roberts lived for a time at 68 Newman Street, London, from where she ran her floristry business, which she called Bruska. See *Diaries, Letters and Recollections*, p. 204.

Dorian Mode
A manuscript dates the poem summer 1949, Laugharne.
Dorian Mode: usually refers to several historically different ways of organising musical pitches into a compositional system, but here perhaps is referring to the Dorian people of Ancient Greece.

Easter Madrigal
dunnock: small bird, sometimes called a hedge-sparrow, with a warbling song.

Eisteddfod
A manuscript indicates the poem was written at the caravan, Laugharne.

Cow, white as lime: another poem inspired by the Welsh white cattle.

Gorsedd: is a society of Welsh writers, musicians and artists responsible amongst other things for presiding over artistic competitions at the National Eisteddfod of Wales.

Eternal Love
On the manuscript of the poem that Roberts sent to Robert Graves she added a handwritten note: 'I am not satisfied with the title ['Eternal Love'] but at the same time wish to make it quite clear that this figure is waiting for either a love she has had and the lover is dead or is waiting for love which she has never given and received.' A later note on a manuscript-list of her works in the Lynette Roberts family papers says the poem 'Eternal Love' was 'written about the enigma of my mother who died when I was thirteen'.

Chained Molossus: the name is taken from an Ancient Greek breed of ferocious dogs.

Experimental
grisailles: see notes to Part IV of *Gods with Stainless Ears*.

corymbs: 'A species of inflorescence; a raceme in which the lower flower-stalks are proportionally longer, so that the flowers are nearly on a level, forming a flat or slightly convex head' (*OED*).

Found Written on the Moon
A manuscript dates the poem January 1939, Madeira.

The Lady of the Fountain: the name of one of the Welsh Romances in the *Mabinogion*.

Nightjar's Chatter
A manuscript has the handwritten note: 'a true event'.

Oh Max
Roberts sent this poem to Alun Lewis, who replied 'Max is nice and very grateful and well considered, especially the charming stage directions.' 'A Sheaf of Letters from Alun Lewis', *Wales* 8:28 (1948), 412.
Elisha and the bears: the story of Elisha, and the two she-bears who kill forty-two children from the city of Bethel, in some kind of divine vengeance, is told in the Bible, II Kings 2.

Solomon's Seal
Solomon's Seal: flowering plant with green foliage.
Cabra: Cerro Cabras is a mountain near Mendoza, Argentina.

The Black Collared Dove
The collared dove is a relative newcomer to the UK, and Roberts's poem is responding to its first arrival, reported in the *Manchester Evening News*, 20 September 1952: 'going under various names – the Indian ring-dove, Eastern ring-dove, Eastern collared dove – a new bird has been identified in England for the first time ever. A solitary male has for some time been heard singing in Lincolnshire and several ornithologists have seen it. Until the beginning of this century the collared dove belonged largely to Asia – to Korea, China, Burma – although it has been spreading gradually west.'

The Warrior and the Harlot
A poem written for Wyndham Lewis in 1951. See Epilogue for further details.

The Witnesses
A manuscript dates the poem 3 August 1949, 12pm, graveyard, Laugharne, 'under fresh night breeze'.

Transcendental Domain
A manuscript dates the poem 1948, Llanybri.

Sacred White Cattle
Another poem inspired by the Welsh white cattle. Roberts had read Reverend John Storer's *The Wild White Cattle of Great Britain* (London: Cassell, Peter and Galpin, 1879).
The Lady: a reference to the myth of Llyn y Fan Fach.
white bull of Connaught: a reference to the Irish myth 'The Cattle Raid of Cooley', and Finnbennach the white bull.
Pwyll's Hunting Woods: in the *Mabinogion* the story of 'Pwyll Prince of Dyfed' is the first of 'The Four Branches of the Mabinogi'.
Dalkeith and Gisburne, Chartley, Dinevor: places where Storer identifies famous herds of white cattle. Dinefwr Castle is next to the town of Llandeilo in Carmarthenshire.

Invocation
This poem is included as the conclusion of Roberts's unpublished radio drama 'O Lovers of Death'.

And They Had for Their Grave Plague Bones Ground to Dust
A manuscript indicates the poem was written at Tygwyn, Llanybri.

As You Were
A manuscript dates the poem 26 February 1949, Ivy Cottage.

Fieldfare
A manuscript indicates the poem was written at Ivy Cottage, Llanybri.

I Will Have None of It
A manuscript dates the poem 1945, Tygwyn, Llanybri.
Two-roomed cottages: in 'TB Windows', her diary entry for 17 August 1946, Roberts discusses the ill effects of badly ventilated houses with tiny windows. See *Diaries, Letters and Recollections*, p. 72.

Mysticism
A manuscript indicates the poem was written at Tygwyn, Llanybri.

Tea Leaves
A manuscript dates the poem 15 August 1949, the caravan, Laugharne.
Pendine face: see Roberts's poem 'Pendine' and its associated note.

The Tablet of Aphrodite
A manuscript of the poem has a typed note: 'I wrote this at Oxford Feb. 22nd after spending an afternoon studying the early tablets of stone.'

The White Heart
A manuscript dates the poem 3 April 1950, Bayford.
Roberts's close friend Norman Lewis travelled in Mainland Southeast Asia, including Saigon, in the early months of 1950. See Lewis's *A Dragon Apparent: Travels in Indo-China* (London: Cape, 1951).

Tinamou
Sansevieria: flowering plant, sometimes called the snake plant.
Marouska: the name of one of Roberts's childhood friends in Argentina.

Quintas: a Latin American term for a large house or estate.
Lachesia: Lachesis is the name of one of the Three Fates in
Ancient Greek religion, responsible for spinning the thread of
life. Lachesis is also the name of a group of venomous vipers
which include the South American Bushmaster.

El Dorado

This verse-play was broadcast on the BBC Third Programme on
1 and 5 February 1953 and repeated twice. The story is taken
from an article, among Roberts's papers, from the *Buenos Aires
Herald*, 28 July 1936. The article was sent to her by T. Hughes
Cadvan, the son-in-law of J.D. Evans, the sole survivor of
the massacre of the Welsh colonists, and one of the original
colonists who landed on the Patagonian shores in 1865.
Cadvan Hughes had read Roberts's piece 'Patagonia' in *Wales*,
and in his letter he tells her that the article is written by him
from Evans's own account:

> His version, *to me*, is stirring in its simplicity; a story
> told without any effort to colour or exalt his own
> participation nor to justify his actions. His sole purpose,
> as he told me, was to leave to posterity a true and exact
> account of what had happened. [...] I have no time to
> translate in all its detail the story as he dictated it in
> Welsh but I am sending you a clipping from the B.A.
> Herald of July 28th 1936 in which you will find the
> story almost complete as I wrote it at the time (Letter
> of 14 January 1946).

Hughes ends the letter by adding a couple of *englynion* from a
friend of his in Chubut 'to show that there are Welshmen with
poetic leanings living in Patagonia'.

There are also among Roberts's papers two letters from a Geoffrey Parry Rhys of Weston-Super-Mare, great-grandson of the Parry who was killed in the Kel Kein confrontation ('I have always been told he was scalped!'), asking for a copy of 'El Dorado'.

The broad outlines of the story are as follows: in late 1883, four young Welsh men went prospecting for gold, following the Chubut river, on a journey to the interior of the territory that would take three and a half months. When, at the end of February 1884, they reached the confluence of the Chubut and the Lepá rivers, they found no gold, but met two Indians, who invited them back to their camp in Súnica. The Welsh were suspicious, and decided to hurry back to the colony, a journey of over 300 miles. It was a dangerous and difficult journey, and two of the men, Parry and Hughes, became so exhausted that they had to be strapped to their saddles. By 4 March they had crossed the Chubut and reached the Kel Kein valley. Evans rode off to hunt for food, and when he returned the men were attacked by the Indians. Only Evans escaped, by riding his horse into a steep gulley, gaining precious time over the Indians, who were forced to make a detour to avoid the dangerous descent. According to the article, he looked behind him and saw 'his comrade Davies falling from his horse speared through, Parry with a spear stuck in his side but still keeping his seat'. Evans eventually reached the Iamacan river, and rejoined the Chubut. When he reached Gaiman, he was taken in by another Welsh settler, and noticed for the first time a gash in his armpit where he too had been speared. When told of the incident, the founder of the Welsh colony, Lewis Jones, refused to believe that the Indians had done this, as relations between the Welsh and the Indians had always been good, and Jones considered himself 'a personal friend of the Indian chiefs'. Jones himself led an expedition to verify Evans's account of the incident, and took Evans with him.

According to the article, 'The bodies of the unfortunate young men lay where they had fallen mutilated in the most cruel and savage manner, too revolting for description'. The bodies were buried there in a single grave, and a short service held. A marble monument, paid for by subscription, was later placed at the spot. Evans later farmed and started the first flour mill in the area, and became known as 'El Molinaro'. In the photograph accompanying the article, Evans sits beside the monument to his horse, 'El Malacara'.

Diving bird, by Lynette Roberts. (Photograph and image reproduced by kind permission of Angharad and Prydein Rhys.)